BREAKING DOWN BARRIERS

To two long-suffering Sallys

Breaking Down Barriers

Practice and priorities for international
management education

Edited by
BOB GARRATT and JOHN STOPFORD

Gower
for the Association of Teachers of Management

Published by
Gower Publishing Company Limited,
Westmead, Farnborough, Hants., England

Breaking down barriers.
   1. Executives, Training of
   I. Garratt, Bob
   II. Stopford, John
   III. Association of Teachers of Management
   658.4 '07' 124   HF5549.5.T7

ISBN 0 566 02122 6

Typeset by Graphic Studios (Southern) Limited, Godalming, Surre
Printed in Great Britain by Biddles Limited, Guildford, Surrey.

Contents

Preface

This book is the result of a conference organised by the Association of Teachers of Management where managers and management educators met to explore together the demands and pressures both groups were experiencing as a direct result of the growing internationalisation of business. The book is therefore designed as a contribution to the thinking of those directly concerned, as suppliers and customers, with international management development efforts. In addition, those managers and government officials who are the consumers of the training should find much of interest here as they reflect upon their own jobs and careers.

International trading and investment are not, of course, new phenomena. Only within the last twenty years, however, have growth rates risen to their present high levels. Though the problems of specifically international education in business were articulated in the United States in the early 1960s, it is only in more recent years that the failures of the early efforts have become apparent.

The central thesis of this book is that there is a need to reconsider in fundamental ways the bases on which both the demand for and the supply of international training are founded. The screens that hitherto insulated most managers in both private and public undertakings from conditions abroad have now been so eroded that few can ignore the state of the world economy. No longer must one be physically abroad to be 'international'. At the purely professional level, managers are exposed to the workings of the increasingly interdependent world economy and are expected by their organisations to respond rapidly and appropriately to its changes. International perspectives on management can no longer be regarded (if they are considered at all) simply as items to be added at the end of 'normal' development activities: they should be an integral part of those activities.

What does this need for change mean in practice? The seventeen contributors to this book attempt to provide answers. They find that progress in creating effective training to reflect changing business conditions has been slow and uncertain. They explore the constraints and blocks to progress and attempt to indicate more productive directions for the future.

We, the editors of this book, wish to thank them for sharing their experience with us and with a wider audience. Neither we nor the contributors have all the answers, but we have learned much from the experience of bringing together widely divergent elements to construct at least a rough map of the terrain. We hope that our efforts will enable what learning is available to be communicated more readily than at present. If we do no more than stimulate a more comprehensive dialogue between managers and educational institutions we shall have achieved our purpose. We would hope that such a dialogue will lead to action, for discussion alone will not resolve the difficulties we have depicted.

Bob Garratt
John Stopford
London 1980

Acknowledgements

We acknowledge with gratitude permission from the Brookings Institution to reprint *The International Dimension of Management Education* and from the American Society for Training and Development to reprint extracts from *Multinational Training for Multinational/International Organisations.*

We also acknowledge our debt to our colleagues and friends in industry, government and academia who helped to educate and encourage us.

Notes on Contributors

Alan M. Barratt is training and OD manager of Mobil Europe Inc. and vice president, Mobil International Consulting Services Inc. Previously, he was training manager of Mobil Oil Company Limited. Among other training posts he has held are seven years with the Furniture and Timber Industry Training Board and five years with Texas Instruments. Originally he read mechanical engineering in the late 1950s, before studying the behavioural sciences in the UK, Europe and US. A visiting lecturer at Cranfield School of Management, he has also lectured and acted as a consultant in Europe, US and Asia.

David Barron is the group manager, development and training, of Cable and Wireless Company Limited. After reading classics he worked with the Electricity Council on industrial relations training and administration. He spend twelve years with ITT in a number of roles and companies working on management development, manpower planning, and organisational development. In 1976 he joined Cable and Wireless. He is a member of the executive committee of the Action Learning Trust and has membership of many Institute of Personnel Management ad hoc committees.

Henri-Claude de Bettignies is professor of organisational behaviour and director of the Euro-Asia Centre at INSEAD. He holds the Diplôme de l'École de Psychologues Practiciens de Paris, Licencié ès Lettres. He has been research assistant at the Institute of Industrial Relations at the University of California and visiting lecturer at the Institute of Industrial Relations at Rikkyo University in Tokyo. He has worked for Miferma (Mauretania) and IBM (New York). He spent over four years in Asia, particularly in Japan, doing research and teaching in Japanese universities and management centres. He has published many articles and a book: *Matriser le Changement dans l'Entreprise?*

John S. N. Drew is head of international affairs of Rank Xerox. He was formerly in the Foreign Service before becoming director of marketing at the London Business School and has designed and taught a number of courses on the EEC. He was specialist advisor on trade and treaties to the House of Lords EEC Scrutiny Committee, 1977–78.

Tony Eccles is professor and director of the Centre for Management Development at the London Business School. Ex-shop-floor fitter and ships engineer, he had ten years' production management experience with Unilever before becoming senior lecturer at Manchester Business School and later professor of business policy at Glasgow University. He is also a consultant to public and private companies and trade unions.

Bob Garratt is a freelance consultant working with action-based interventions in organisations. His educational ideas were developed through live-project based activities with students at the Architectural Association School, London, and the Patrimoine Historique et Artistique de la France during work on community rehabilitation in central France. He was visiting fellow in management education, Ulster College, Belfast in 1974 and returned to London to work on the first developing senior managers programme with the General Electric Company. Since then he has been involved in consultancy work in industrial, governmental and community organisations and has worked extensively in Europe, Bahrain, Hong Kong, Malaysia and Nigeria.

Malcolm Harper is professor of enterprise development and director of The Marketing Development Centre, Cranfield School of Management. He read classics at Oxford, holds an MBA from Harvard and a PhD from Nairobi. His current major interests are the promotion of small-scale enterprises, particularly in developing countries, and the improvement of training of managers and change agents through the development and diffusion of alternative strategies for effective learning.

Judy Lowe is currently research fellow in international management education at The City University Business School, London. Her main interest is in the development of managers operating internationally, particularly within the EEC. Following four years' research in this area sponsored by the Foundation for Management Education and the Social Science Research Council she published *The New Euromanagers* in June 1979 and plans to extend this work in future to look at the problems of cross-cultural executive transfer.

Desmond McAllister is director of management development for ITT Europe in Brussels. When he wrote his chapter he was an independent management consultant working on long term contract with ISVOR FIAT and consulting to a range of other companies and organisations in Europe and the UK. He has been a visiting lecturer at the London Business School and was previously consultant with the Grubb Institute of Behavioural Studies in London and the Giovanni Agnelli Foundation in Turin. He has had a varied work experience in Europe, Far East and USA after studying at the Gregorian University, Rome and the University of Munich.

Alistair Mant is an author, researcher and consultant in management development. He has been internal management development consultant for IBM, consultant at the Tavistock Institute, visiting fellow at Manchester Business School. His most recent book is *The Rise and Fall of the British Manager*

(Pan paperbacks) and he is currently working on a new book on the comparison of Anglo-German political and industrial institutions. He specialises in programmes to enhance managers' awareness of political and societal forces.

Robert M. March is principal consultant, March and March Management Consultant, Nishinomiya, and visiting professor of international business, The Institute for International Studies and Training, Shizuoka, both in Japan. Dr March specialises in management development and training in the Japanese subsidiaries of Western MNCs. He also advises Japanese companies in their overseas business negotiations with governments and private companies.

Lee C. Nehrt is director of the World Trade Institute, New York. He received his graduate degrees from the Universities of Paris and Columbia. After four years of industry experience he began teaching international business at Indiana University in 1962 and held an endowed chair from 1974–78. During the 1960s he was with the Ford Foundation for two years each in Tunisia and East Pakistan. The author of eight books, he chaired in 1976–77 a national task force of 'business and international education' for the American Council of Education. In 1978 and 1979 he was the national coordinator of the AACSB's workshops on 'internationalising the business school curriculum'.

His Excellency Amon J. Nsekela is High Commissioner for Tanzania to the Court of St James's in London and Ambassador Extraordinary and Plenipotentiary to the Republic of Ireland. He was educated at Makerere College, the University of East Africa, where he qualified as a schoolmaster and then taught for four years before going to the University of the Pacific, Stockton, California for his MA in politics and history. On return to Tanzania he was soon appointed Clerk to the Cabinet, Permanent/Principal Secretary in the following ministries: External Affairs and Defence, Industries, Mineral

Resources and Power, the Treasury (also ex-officio Paymaster General). When the commercial banking system and insurance were nationalised in 1967 he was appointed chairman and managing director of the Tanzania National Bank of Commerce and chairman of the National Insurance Corporation (Tanzania) Ltd. He has served as director or chairman of many state and private companies and was chairman of the Council of the University of Dar es Salaam and a member of parliament. In addition, he has written four books, many articles and has broadcast widely on the problems of development.

Gordon Redding spent over ten years as an executive in the UK department store industry before going to Manchester Business School to research for a doctorate. Since 1973, he has been director of the University of Hong Kong's Diploma in Management Studies programme. He has undertaken extensive research into cross-cultural attitudes and behaviour. He is a regular visiting teacher at the University of Hawaii, and for the Asian Productivity Organisation. In 1979 he published *The Working Class Manager — Beliefs and Behaviour* (Saxon House) as a continuation of his PhD thesis.

Richard D. Robinson is professor of international management, Alfred P. Sloan School of Management, Massachusetts Institute of Technology. He is author of *International Business Management: a Guide to Decision-Making* and other books. He is a past president of the Academy of International Management and a fellow of L'Academie Internationale de l'Organisation Scientifique.

Melvin Schnapper is president of Mel Schnapper Associates and is director of development and training at G. D. Searle & Company. He is also a faculty member of the Advanced Management Institute at Lake Forest (Illinois) College. Dr Schnapper's major interests are helping multinational corporations and international organisations cope effectively with diversity and change. Of prime interest to him are training international trainers, training international managers, and preparing people (families) for working and living overseas.

David C. Steel began working in training in 1967, after a career first as a merchant navy officer, then working in transportation and production. During his period in Nigeria he was training/development manager of Dunlop Nigerian Industries Ltd, a subsidiary company of Dunlop Holdings Ltd. He left the Dunlop company in 1977 to become the manpower development manager of Plessey Telecommunications Ltd in Liverpool and rejoined Dunlop as manager, training and development, UK Tyre Group in 1979.

John M. Stopford is professor of international business at the London Business School, president of the European International Business Association and member of the executive committee of the Matrix Group. He was a shop-floor apprentice with Baker Perkins before reading engineering at Oxford and MIT. He worked with Shell, was later a non-executive director of Shell (UK) Ltd, and has worked with the United Nations. His latest book is (co-authored) *Cases in Strategic Management*.

1 Introduction and Review

BOB GARRATT AND JOHN STOPFORD

The workings of global politics combined with startling advances in communications technology have meant that all of us are affected constantly by international pressures and events. These are made manifest to individuals in the rich countries through the discontinuity of energy supplies, commodity supplies and the consequent fluctuating prices which disrupt their previously assumed smooth progress to an affluent, post-industrial future. Such international pressures affect governments and organisations, both public and private, whose work crosses international boundaries. In the forefront of such boundary-crossing are those managers, executives, administrators, politicians, and diplomats, whose job it is to ensure that agreements are made and maintained at each boundary to ensure that organisations can continue to provide their goods or services effectively.

Yet these managers, on whom the relative stability of the rich countries depends increasingly, have been given little serious thought or constructive support in terms of what are their work and personal needs and how these might be satisfied. It is easy to make the case that little encouragement, and even less direct help, is available currently – or planned – by governments, educational institutions or helping agencies. So the people who are to provide the core of the new diplomats, traders, entrepreneurs and industrialists of the internationally interdependent 1980s will have to find their own solutions to the problems of increasing complexity and discontinuity which they face and on which they must take action – unless those who define and provide training at present rethink their priorities, structures, and reward systems,

1

to cope with these growing needs. In this book we acknowledge that the picture of international management development is cloudy and incomplete at present. We have set out to draw the best map that we can, with the help of colleagues who have seen other parts of the territory. Our map is an early edition — Ptolomeic rather than Mercatorial — which we hope will encourage others to venture into these difficult but increasingly important areas to produce their own improved maps and charts until such time as we can establish some international cartographic and hydrographic standards. We accept that our map looks peculiar as *terra incognita* lies not only on the outer fringes of the sheet but also at the centre. Our studies, and the collected experiences of many colleagues at the Association of Teachers of Management conference in April 1979, have shown that the conventional assumptions about the forces at work to shape the 'management' map are sadly misplaced when tested against the practical needs of the individuals concerned. International management education may perhaps best be considered, as we argue later on, a specific context within which to test the generalities.

The seventeen chapters that follow this introduction examine both the nature of the demand for international management education and the current 'state of the art' in creating supply, both within and outside the organisations involved. Each author writes from his own perspective on the issues, yet all share the same concern to improve on current performance. In assembling these chapters we, the editors, have attempted to link the rich variety of ideas into a coherent whole that itself provides a guide to where future efforts may productively be directed. We have found it necessary to confront directly the contentious issue of whether or not 'international' is different from normal or traditional education, and then derive a rudimentary demand-and-supply model in which can be located the full range of environmental demands and constraints that make breaking down the barriers to conventional thinking so difficult.

Are there basic differences?

Does the international dimension fundamentally alter the 'normal' needs and processes of education, or does it merely add further complexity to an already complicated scene? There are many answers, for much depends upon whose needs are under discussion. For some, international issues are of minor consequence, though few managers can today totally exclude them from their thinking. For others, a clear understanding of what is happening abroad, either in other parts of their firm or in their competitors', is vital for an adequate assessment of how they should be acting at home. For yet others – probably a smaller group – the urgent needs of managing technological transfers, or exerting control across national or cultural boundaries, cannot adequately be considered within a uni-national framework. Though Mant's chapter provides an alternative argument, it would seem that, if one adds the full set of international transactions to existing domestic conditions within an organisation, there are quite clear distinctions that have been found helpful in generating concepts sufficiently rigorous to be of practical use. In other words, the debate is about when a difference of degree becomes a difference of substance.

Though falling short of providing a comprehensive discussion of all the possible discontinuities, the chapters in this book identify some of them and the related conceptual problems. Each chapter focuses on one set of issues and one group of managers. To link together the discussion and the findings, the reader will need a general classification of the different types of manager about whom we are talking.

Judy Lowe's chapter provides one list, which can conveniently be expanded and generalised as follows:

Ambassadors	– senior general staff on peripatetic missions;
Diplomatic technicians	– senior functional specialists on visits or short-term secondments;
Expatriate residents	– medium to long-term stay career-builders living abroad;
Home country nationals	– indigenous local managers of multi-national organisations;

Third country — managers in international organisations
nationals who are from neither the headquarters
country nor the local home country;
Home country — managers of any organisation who
hosts receive foreign clients, and guests, and
ease them into the local business and
social environment.

This list is not exhaustive, nor is it exclusive: managers
may hold several of these roles simultaneously. It does not
include all those people indirectly affected by international
pressures at work, nor does it include the body of international
'mercenaries' of big business with their constant job changes
and capital acquisition objectives. But it does cover the main
groups we see as directly affected by the new international
demands thrust upon them.

Cutting across this typology of international manager is a
typology of subject matter. We approach the question of the
intellectual content of the subjects by considering 'international' as a *context* within which one can emphasise certain
features of managerial life. We resist the notion that there is
something *sui generis* about life in foreign countries that
requires quite separate educational treatment. Indeed, it
has become a reasonably well recognised consequence that
teaching about foreign conditions can illuminate students'
perceptions of their home environment. Even though this is
a book about the design of the curriculum and not its content,
the reader should bear in mind that content can vary considerably in its domestic/international application. Some subjects
have universal application, others apply principally in a
particular country, while yet others have a mainly international
setting. In the first category, there are the calculations using
mathematics or procedures for such basic activities as double-
entry book-keeping. Even here, though, one must be careful
about claims for universality. As de Bettignies points out, the
application and interpretation of the results of standard
procedures can vary considerably from one culture to another.
In the second category there are the familiar set of purely
descriptive subjects. For example, the Trades Union Congress
and its impact on industrial relations usually concerns only
those whose interests lie in the UK. The third category

includes technical issues such as the specification of currency risk as well as all the less definable issues introduced by considerations of managing in more than one culture. Managers in each of our categories have differing educational needs in each of these subject categories.

Added together, these classifications of job and subject indicate the complexities involved in the international context. Education that directly confronts this complexity must itself become on occasion quite distinct from education in a 'normal' domestic organisation. There is a sense of a quantum jump in educational complexity for some aspects of the task. Consider, for example, the needs for internationally involved managers to be able to cope with cross-cultural issues, the problems of the imposition of an HQ country's values on local operating countries' growing national awareness, the politics of each indigenous operating unit, the balancing of the need to take local decisions quickly against apparent flouting of the HQ's policies, and the problems of reliable international information transmission. The attention and expense given to the sensitive development of a meta-culture in the IVECO and Mobil cases should be sufficient example of the growing need to consider the field worthy of separate treatment.

It is to the problem of how to operate in the meta-culture whilst maintaining a strong personal and national identity that this book is addressed. We believe that lessons learned here are transferable back into the uni-national organisations to improve in turn their effectiveness and efficiency.

The supply and demand model

The sheer diversity of mechanisms whereby international pressures and changes become translated into developmental needs for managers presents a patchwork of demands on the prospective educator, regardless of whether he or she is within the managers' organisation or outside it. We have found it helpful to use familiar concepts of demand and supply to interpret the chapters that follow. On one side there are the varieties of perceived need for training for each category of manager. On the other there are all the possible methods of supplying training, and the challenges that managing the supply pose for the various types of institution and organisation active in this market.

Our demand and supply model is rudimentary because of the difficulties of defining the discontinuities mentioned earlier. Matching each segment of demand with each source of supply cannot yet be achieved within a general model of the market. On the demand side we need to make explicit the distinction between the customer and the consumer. In this model, the 'customer' is generally the firm or its managers responsible for the provision of training and development. The 'consumer' is the individual manager or student who is the final user of that supply. We consider, and most of the contributors to this book seem to agree, that there is a wide gap in perception between customer and consumer, even within a single organisation. The nature of the consumer demand needs to be determined in much greater detail than is possible at present, otherwise supply-and-demand models will continue to be misleadingly constructed on the customers' inappropriate assumptions of demand.

There is yet another difficulty in the construction of a general model. The current debate about *any* form of management development activity challenges many cherished notions about how people learn. Though we have avoided tackling this debate head-on, we cannot ignore the fact that much of the discussion about the form of training best suited to matching demand with supply in our chosen territory is based upon individual preconceptions about training in general. The reader will form his own conclusions as to whether or not we have succeeded in at least illuminating the specifically international components.

Measuring demand and supply

Robinson's chapter takes a hard look at what companies in the United States think they want by way of international training and what the major business schools offer. This survey provides little comfort for anyone interested in developing the area as an easy extension of their present activities. The companies are seen to be uncertain of their own needs. They respond only slowly to changing circumstances and few have any *general* programme of action. Many of them are shown to be ignorant of available, even when nearby, sources of supply and research. For the schools, the position is equally dismal. Little effort has been made to find out what demands are being made, whether by customer or consumer. There is an absence of conceptual leadership in the field. What efforts have been made to change patterns of faculty behaviour to improve the chances of creating new thinking have largely been dissipated by internal dissent. For a country that has had nearly twenty years of public debate on the issue, progress has been surprisingly constrained on both sides. Robinson is, in effect, describing a 'dialogue of the deaf', and raising issues that are picked up in other chapters by those whose concern is to remove or reduce the constraints.

The cumulative impact of those chapters is a description of demand conditions where individual managers, much more than their firms, are asking for help. They want to share ideas, swap experience and knowledge so that as they cross international boundaries they can maintain or develop their spheres of operational ability and influence in their organisations. Within the organisation there is usually little relevant knowledge or experience which can be passed on easily; there are not sufficiently rigorous systems of learning built into organisations to capture and reinterpret what experiences do exist. Consequently, trainers, developers, and personnel people are not rewarded for work in this area so they tend not to empathise with the sets of attitudes, skills, and knowledge for which many international managers are rather incoherently asking.

On the supply side there is turbulence, confusion, and a high level of ignorance. Instructors seem to make little attempt to adapt their standard offerings to cope with the new demands. Little research is undertaken in the area of international management development, and few of the faculty have relevant international experience on which to build. Thus the connection is rarely made between the demand and supply sides of our model in any way which can contribute to the effectiveness of any organisation.

This lack of connection is particularly disturbing in the context of planned developments in business schools for the 1980s. A recent survey [1] of the deans of business schools in the USA, Europe and Latin America showed almost unanimous agreement that international business courses were being or about to be greatly expanded as part of the general response to current trends. We sense that the academic planners are in the grip of a fashionable fever and do not welcome pointed questions about the nature of the demand to which they claim they are 'responding'. We wonder from where the resources and skilled faculty will emerge? Their analysis seems reasonable, so why do they hesitate at taking action?

Mant's chapter provides a completely different approach. He argues that the most urgent problem facing teachers on the supply side of the model is to develop more effective means of stimulating managers to translate their acquired learning into action. He does not recognise 'international' as a useful distinction in this context. In other words, he challenges the whole notion of our supply and demand model in the international context. He raises the very real possibility that training can have the effect of making the already difficult process of translation into action even more so when it is pitched at a global level and devoid of cultural content. He argues that one needs to emphasise history and culture if one is to increase managers' awareness of their own and their organisation's capacities to understand and accept change. This point is also made by Drew in his consideration of European cultures. Mant argues that only by resisting the possible loss of cultural identity when crossing national boundaries can the individual remain effective as an initiator of action. Yet the very recognition of cultural roots and differences among cultures suggests that international boundary-crossing jobs involve specific complexities absent in purely single culture ones, as was argued earlier.

A third view of the demand side of the picture is painted by Barron, who considers the impact on training needs of changing career structures within international firms. He points to the decline of the expatriate career as costs rise and legislation increasingly requires the employment of

local executives. Foreign postings are becoming of shorter
duration and executives are likely to spend time in more
countries than hitherto. This increased mobility provides
little time for anyone to establish close working links and
understanding of each local culture and at the same time adds
demand for educational qualifications that are immediately
recognised everywhere. Under such conditions, systems for
the central management of international careers and the
required training are beginning to break down. The consequence is that individuals take more personal initiatives in
specifying their own career moves. This view corresponds to
the more general one, mentioned earlier, in which it is the
individual consumer more than the organisation that specifies
change in the demand for international training. The unanswered question is how these individuals are to acquire
the perspective and knowledge necessary for taking the
initiative intelligently?

Regional perspectives

There are eight chapters giving a view on some of the particular
demand characteristics and supply difficulties in different
regions of the world. Taken together they raise many of the
detailed considerations and difficulties in matching supply to
demand that have so far prevented major initiatives from
being successfully undertaken. Taken separately they suggest
just how widely training needs vary from one region to
another. Four chapters deal with developed countries and
four with the adaptation of thinking required when transferring attention to developing countries.

Drew emphasises the absence in almost all European
programmes of an adequate treatment of the institutional
and cultural environments within which European activities
are conducted. He cites businessmen's awareness of the
need for a continental perspective, though he does not
speculate about why such awareness has not been followed
by action. Like Mant, he insists that a working knowledge
of the historical and contemporary forces in the environment
is a prerequisite for an adequate assessment of how business

is conducted. He espouses the use of information-transfer courses to remedy the glaring gap in the content of European programmes, and suggests how management teachers can educate themselves for this task. The implication of Drew's approach is that such 'taught' courses should precede others, perhaps of the more experiential variety, adding flesh to his bare bones.

Lowe appears to accept Drew's strictures as one of the starting points for her examination of why British courses are so insular. She considers that European schools are ahead of Britain in the provision of training in international skills. Travel and language are identified as two key items normally overlooked or underemphasised in Britain. Living abroad and learning the language while at the same time learning about management can, she argues, go far as a means of gaining understanding of foreign cultures and different managerial practices. Rather than concentrating on adapting the curriculum, one also needs to consider the setting for the training. The British, for a variety of historical as well as financial reasons, appear to find this balanced type of approach more difficult to achieve than do others in Europe. Yet, even in Britain, demand from individuals, as she cites at the end of the chapter, is emerging noticeably to outstrip the possibilities of generating adequate supply.

In the United States the need for international awareness as an explicit objective of management education is widely accepted by the leading academics. The Brookings Report provides their collective wisdom on the issue as it was articulated in 1975. What makes this report of interest in 1980 is that the awareness has remained high, yet the practice has hardly changed. Nehrt describes the lack of progress despite major investments of money and effort on a national scale. International business as a subject still remains largely an afterthought to be tacked on at the end of conventional courses, if it is taught at all. Nehrt considers that this situation will most likely persist until faculty members first widen their own international horizons. In what ways wider faculty perspectives will widen their teaching has yet to be clearly established, though both Harper and de Bettignies provide some useful clues. To some extent the difficulties for the

Americans must be due to their continental isolation and continuing sense of an academic version of the 'Fortress America' way of viewing the world. The costs of changing this bias are enormous, as the budgets of the current efforts described by Nehrt indicate. By comparison the British problem, as seen by Lowe, pales into insignificance. At a time when university budgets are under pressure and when government support on both sides of the Atlantic for further initiatives in this direction seems unlikely, the prospects of Nehrt's solutions being realised are decidedly poor.

Africa faces an altogether different type of problem. Nsekela dwells on the width of the gap in understanding that exists between the foreigners's perceptions of Africa and what Africa needs. Based on his wide experience as educator, civil servant, manager and diplomat, he provides a reasoned and balanced yet thoroughly damning indictment of the failure of training in both Europe and America to prepare managers to adapt to African conditions. Not only do managers arrive ignorant of basic facts but, more importantly, they arrive unaware that different philosophies and approaches to business prevail. Further failure is apparent from Harper's more general evidence on the provision of training for the poor countries. Harper considers that training approaches developed in the industrialised countries are entirely inappropriate and an expensive waste both when they are used locally and when nationals are sent to courses abroad. His concern is not so much the provision of international training as the adaptation of existing models to new conditions. In this, his canvas is the same as that of Steele's Nigerian programmes. Both authors reach similar conclusions about the difficulties of adaptation and the need to provide carefully prepared, complete 'packages'.

Harper goes on to look at the teachers themselves. He considers that neither do they really wish to invest in the laborious process of learning how to make the necessary changes nor are they prepared to admit they need help. The teachers' amour propre in Africa is as much a barrier to change as it is for others!

The two chapters on conditions in the Far East present evidence and analysis that bear on the demand/supply relationships only indirectly. They earn their place in this book by adding to the stock of issues discussed elsewhere.

March takes a look at the workings of the managerial systems within multinational firms and focuses attention on the demands those systems make on managers' learning and control abilities. March's approach is that of the academic researcher who uses questionnaires to collect data on a large sample of multinationals active in the Far East. His data suggest that behaviour is conditioned as much by the nationality of the parent firm as it is by any other factors. This suggests that 'company culture' needs to be taken into account explicitly when assessing the training needs of a firm, a point that Eccles reinforces later. March also corroborates Barron's statements about the shortening of foreign postings and the difficulties many managers have in learning about each new environment. On the issues of communication, control and staffing policies, March's findings are more speculative. Questionnaires are not perhaps the best means of determining how, for example, control is really exercised. Yet his findings are quite consistent with those of other studies in other parts of the world. [2] Such consistency suggests a degree of universality rather than regional idiosyncrasy in the underlying problems of designing effective international management systems. Thus training to help improve on the current situation demands a global perspective.

Treating the issues at the level of the system can readily have the effect of imposing the resulting universality. It is clear that firms are unable or unwilling to attempt to adjust their international mechanisms to all the particular local circumstances they encounter, because when added together local tailor-made systems unrelated to company-wide policies yield more confusion than control. The chapters on company programmes take this problem as a point of departure. Nevertheless, at the level of the operations of the firm within any one country, it is equally clear that offsets to the general system are imperative if effective action by local managers is to be induced.

The local chief executive can be regarded as a lynch-pin in the system. For headquarters he must interpret his local actions in terms of the common language of the system. For his subordinates he must provide some insulation from the general system, because it is not likely to be understood in its 'pure' form. Simultaneously he must educate his team in the methods, procedures and skills that together provide the distinctive strength of his international firm, as was the case for Dunlop in Nigeria. There is a dilemma. If he is a local national, how does this man learn enough about the world system and his parent company to provide for the first part of his dual task? If he is an expatriate, and especially if he is resident for only a short span, how does he learn enough, quickly enough, to provide for the second part? The Mobil programme confronts this dilemma, but does not entirely resolve it.

Redding picks up some of the issues involved in the dilemma by examining the philosophical premises on which educators from the West (and hence by inference the managers as well) approach the oriental mind. He demonstrates the ineffectiveness of Western logical premises ./hen faced with Confucian philosophies. In particular he points to two oriental behavioural characteristics that inhibit the successful communication of ideas. First is the 'modest behaviour' of the student (subordinate) when faced with the teacher (superior) whose word is taken as gospel. Second is the tradition of learning-by-rote that gets in the way of experiential methods of instruction.

Redding argues that the apparently fundamental differences between the philosophies are eroding slowly as Western concepts change by discarding deterministic, logical models in favour of more contingent and pluralistic descriptions of managerial behaviour. In other words, the next generation of Western managers as well as teachers may find that their ability to communicate and instruct in the East will be enhanced as will, one hopes, their ability to listen to and learn from their hosts. Redding may be too optimistic in his sense of convergence but nevertheless he implies an important challenge for the institutions adequately to adapt their programmes, and their capacity to generate adequately robust philosophies.

Company programmes

Some companies are attempting to cope with all the multi-faceted demands by developing their own in-house programmes. The three chapters on specific company initiatives suggest the extent to which the 'customer' is beginning to eschew traditional sources of supply. To some extent they describe a logical response to the supply difficulties described by Robinson. All three studies – on IVECO, Mobil and Dunlop – show remarkable consistency in accepting that the organisation needs to learn from the experiences of the individuals who together define the system. This point is really yet another way of saying that the demand side of our model is perhaps best defined by the consumers not the customers.

The particular training tasks described in these studies are quite distinct and occur at different levels in the organisation. Together they suggest the range of training tasks. For IVECO, the central problem is the creation of a brand-new company in which formerly independent national companies in Italy, France and Germany need to be welded into a coherent whole. To do this effectively, there was a strongly felt need to develop a new 'meta-culture'. This need provided the objective for the programme. The setting is the broad band of senior management and the process, to be effective, is soon seen to require the active participation of board members in an evolving learning system. For Mobil the canvas is broader in that more countries are involved, but the task is simpler as only one set of training needs is being tackled. Here one sees the conscious attempt to superimpose another version of a company culture upon national operating units as part of a wider policy of improving communications and the effective functioning of individuals within the established system. Whereas both the IVECO and Mobil programmes span many countries, the Dunlop programme is concerned with a single country, Nigeria. For the Nigerian subsidiary, the training task is the local inculcation of technical and managerial thinking in a form that both respects the local way of doing things, so as to be acceptable and useful, and at the same time enchances the ability of Dunlop to transfer technology [3] and so provide in Nigeria commercial strength that purely local firms find hard to achieve. By observing this general process in the setting of a developing country lacking much of the infrastructure taken for granted elsewhere, this chapter highlights many of the problems of managing effective transfers of thinking that exist elsewhere.

Of particular interest in all three companies is the changing role of the trainers; the 'internal' educators as opposed to 'external' ones from academic institutions or consulting firms. McAllister's work with IVECO on long-term contract can perhaps be described as internal once he had built the necessary bases of trust and friendship. As the credibility of the learning process in these companies has increased, so the training has tended to become a *line* function rather than a peripheral staff, personnel one. The trainers become part of a management team tackling current problems and being measured, most noticeably in Mobil, by standard principles of performance against budget like any other manager. Their success is affected by their own managerial skills as much as by their abilities to teach and train.

The three chapters show how these organisations have learned to use the ranks of external helpers in highly discriminating and sparing ways on the assumption that the knowledge, attitudes and skills needed to cope with their problems is already within the total experience of that organisation. What is needed is a rigorous process by which such experiences can be released and put to work on solving the problems. Therefore, knowledge, attitudes and skills existing outside the organisation might help set the context in which, or process by which, an organisation starts its self-learning activity — but it is not necessarily crucial to it. Moreover, knowledge needed to solve specific problems tends to be generated increasingly in-company once such a learning activity gets under way. The use of consultants from outside therefore tends to be infrequent, of very short duration, and highly demanding. This seems to pose a series of related problems about the future roles of educational institutes and consultants; the logic of this development is to contain the supply and demand functions within each organisation, with only specific and short-term demands being made outside the organisation. Perhaps this is one of the few ways that the educational institutions could cope with the new demands at present?

Internal problem-centred activities point to the use of such approaches as action learning. Indeed McAllister explicitly advocates them, as does Harper in the context of developing countries. Such advocacy, however, needs to be evaluated very carefully. Blind rejection of conventional 'content' rather than 'process' approaches merely replaces one dogma with another.

On this issue the reader is no doubt immediately aware that the general debate is probably of more consequence than its application to the special case of international training. As we stated earlier, we do not consider this book the appropriate setting for a rehearsal of all the matters at issue. We would point instead to two items. First, as Eccles suggests in his chapter on the design of programmes, the distinctions between the 'process' and 'content' approaches tend to become blurred in the classroom or wherever the learning is taking place, particularly when the instructor is highly skilled. Second, it is noticeable in McAllister's description of the IVECO programme that international content is taught in conventional ways as a *prelude* to the more process- and problem-centred activities that occur at later stages of the desired organisational learning. In other words, a blend of different approaches seems both desirable and possible. Nevertheless one must recognise the very serious obstacles confronting trainers and educators who might wish to create such a blend of approach. As Robinson and Harper among others point out, conventional academic career and reward systems do not encourage such activity. Besides, the administrative complexities can rapidly increase beyond the capacity of most existing systems.

Adapting the 'traditional' supply

Three chapters look at different aspects of the need to consider new methods of supply of international training. Eccles takes the position of the designer of a range of programmes to meet a wide range of types of need. De Bettignies describes a

France-Indonesia initiative in 'packaged' instruction and its impact on the teachers and their home institution in France.

Schnapper is an independent trainer, tied neither to an academic institution nor to a company, who has developed a new approach to training for cultural sensitivity and personal change. Eccles makes a number of valuable points about what designers of international programmes need to take into account. He concentrates on the need to balance all the ingredients in the assembled 'package' so as to provide an appropriate mixture of subjects and context for the individuals in question. By placing various standard types of programme on a continuum that ranges from a mono-cultural context to a pluralistic one, Eccles demonstrates that none of them meets all the international requirements for training where the main objective is to induce effective post-programme behaviour. In so doing he raises fundamental questions about the nature of the required supply of teaching and the capacity of institutions to manage the supply. Institutions need to consider more carefully than hitherto the timing of various types of inputs in the mixture of standard approaches he advocates. Yet quite how they should do so remains unanswered.

Eccles also poses the question of what type of training the faculty should themselves undergo to become more effective. Just as Barron identifies managers' career structure as an important ingredient affecting the changing nature of the demand, Eccles indicates a need for a more carefully considered approach to the career and developmental needs of the suppliers. He is in effect echoing Nehrt's plea and beginning to specify component pieces of the need for different types of programme.

De Bettignies takes one aspect of the supply problem in his description of the design of the INSEAD programme for senior Indonesian officials. He starts from the proposition that our conventional approaches to the transfer of management 'know-how' are probably asking the wrong questions and are thus ineffective. He rehearses at some length all the considerations he and his team at the Euro-Asia Centre have attempted to take into account so as to 'increase participants' capacity to define issues and problems in ways which make *culturally acceptable solutions* easier to identify clearly and to implement'. His purpose was not merely to hand over techniques that have proved successful elsewhere. His chapter elaborates the arguments articulated by Harper and Redding and then places them within the context of a specific supply requirement.

Implicit in de Bettignies' treatment of how his programme was designed is the effect upon the faculty involved. He concludes that, to be effective, the designers must 'unlearn' much of their prior perceptions. 'Unlearning' is, of course, merely another way of saying that new learning is needed. By taking to heart his strictures on the limitations of conventional wisdom, one can begin to see glimmerings of what is needed by way of career development for those faculty members who are going to be increasingly involved in international programmes.

There is another aspect of such possibilities for new learning. Those who teach on international programmes also teach on purely domestic ones. They can bring back to their home environment new insights and approaches that can improve their own teaching. The University of Montreal, for example, has had considerable exposure to foreign conditions as a result of developing management programmes in Algeria. One recent report summed up the benefits. 'Plunged into a totally different environment, they (the faculty) often returned with a far more rigorous and less complaisant attitude to their own science or art.' [4]

Transferring managerial techniques and approaches from France to Indonesia, or from Canada to Algeria, involves the crossing of wide cultural distances. The very width of the gap to be bridged makes it perhaps easier to perceive the need to recognise explicitly the cultural dimension of the training requirement than it is when one is dealing with much more proximate cultures. Yet is the need any less within Europe? Drew and Mant among others would answer with a clear 'No'. That perception is, sadly, not widely recognised and its absence is likely long to remain a constraint on the development of appropriate culturally-based training.

Schnapper examines another version of this constraint. His concern is the design of programmes to be run within a

single organisation, where managers typically do not recognise
the need for cultural awareness. He starts from the premise
that there is a need for a balance between thought content
(*vide* Drew's argument) and the experiential process. His
chapter does not elaborate on the first part of the balance as
this is not his area of expertise or concern. His objective, like
Mant's and de Bettignies,' is to provide training that helps
the individual to learn to adjust to different cultures without
at the same time losing his own cultural identity. He dwells
on the processes by which the particular needs for training
in any one organisation need to be properly identified and
elaborates on the specifically international aspects both of
that process and of the training that follows. Though he claims
great effectiveness for his approach he admits that most
organisations remain resistant to the basic idea. He attributes
much of the resistance to the fact that few senior managers
have a clear understanding of just how far cultural differences
can affect economic performance. His sense of resulting
confusion and relative lack of a clearly perceived demand
function — by the customer, *not* the individual consumer —
echoes Robinson's view. In effect Schnapper's analysis brings
the argument back full circle. He does, however, indicate
that new supply possibilities abound and that priority should
be given to the demand side of our equation. We remain
somewhat sceptical: Schnapper's prescriptions for supply
are unlikely to be adopted by most of the institutions providing
the great bulk of available training, because of their internal
rigidities described above.

The challenge

Implicit in all these chapters is the sense that neither suppliers
nor customers feel as much urgency as do the consumers for
change in current approaches to international management
development. New training initiatives are likely only when
the customers perceive clear economic or political gains from
the required investment in new approaches and new training
skills. Those perceptions, despite all the increased internationalism of contemporary economic life, are in their

infancy and are likely to grow only slowly as industry, true to its usual form, reacts sluggishly to past changes. Our concern is that sluggish responses are not good enough for the 1980s. Rapid change, turbulence and discontinuity in the global environment makes it imperative that ways be found quickly for organisations to learn to keep up to date. As Reg Revans once said, an organisation has to design its systems of learning so that its learning is equal to, or greater than, the rate of change in its environment. It is no longer any excuse to say that the other organisations are not changing.

Yet individual managers and a few organisations do see the new demands clearly. Individuals provide the base for new forms of demand for international training. They feel, as so many chapters in this book show, the need for help. Given adequate encouragement and appropriate experience-sharing mechanisms, they could push both their own organisations and the traditional institutions in new and productive directions. Can the suppliers preserve their existing strengths and add extra ones? That is the challenge. Much still needs to be done to sharpen the concepts and focus the needs so that the challenge may assume tangible form. We hope that this book makes a contribution to this developmental process so that our map may begin to take on the precision of the Ordnance Survey and dispel the uncertainties that surround the existing Ptolomeic version.

Notes

[1] S. Altman, D. Kujara, G. Sutija, 'A survey of academic deans in the US, Europe and Latin America on trends in management education over the next decade', paper presented to Academy of International Business, June 1979.
[2] March provides an extensive and useful bibliography in which he cites some of the evidence, but omits reference to some studies that give powerful support to his tentative conclusions. The reader interested in European evidence might wish to consult the classic and largely ignored study by D. Van Den Bulke, *Les Entreprises Etrangères dans l'Industrie Belge,* Gand, L'Office Belge pour l'Accroissement

de la Productivité, 1971.

[3] The general debate on the transfer of technology to developing countries concentrates (wrongly) on the purely scientific or engineering aspects. Properly speaking, management ought to be included as an integral part of the technology transferred in a form capable of creating local wealth. See Chapter 17 for an elaboration of this point.

[4] Editors' translation from the French in A. Poirier, 'Reflexions sur la Gestion du Projet HEC — DPGE', HEC Montreal Working Paper, 1979.

PART I
THE DEMAND:
ISSUES AND ENVIRONMENT

2 The US Market for International Business Teaching

RICHARD D. ROBINSON

The purpose of the inquiry reported here was to develop a more precise notion of the quality and relevance of international business management education at the graduate level in the United States. Initially it was hoped that international personnel executives in a sample of relatively large internationally-active firms scattered across the country would be able to rate programmes and describe very specifically what they liked or did not like about them so that some measure of relevance could be developed. It turned out, however, that these executives possessed little information about such programmes. Indeed few corporate executives, other than in some of the large banks, reflected more than casual interest. The corporations simply did not recruit international business majors as suggested by prior research.

Questions about what business schools should be doing in the international area generated somewhat more response. Although many opinions were voiced on the subject, those responding seldom indicated any insight into what schools were in fact doing. Nonetheless, the interviews, which were completed in Janaury 1978, provide some market measures of relevance. Hence, the chapter begins with an analysis of the demand side of the equation.

Survey of perceived business needs: the demand side

Perhaps the best way to define the apparent market for those coming out of graduate schools of business and management with majors or concentrations in international business is to describe the responses of some of the 18 companies in which interviews were conducted. The consistency of these responses seemed to rule out the need for a larger sample.* Due to promises of confidentiality, the identities of the firms are not disclosed.

In each case the purpose was to solicit information on corporate hiring policies (with special reference to international operations) and attitudes possibly relevant to those policies; on the extent of corporate training programmes to prepare employees either for overseas assignment or for positions with international content; on executive views of international management training offered by graduate schools of business; on the identification of any special educational needs not being addressed by the schools.

The banks seemed to be the only category of institution specifically interested in MBAs with a concentration in international business. Even so, they were not enthusiastic about the business school products. A serious deficiency in financial accounting was identified, particularly that required for credit analysis. It was felt that some schools had a tendency to lose the management perspective, particularly Harvard and Sloan. This defect was present in the international courses as well as elsewhere. Some executives felt that the 'better' schools were prone to permit professors to use classes to explore their research interests rather than to develop what students needed to know. On the other hand, schools such as The American Graduate School of International Business (Thunderbird) were criticised for spending too much time on language, too little time on technical business courses.

Executives in one bank believed that schools should offer international courses carefully differentiated from on-the-job

---

* The sample consisted of four financial institutions (two east coast, one south-east, one west coast), two engineering construction firms (one east coast, one west coast), one raw material processor (west coast), nine manufacturers (one west coast, five mid-west, one east coast, two south), one oil and energy-related firm (east coast). In most instances at least two, and frequently more, executives were interviewed.

All were major corporations (top 500) except two of the financial institutions. One of the engineering construction firms was a semi-autonomous subsidiary, otherwise all were independent.

training, but not too general so as to carry little content. They felt that emphasis should be placed on an understanding of the international economic and monetary systems, on balance of payments, on sovereign risk, on trade flows and their meaning, comparative business practice, public finance, inflation accounting: not on 'management science'. In one instance, a 'silent performer' did not do well. The art of making presentations was of signal importance, likewise writing skills. These were felt to be a communicable skill. The implication was, given the context of the discussion, that these skills were of special importance in the international area.

Spokesmen for the bank recognised that there was a visa problem in hiring foreign nationals for permanent employment in the US. Headquarters hoped to find foreign students who could qualify for permanent residency, particularly in that part of the organisation serving US-based 'multinational corporations'.* After a foreign national was hired, the bank would go to work immediately to secure the 'green card'. In one division some 40 per cent of the headquarters' personnel were non-American; in the UK about 40 to 50 per cent non-UK nationals. The objective was 'to hire a multinational *talent* base to handle a multinational *client* base'. Prior to overseas assignment (a 90 to 180-day lead time was attempted), the executive received intensive language training if the business language was non-English. Other than Japanese and Chinese, the assignee was generally fluent in the language before departure. The bank was happy with Berlitz in that the training was one-on-one, done by native instructors, and worked cultural mores into the training. The bank also arranged for wives to meet with bank wives who had lived in the area of assignment.

One bank executive observed that there had been a slowdown in the bank's international growth rate over the past decade. Did people now feel that the challenge was gone and, hence, were not as motivated as before? He was uncertain,

---

* In quotes, for the use of the phrase multinational corporations was not technically correct in that international, transnational, and international service organisations were included.

but did observe that the average age and tenure in the job was going up. This bank had a special 'international staff' consisting of approximately 1,000 US expatriates and third country nationals who were willing to work up to two years outside their home country. It was claimed that this corps 'glued the corporation together worldwide' in that it consisted of a special set of people – mature, knowledgeable of the corporate ethic, highly mobile. Until recently, virtually all had been US nationals, but the influx of non-US nationals had increased during the past five years. A recognised problem was that such an organisation generated a sharp distinction between international and domestic. It was expected that top corporate executives would emerge from this international staff. The bank's UK subsidiary had begun hiring UK nationals from Oxford and Cambridge – 'liberal arts types' – for the UK management. According to bank spokesmen, this was the first time that a UK bank had hired college graduates.*

A second bank, like the first, had drawn fairly heavily on graduates from the Thunderbird School. The reason seemed to be that such people had demonstrated a commitment to international careers and had working knowledge of at least one foreign language. 'For banks particularly, the top quality MBA often has more difficulty in adjusting, particularly those from Harvard. Expectations are entirely too high.'

This second bank seemed to be looking for a demonstration of interest and ability on the part of young men and women to get along in a foreign culture, plus intellectual capacity and maturity. 'What we are really looking for is one who can become a qualified banker and, on top of that, has the personality and interest to work satisfactorily in international. We do not assume, or look for, expertise that can be put to work immediately.' In respect to the desired international content of a business school, the executive observed, 'most important to us is (1) general understanding of how the world operates (including an historical perspective), (2) knowledge of the international economic and financial sys-

---

* Editors' note: This is so far from the case that it provides another instance of ignorance.

tems. Thunderbird does not do this.' As this statement contradicts those in the previous paragraph, the presumption is that weight is given to personal mobility and language ability, not knowledge.

An international executive for a large west-coast bank observed that what his institution really looked for was those who had completed solid courses in accounting and finance. Knowledge of international finance would give them a small edge. With more and more units overseas, he felt that the bank was giving more emphasis to managerial ability. 'We are hiring potential managers, those with the ability to get along with people and can communicate well — people-oriented individuals'. Exposure to a superior international business programme was considered a plus, but was not critical. Educational needs would be an understanding of what was involved in an international career and of the international economic order, a definition of issues. The chairman of a relatively small west-coast bank, but one of regional significance and which had been expanding rapidly into the Pacific basin, observed that a demonstrated international interest on the part of a job applicant would be given some weight. However, almost all overseas positions were filled by foreign nationals.

In general, spokesmen for the engineering and construction firms echoed similar views. Neither hired MBAs. The first did not hire in the US for its overseas offices, and a young engineer hired in the US would not be sent overseas for many years. A vice-president observed: 'If a man with a relevant technical background had some international management training (or an MBA) plus a language, we would be interested'. (But the firm had not recruited in a nearby academic institution with precisely that mix.) It was felt necessary to bring foreign nationals reaching top positions to the US for a management course, such as that offered by Columbia. This experience, it was felt, gave them more confidence in dealing with Americans. 'A foreign national who finds himself in a senior position in a foreign company tends to worry, to feel somewhat threatened'. It was recognised that the company lost technical expertise as some of its more senior engineers moved into project management and departmental administration. On the other hand, it was felt that having non-engineers managing engineers, including the more senior, would cause friction and loss of morale.

A larger, west-coast engineering construction firm was hiring new technical personnel to go overseas within a relatively short lead time. It would prefer to send experienced company employees and, indeed, some clients specified such, but that was not always possible. When possible, the firm brought people to headquarters first to become oriented with the company, during which time they were used on various tasks in the personnel division. Language training was provided if there were enough time. One of the problems arising quite frequently, it was claimed, was that many people were sent overseas for relatively short periods of places with no facilities for families and no recreational opportunities. The one motivating factor had to be compensation. 'But once a person is there, money is less important.'

Major academic deficiencies perceived in the international area were the absence of work in international construction management and inattention to the problem of lack of mobility. This firm had an older, highly mobile cadre of craftsmen (iron workers, pipe fitters etc.) often used overseas in a teaching capacity, but among newer people, the esprit de corps relative to overseas work appeared lost. 'There is a different attitude.' The younger generation seemed to be less mobile.

As for the engineering construction firms, the one west-coast raw material processor in the survey used largely technical personnel in its overseas operations. It did not hire directly for international operations. This corporation had passed through the international division phase into global product lines which in turn maintained regional headquarters. The 'international division' remained as a corporate support group and policy co-ordinator. Although at corporate head-quarters some expertise was employed in international finance (a Stanford MBA), economic forecasting and inter-national tax law, it was very unlikely that MBAs would be directly employed in international operations. Those sent overseas must rate high in inter-personal skills and flexibility and must have demonstrated a high level of technical expertise ('we do not want second rate people overseas').* As one executive commented, 'Unless a person has a language or life experience in an area, international business education is not relevant; one can learn the basic business skills'.

How should educational resources be allocated within the international management area? Responses to this question suggested the objectives should be to create an awareness of the strategic alternatives and the range of relevant variables, to develop knowledge of the basic principles and issues, to generate familiarity with the different concepts of what the law means and how it is used, to teach how to work effectively within any system and not to be surprised by anything.

Executives in a west-coast manufacturing firm expressed no interest in the general preparation provided by international management courses. 'But continuing education is another matter. There is a need for management to be aware of, and sensitive to, major issues.' As in the preceding case, this firm had gone through the international division phase to worldwide product organisation, with each operating organisation in charge of its own international operation. In this company, all overseas personnel had to acquire, by operating experience, a unique set of technical skills. Family stability, plus some language, were seen as secondary criteria. The company provided language labs. As one executive observed, 'We keep Berlitz in business'. The company was running training programmes for individuals and their families prior to overseas assignment. Business schools were seldom used for this purpose, but Thunderbird and the Universities of Syracuse and Columbia had been used to train people for specific assignments (i.e. area study plus language).

A mid-western manufacturer of technologically-advanced

---

* The backgrounds of headquarters personnel in the 'international division' was as follows: a senior VP in charge, who was likewise head of an operating division; a Harvard law graduate who had become involved in a number of international projects during his career with the company; his principal assistant who had come up through a product division, and had asked for overseas assignment in the Far East; and a second assistant who was a graduate in international affairs, a former political science professor with special expertise in Latin America.

equipment specified 'no Americans overseas' as company policy. There was a tendency to bring foreign nationals to the US to be socialised in the company. Later, they might return in top corporate positions in the parent corporation, although this had not yet happened. Periodically US nationals were assigned overseas for purposes of personal development, but this was not part of a formal career development programme. International experience was considered desirable but not essential for top management. There was allegedly a 'closed mind attitude to outside training and the use of consultants'. A short time before, foreign manufacturing had been organised into product groups because of a world-wide sourcing strategy. This reorganisation had created a serious problem in that managers had been assigned global responsibility who had no prior experience. If a person were promising and had indicated a strong preference for international, he would be given some consideration, but there was no career development path involving international; job content was considered the same world-wide, and each country manager was responsible for recruiting his own people. Even though no formal preparation was given when overseas postings occurred, the failure rate was alleged to be very slight. What was usually involved, however, was a senior management assignment, for a person very likely to have travelled extensively before hand. Language knowledge was an asset, but not deemed important.

In the case of a southern-based corporation involved in the manufacture of closely related lines of consumer goods, overseas companies asked the parent company to fill positions only if they were unable to find appropriate people locally. The parent firm would be involved only in the appointment and transfer of plant, marketing, financial and technical managers. Previously, the company had been divided into a number of zone offices, located in various places, which reported to an export corporation. Subsequently, these offices had been disbanded and the world divided into three 'groups', all of which were headquartered in the parent corporation. One consequence was that foreign nationals were beginning to appear in headquarters' positions. In international operations, training was generally of an on-the-job nature. It was felt that it was very difficult for a school to prepare a young American for international service who had never been outside the US. 'The most important thing a young guy can have is the language, at least to some degree', one executive observed. When the 'intercultural communications' sequence offered at one graduate school was described, the response was, 'That is the sort of thing that really pays off. To us this is one of the most important things.'

A mid-western manufacturer of heavy industrial equipment, whose foreign operations were managed by an international division, had an explicit policy of having all overseas operations managed by foreign nationals. At the same time it was explicit policy that to advance to the top required international experience. About four years before, the company had begun an international recruiting programme in Europe. An executive explained, 'We designed the system, selected the schools and recruiters and picked the pre-screening candidates'. Active recruiting of foreign nationals was done at INSEAD, Stanford, Harvard and London. Some recruiting was done at Thunderbird, but 'it has more Americans'. The firm had a long-term recruiting relationship with Harvard and Stanford, both of which had many foreign nationals. A few years ago, the firm had looked at a number of European schools. It ruled out IMEDE because its people were already spoken for. INSEAD was seen as having a 'super programme'. London was rated as 'questionable', but it was used occasionally. Foreign nationals were hired in the US at a US salary. Normally they would work for two years in the US and then be assigned for employment elsewhere. If they were hired in Europe, they were sent to the US for 18 months' training. If they wanted to stay, the company sponsored them for permanent residence. The standards for US and foreign nationals were the same – technical skills, language capability and cultural familiarity. There was a special problem with UK personnel, who all wanted to stay in the US. Insofar as US nationals were concerned, the firm was interested in language skills and a strong commitment to international, plus the relevant technical skills, 'the Peace Corps type'. (Interestingly enough, one of the banks and one of the engineering construction firms had reacted negatively to the

'Peace Corps type' as being incompatible with their respective organisations; they were seen as a possible source of friction.) Although a foreign subsidiary could refuse to hire job candidates suggested by the parent company, it 'better have a damn good reason'. Apparently, this problem had arisen particularly in the case of the UK subsidiary, whose managers were biased against hiring MBAs.

This particular firm was one of the few which had formed an 'international cadre', membership of which was insensitive to nationality. Those indicating a desire for a career for a period of time which involved living overseas had a good chance of acceptance into the cadre, provided they had the potential (technical skills etc.). 'There is always a trade-off between technical skills and cultural skills and adaptability.' The director of development and training knew of no institutions trying to generate cultural skills in the US. At one time Indiana University wanted to sell a programme of cultural training, but the company was not convinced of its quality. 'It sounded naive. . . What we look for are people who are brighter than hell', 'have a high personal energy level', 'have language and cultural skills (an understanding of the literature, customs, history)', 'have a sense of ethics and a value system which treats people with dignity and respect.' He added, 'If a programme reinforces these things, great. Any school can teach financial analysis and the like, which are critical and have to be taught, but what about the social sciences? Also, what sort of people are brought into the programme? I am very dubious about those who were in business as undergraduates and then go on to business school. We prefer other backgrounds, breadth. A person has to be able to adapt to a rapidly changing environment and to ambiguity, and to like it'. The corporation had used the Sloan programme at Stanford, the Aspen Institute, and the Salzburg seminar as growth experiences for top executives.

A large southern-based corporation, a supplier of high technology goods and services to the energy and resource industries, was organised into some ten or so product groups with global responsibilities. It also maintained three overseas regional offices for coordination and marketing purposes. It did not have a formal career development programme, and international experience was not a necessity for advancement to the top. Recruiting was done at the group level, each of which was largely self-contained. In discussing the educational problem, the director of international planning observed, 'The US does not grow international businessmen. We are not an exporting country. In some other countries they think exports. You can train people in international finance and the like, but how do you train a person to be an international exporter? Generally, the graduates of US business schools are not prepared for international business'. In selecting personnel for overseas assignment, the firm looked for technical competence, experience, adaptability, understanding of other ways to do business. There was an explicit policy to reduce US expatriates to a minimum, and, with very few exceptions, no foreign nationals were recruited within the US. Foreign nationals were sometimes brought to the US for training, particularly for a new operation overseas. For example, the top management cadre for a new European plant was brought to the US for six months, but they were hired out of related industries within the country concerned.

Executives in a large mid-western, multi-product manufacturing enterprise professed an explicit corporate philosophy that familiarity with international operations was needed for all top corporate executives. There was, however, no career development planning except at the very senior level, and it was a corporate objective to have all off-shore subsidiaries managed by local nationals. One major product division of this corporation had had over half of its business overseas and had long used a system of a 'corporate foreign service'. A major problem however with permanent foreign service personnel was that they lost any direct contact with headquarters in the US. For example, a US national was leaving a Latin American assignment and being replaced by a local national who had no direct personal links with headquarters. Another problem arose because the corporation was beginning to develop products for the world market, not merely for national or regional markets, yet only about half of the corporation's executive VPs had had any international experience. As production and markets were integrated, there would be opportunity for more top management candidates to get international experience and there would be fewer and fewer foreign service people.

The manager of the management personnel planning department observed 'Anyone coming out of an MBA programme would be out of his mind if he did not have international exposure, a major exposure. Perhaps that is an answer to the dilemma we face. There is no longer any such thing as designing (one of our products) without considering the international aspects. The new guy coming in should recognise that his management concerns are going to be with international issues'. He added that in his judgement the Thunderbird School did not meet this requirement and that eventually it would disappear.

The European subsidiaries of one corporation had gone from semi-autonomous companies in each country to more of a regional product orientation. The international division in headquarters had become an administrative support unit leaving manufacturing in Europe to be run from the major European subsidiary, and sales to be run by the global product management. One effect of this new organisation was to cut down on jobs through which US nationals could gain experience overseas. The trend was to look for management candidates with US experience. There was also a real need to develop a better system for transferring people back into US operations. The company had a long history of taking specialists from domestic operations and assigning them abroad where needed, but reabsorbing these people once the need overseas expired was another matter. As the re-entry difficulty became known, it became difficult to find good candidates to fill the overseas needs which remained.

In a large eastern-based manufacturer of high technology products, which were sold globally with little modification, marketing, service support, and general coordination were the responsibility of several regional headquarters. Corporate headquarters, itself becoming increasingly internationally minded, was still managed essentially by US nationals. The objective was to develop local national managers overseas and the percentage of US nationals with foreign experience was dropping. For example, in one region 33 of the 45 countries had local nationals as country general managers.

There was also a growing tendency to bring foreign executives into US headquarters in significant jobs. The corporation had set up no programmes to prepare US nationals for overseas assignment. Nor had any programmes been designed for the executive with new international responsibility, even though, in percentage terms, fewer and fewer US executives were being sent overseas on long-term assignment. Many were working constantly with various countries, travelling extensively, and occasionally given the opportunity for some external training. Mentioned were the Aspen programmes on Asia and Japan, the CEI, Columbia's four-week programme for international executives, and a three-week international executive training programme to which sessions on 'cultural patterns' were added.

One manager pointed out that 'most US businessmen do not realise how complicated the national economic systems are (e.g. Brazil, Mexico), particularly in view of the role played by government'. Listed as emerging issues were nationalisation, balance of payments, equity considerations, cultural customs and a need for external affairs training. The external affairs staff in his firm had at least doubled in the last few years.

Similar experiences and attitudes were described in the other companies. Clearly there is no unanimity of view, but many issues relevant to the design of educational programmes in the international area emerge. These can be listed under three broad headings.

Issues of moving people internationally

The declining percentage of US nationals given long-term assignment abroad versus the need for language skills, cultural understanding, and adaptability. The requirement that substantial international experience is needed for promotion to the top versus the dwindling opportunity for American managers to accumulate meaningful overseas experience. The preparation of US nationals, often technical personnel, for relatively short-term assignment overseas, often with little lead time, or for assignments to develop local national replacements. The assignment of executives to global responsibility who have no prior international experience (such as occurs with the organisation of global product lines to replace an international division). The difficulty of training young Americans for international service without in-depth experience abroad. The legal (visa) and psychological problems of introducing foreign national managers into corporate headquarters on long-term assignment. The relative immobility of managers internationally.

General communication issues

The communications gap between a headquarters dominated by US nationals with little in-depth experience abroad and foreign subsidiaries managed very largely by local, or third country, nationals. The need for cultural empathy, to step outside one's own framework.

Problems with, and needs in, curricula

The loss of the managerial perspective in courses, particularly at the more prestigious, research-based graduate schools. Weakness in basic managerial skills — financial accounting, statistical analysis, written and oral communication. The fact that international management training at the MBA level is not likely to be relevant to one's job for several years after entry into corporate employ. Determining the appropriate apportionment of training between school and the corporation; the need to differentiate vocational training from professional academic preparation. Need on the part of all managers to understand the dynamics of the international economic and financial system, the implications of sovereign risk, comparative business practice, government finance, forms of government intervention, political ideologies, cultural differences and their implications, how the world operates (including an historical perspective).

It is also important to note the emergence of formal management training programmes (exclusive of the purely technical) within the corporate context. Eight of the 18 firms in which interviews were conducted had instituted such programmes, one of which was an accredited MBA course designed and manned by a local university exclusively for corporate personnel. None of these programmes as yet offered international business management as a separate and distinct subject of training, although there was serious discussion about this in two of the corporations.

Educational institutions most frequently mentioned as a source of internationalised managers were the Thunderbird School, Columbia Graduate School of Business (its one-month course for international executives) and INSEAD. Virtually nothing was known about the international business content of the curriculum offered by nearby (or more distant) schools. Nor was there any evidence, with but minor exceptions, that corporate officers were familiar with the names of the leading academicians in the international management field, nor with the relevant literature. Even in some of the very largest corporations in the sample, the principle international personnel officers had never heard of the Academy of International Business.

Three earlier studies of the demand side of the international business management education market complement the findings here.

Jesse Tarlton polled corporate views on the subject in a questionnaire-based study in 1976. [1] The answers presented an extraordinarily muddled picture; the one generally common experience reported being that very few, often none, of the MBAs recruited by the firms had been given any international responsibilities. Yet the study concluded that 'most of the respondents seemed quite interested in, even enthusiastic about, increasing the internationalization of the MBA program'. [2] The basis for this statement was not clear, nor was it clear whether the alleged enthusiasm reflected general corporate enthusiasm or merely a personal one. The author did admit, 'However, there was a significant and somewhat surprising number of responses which, while not negative, were at best neutral to any such trend, Apparently, some executives do not perceive there being very much value in having an international perspective in graduate programs from the standpoint of making the MBA more useful or valuable to their companies'. [3] Did these same people see any value in the MBA programme itself? We do not know.

Finally, the study concluded, on the basis of the responses, that if a school were to require only one IB course it should be international financial management, international finance, or international economics and finance. (It was not clear how these were differentiated in the minds of the respondents.)

If career patterns including foreign experience are related to demand for international business education a survey undertaken by the Task Force on Business and International Education in 1976 [4] is slightly more optimistic. Survey questionnaires were sent to the presidents and chairmen of the 100 largest industrial firms in the US, from whom 73 usable responses were received from 55 firms. Results showed that 25 per cent of the respondents had spent five or more years abroad for their companies; a 20 per cent increase over a similar survey in 1965. 'Of the 28 individuals who had had international responsibilities either in the US or abroad, only two (5 per cent) felt that their university courses had helped to prepare them for such responsibilities, while only three (11 per cent) had attended a management development programme with international content.' [5] It was also pointed out that whereas some 90 per cent of the firms represented had extensive international activity, only 35 per cent had in-house training programmes with any international content.

In a study of nine large companies with extensive international operations, the task force queried, via questionnaire, ten persons in each (four top managers, three middle managers and three lower managers). From formal records it was found that all of them had had at least one assignment with international responsibility in corporate headquarters or an overseas assignment. Eight of the nine companies responded with 73 usable replies. These indicated that none of the eight companies had a 'specific policy' of rotating people through international assignments on their way to the top although one did so as a matter of 'explicit practice'. The majority of the 73 executives involved had relied solely on on-the-job learning. [6]

Members of the task force used a Delphi process to arrive at a concensus on a number of questions relating to the types of international training and skills required by businessmen. The results indicated that: (a) the number of overseas managers will not be decreasing; (b) a very high percentage of all US business managers, at all levels and in all types of companies, whether or not they have international operations or are directly engaged in exporting, have need for knowledge of international business; (c) there will continue to be a growing need for both specialised and generalist types of international business skills; (d) 'solid' training in one of the functional fields of business should be understood to include the international aspects of that field; and (e) most of the generalist skills in international business are preferably taught in universities, while most of the specialist skills are best learned in executive development programmes or on the job. [7] Among the generalist skills considered important were such subjects as knowledge of the economy, politics, business practices and culture of a foreign country or region, international management skills, and working knowledge of a foreign language.

Survey of schools: the supply side

In order to select those US graduate schools of business and management deemed to have the best programmes in international business, past presidents of the Academy of International Business were asked to rank the ten best in their opinion (excluding the Sloan School at MIT, to avoid bias). Each was also asked to rank the ten North American academicians who had contributed most to the international business field.* Seven individuals, other than AIB past presidents, were named with sufficient frequency to warrant soliciting their ranking of schools, The result was that six of seven AIB past living presidents and five of the seven other scholars responded. Table 2.1 shows the result.

In order to report the quality and relevance of the international business management programmes offered by the 12 graduate schools (the 11 listed in Table 1, plus Sloan), a number of measures were developed. Conceptually, it proved impossible to separate quality from relevance unless one were

---

* The author was excluded from this ranking.

to impose a personal definition of quality. Or one could use the collective judgement of the 11-man panel by assuming that New York University, Harvard Business School and Columbia University programmes are the 'best' in some

Table 2.1

Ranking of the ten US graduate schools of business deemed to have the best international business programmes (excluding Sloan)

Rank	School	Score*
1	New York University	7.50
1	Harvard Business School[†]	7.50
3	Columbia University	7.33
4	University of California at Los Angeles	6.25
5	University of Pennsylvania (Wharton)	5.00
6	Georgia State University	3.17
7	University of Michigan	3.08
8	Indiana University	2.83
9	George Washington University	2.50
10	University of Washington	2.25
11	University of California (Berkeley)	1.33

* The score was calculated as follows: a ranking of first was scored 10, second 9, etc. The scores for each institution given by the 12 respondents were added and divided by 12.

† Technically speaking, Harvard does not have a 'programme' in international business.

Note: After the University of California, the scores dropped off abruptly.

generalisable way against which other schools might be compared. The difficulty is that the programmes in these three schools are very different and, indeed, Harvard does not even have an international business programme. A third approach would involve actually attending a sample of classes in all schools, which was clearly impossible. Therefore, in the measures used here there is no effort to separate quality from relevance. Each school was rated along ten dimensions, which were defined as follows:

1   Coverage of subject matter in a formal sense, specifically the listing of courses in international economics, international finance, international accounting, international business management, comparative organisational behaviour, comparative or international industrial relations, international marketing, private international law, language and area studies, international business policy, international technology transfer, environmental analysis (comparative economic and political systems). Scoring: (1) one to three areas covered; (2) four to six covered; (3) six to eight covered; (4) nine to eleven covered; (5) all twelve covered.

2   The degree of coherence or integration of the IB programme (i.e. degree of leadership, frequency of IB group meetings, physical proximity of IB faculty offices, existence of a special write-up of the programme, presence of joint research, absence of internal discord, presence of IB research seminars, existence of special IB facilities such as an IB seminar-library). Scoring: (1) weak (no IB programme or group as such); (2) below average (report of internal discord); (3) average; (4) above average (special IB facilities of some sort and/or frequent meetings); (5) strong (special IB facilities, an IB office suite, strong leadership, frequent interaction among IB faculty).

3   The extent to which the school seemed to avoid the 'trade school' or vocational approach (apparent in course titles; by definition the offering of an undergraduate IM course was evidence of some tendency in this direction). Scoring: (1) essentially vocational; (2) some vocational courses; (3) not more than two such courses; (4) no vocational courses, but does offer one or more undergraduate IB courses; (5) no apparent vocational courses, no undergraduate IB course.

4   The ability of the IB faculty to influence hiring and promotion. Scoring: (1) no influence; (2) weak influence; (3) moderate influence; (4) veto power; (5) IB faculty in control.

5   The existence of a language-area studies track. Scoring: (1) none; (2) one regionally-oriented course; (3) several regionally-oriented courses (re different regions); (4) only via joint degree route requiring added time; (5) a developed language-area track within the normal MBA programme.

6   The relative importance of management-related IB research. Scoring: (1) none; (2) modest amount; (3) average; (4) above average; (5) impressive (faculty time freed for research, independent funding).

7   The degree to which the IB group or department had succeeded in influencing the internationalisation of other groups or departments within the business school. Scoring: (1) not at all; (2) at least one other group or department; (3) two other groups; (4) three groups, plus a core IB course required for all students; (5) more than three groups, plus the required IB course.

8   Involvement by the IB group or department in continuing education programmes for practising managers. Scoring: (1) none; (2) sporadic, short-term; (3) involvement in one or more continuing programmes sponsored by the school, but limited to a minor role; (4) a major role (i.e. a distinct 'course') within such a programme on a repetitive basis; (5) involvement in executive training courses sponsored by the IB group or department.

9   The degree of student/faculty exposure to the international business community. Scoring: (1) virtually none (case writing only); (2) occasional (e.g. seminars or an international business club which invites practitioners as speakers); (3) presence of a business advisory committee; (4) required student projects which place them in direct contact with a business firm; (5) student internship within a business firm and/or high percentage of working students.

10   Degree to which students are discouraged from majoring in IB. Scoring: (1) encouraged; (2) encouraged, but with a minor in a functional area; (3) encouraged, but with a second major in a functional area; (4) required to have a dual major; (5) encouraged to major in a functional area and minor in IB, or no majors as such.

A reasonable rating of the 12 schools, based on personal interviews with two or more IB faculty members in each case on their respective campuses and study of written materials provided, would appear to be as indicated in Table 2.2. As in the company case, the identity of each school remains unspecified, for much information was collected on a confidential basis. All interviews were conducted between July 1977 and January 1978.

Admittedly the ratings are not objective measures. The rating process took place after completion of all field work and after studying notes and materials relating to each campus visit. It is clear that a prior judgement had been made that programme quality and relevance was a function, at least in part, of high scores along the ten dimensions listed above. At best, such an analysis is a mere proxy for direct measures. The excuse is that no way to effect such direct measures suggested itself, particularly in view of the admitted ignorance of corporate executives of programmes and the absence of any real consistency among the top-rated IB programmes. The only test of validity v·ould be to compare this subjective, one-man rating with the aggregate ratings (Table 2.1) given programmes by the leading scholars in the field. In fact no clear correlation was apparent. In any event, the problem in

Table 2.2

Aggregate ratings for the eleven schools on the ten dimensions (Sloan excluded)

School	Maximum 50
University of Pennsylvania (Wharton)	33
Columbia University	33
University of California at Los Angeles	33
Georgia State University	32
New York University	30
University of Washington	29
Indiana University	28
Harvard Business School	27
University of California (Berkeley)	26
University of Michigan	26
George Washington University	24

making such a comparison is, of course, the lack of an objectively-defined weighting scheme for the ten dimensions along which the schools are rated in Table 2.2. Lacking a compelling rationale for doing otherwise, the factor ratings have simply been added, which implies that all are equal in importance.

As can be seen readily, the spread is relatively minor. What are perceived to be strengths and weaknesses are relatively evenly distributed.

Table 2.3
Average score of all twelve schools along the ten dimensions
(Sloan included)

	Dimensions	Mean score	Range	Modal score
1	Coverage	2.5	2–4	2
2	Coherence	2.9	1–4	3/4
3	'Vocationality'	4.1	2–5	5
4	IB administrative influence	2.3	1–4	2
5	Language-area studies	2.0	1–5	1
6	Research	3.5	2–4	4
7	Internationalising influence	2.7	2–5	2
8	Continuing education	2.8	2–4	6
9	Business exposure	3.5	2–5	2/4
10	IB major	4.0	2–5	5
	Mean for all dimensions	30.3		

The conclusions to be reached are that the schools are consistently weak in coverage and in language-area studies. From an administrative point of view, the IB area in most schools seems to be weak in administrative influence, coherence, and participation in continuing education programmes. The schools seem generally responsive to market pressures in regard to discouraging an IB major without linkage to a functional area. The degree of business exposure seems relatively high, likewise the resistance to offering vocational-type courses. Research, as one might expect among these institutions, stands quite high.

Curiously, some of the subjects missing most frequently from the curriculum of the schools are among those mentioned most often by corporate executives as being desirable, specifically some variety of comparative organisational study, exposure to area-language studies which might sensitise students to both the differences and similarities among cultures, and international accounting. Only one school offered a fully-credited area studies-language option. One other held it out as an option via a joint degree which required an additional year. Only three US institutions are known to concentrate on this area of international business, the American Graduate School of International Business (Thunderbird), the Monterey Institute of Foreign Studies and the University of South Carolina. One suspects that the main obstacles in this case are time and money constraints, for in about half of the schools complaints were heard from the IB faculty about the rigidity and load of required core subjects. The lack of offerings in the comparative organisational field is clearly due in part to the non-availability of social psychologists concentrating in this area. Another area of weakness which showed up was the absence of political scientists active in IB programmes. Yet there is great need for a more sophisticated analytical approach to comparative political systems and assessment of political risk. Only one school seemed to have a strong offering in the international accounting area.

The ratings for coherence or integration of the IB programme was very much a function of leadership. Some of the obvious manifestations were the absence of 'backbiting' (which surfaced very quickly in three or four of the schools), the existence of special physical facilities (three schools), the frequency of meetings among the IB faculty (whether formal or informal), and of joint activities (such as an IB research seminar). Other than in one case, schools which rated relatively low on this dimension came out well down the list in terms of aggregate ratings. In three schools there was no IB group in any formal sense, either IB was not a recognised programme or the group was subordinated to a functional department, either policy or marketing. A strongly coherent IB group might either exercise considerable influence in internationalising other departments or isolate itself from the rest of the faculty. The mere physical distribution of the IB faculty offices, whether grouped together in a suite or scattered throughout the school, might be significant, but much depended, of course, on the personalities of the people concerned. In two cases the most respected senior IB faculty member had almost withdrawn from active interaction with the rest of the IB faculty. A safe generalisation, however, was that for the IB group to exercise a strong internationalising influence on the faculty generally requires some degree of coherence within the group.

Despite pressure from the American Assembly of Collegiate Schools of Business to provide training for 'domestic and worldwide' business needs, only two schools had what might be considered a required international course in the core curriculum. In one other case an international course was one of two or three options with which students might satisfy a core requirement in 'business and environment'. Nor had any school succeeded in internationalising any of the functional areas to a significant degree.

Several schools had attempted seminars for practitioners in the IB area, but had subsequently dropped the effort as being unrewarding; too few attended. With a few isolated and short-lived exceptions, no school had mounted any effort to market courses for the executive who is being given international responsibility for the first time or for the foreign national subsidiary manager to learn about the USA.

It seemed quite clear that the schools generally were not addressing themselves to the problems inherent in the increasingly common corporate situation where the parent headquarters is managed pre-eminently by US nationals with very little in-depth foreign experience, but who are supposed to deal effectively with overseas subsidiaries and affiliates managed almost entirely by local or thirdcountry nationals. Nor was anybody, except Monterey, offering courses for the engineer or technician being sent overseas on relatively short-term assignment.

Despite this apparent non-responsiveness of the schools to specific business needs, there were other forms of exposure to the international business community. Internship programmes and field projects were used on occasion. One school had an IB advisory group recruited from the surrounding business community and another was in the process of following suit.

Given the fact that very few business firms were specifically recruiting IB majors, schools which were actively encouraging a major in a functional area with only an IB minor were rated most responsive along this dimension. In fact only one school went so far as actually to encourage an IB concentration with only a minor in a functional area. All others at least encouraged a dual major, IB and a functional area. One *required* a dual major and six encouraged a functional major with IB as a minor. The tendency was definitely in the direction of at least a dual major.

In speaking of the relevance of an academic programme to the real world, there is always the danger of suggesting that academia should merely respond to the market rather than leading it. This study suggests that the IB programmes in the schools visited were doing neither very effectively. Insofar as the quality of IB programmes could be ascertained, in general they lacked integrated and consistent inputs from the functional specialists, i.e. the economists, political scientists, social psychologists and cultural anthropologists. Very frequently those who had become involved were inadequately aware of the other dimensions of international business management. Such an integration process is obviously difficult at best, but team-teaching suggests itself, team-teaching in which all members of the team attend all sessions of a given course. In no school was this approach being employed.

One also comes away from such a study as this with the strong suspicion that scarce educational resources are being wasted in the 'shot-gun' approach used by all the schools. That is, all students — many with but vague ideas as to their career paths — are required to take a myriad of courses, very few of which, incidentally, have an international content. One suspects that much more of a school's resources should be expended on mid-career programmes, or at least on programmes designed for the young manager (say, after five years of experience) who knows what he wants and needs.

In that case, of course, the programming response would have to be much more flexible so as to accommodate the student client. The IB area is not immune to the same charges. It may be useful to provide all students with some exposure to the nature of the international economic, financial, and political systems and to the impact of national economic, political, social, and cultural systems on organisational behaviour, but to go much beyond that until one knows what the student will actually need in his work life may lead to excessive waste of resources. This view was expressed frequently in various forms by both managers and academics during the course of this survey.

Finally, it came out quite clearly during this study that the importance of having a distinct IB group within a graduate school of business lies in the internationalising pressure on the system which it exerts — or could, if the group perceives of itself as occupying this role and not that of autonomous empire building. The internationalising role implies stimulating inter-disciplinary research projects by getting faculty in other groups or departments involved. It also involves developing and spinning off course, or stimulating their development, bringing visiting foreign scholars to the campus and generally arousing student interest in the international dimensions of business. In the one school in which the IB group had lost its identity, the entire curriculum and faculty seemed to be lapsing into a more domestic orientation.

A thought which came out of this study was that for the usual two-year MBA programme, a school might be well advised to separate the two years by five years or so of job experience. The student would then return with a much better idea of what skills and knowledge would be needed on the job. More intense international treatment would then be justified.

Appendix: four evolving models of international management education

One of the few institutions giving a masters in international business studies (MIBS) is the College of Business Administration at the University of South Carolina. The MIBS programme is divided into six segments:

1   Language instruction (June-August).
2   Business foundation course (September-May) — acquisition of fundamental business skills, during which time the student takes 'The Manager of the International Enterprise'.
3   Environmental variables course (June-July) — the study of the cultural and political background of the area which the student has selected for study and overseas job experience.
4   Additional language study — achieved overseas. The college has overseas language training centres in West Germany, Belgium, Colombia and Brazil. Students pay regular university tuition for this training.
5   Internship (September-February). The student is assigned to a firm overseas (the non-US student to a firm in the US) at no cost to the firm and no long term commitment. The nature of the internship assignment is subject to agreement by both the MIBS internship coordinator and the student. A performance appraisal is given by the firm.
6   Integration of concepts and skills development (March-May). Undertaken at the university, it includes a course in the overall strategy of the multinational firm, with emphasis on policy formulation and corporate planning. Also the student is given the opportunity to specialise in a particular area of business.

Another unique programme is that offered by the Monterey Institute of Foreign Studies, a privately-supported institution offering both BA and MA degrees in international economics and international management, international studies, languages and civilisations. The institute is departmentalised accordingly, the first being much the smallest in terms of students and faculty. Total enrolment is about 450, with a graduating class each year of about 100. Of these, only about 10 or 12 are in international economics and management. In addition the institute runs a special studies programme which undertakes to meet the specific needs of corporations and other institutions. For example, it has developed the capacity to give intensive work in English as a second language, coupled with some exposure to management. The course starts exclusively with English and then shifts to management as students build up an appropriate vocabulary. Students receive an introduction to analytical decision making, management information systems and quantitative reasoning. Instructors are recruited from area schools — Santa Clara, Santa Cruz, Stanford and the nearby Naval Postgraduate School. The institute is equipped to set up special courses in some 20 languages for corporate executives and their families. It is reported that Bechtel has been the largest user in preparing personnel for overseas assignment. The institute has also trained peace corps volunteers.

It is quite clear that the strength of the institute lies in its language and area studies programmes of varying lengths, not in the more substantive economics and management offerings. The point is that the total orientation of the institute is international, with the primary emphasis on languages and area studies. One can get a BA degree in international studies and then go on into the international management programme. The institute, however, prefers to take students with good liberal educations at the graduate level, which is a two-year programme. The work in intercultural communications leading to an MA degree is said to consist of highly sophisticated training and may well be the best available within the US.

Two other educational models relevant to international business management education are the Oxford Centre of Management Studies and the Administrative Staff College, both located in the United Kingdom. The Oxford Centre mans a small B. Phil management programme for Oxford University (10 students a year), a two-year graduate programe. But the main focus of the centre's operation is to serve the needs of some thirty corporate 'associates'. It does so by organising special programmes for groups of executives from individual companies, for multi-company groups, or for individual executives. These programmes involve anything from lecture series or workshops to consulting. An example of the latter would be meetings of higher level executives or directors from one corporation in which the centre's faculty participate as observers and commenters. Although it has not developed any specific international programmes, at least one faculty member was pushing in that direction in 1978.

Among the various programmes run by the Administrative Staff College at Henley-on-Thames is a one-month, mid-career executive programme called 'Directing Foreign Operations', which is perhaps something of a misnomer.* Course participants include individuals from LDC governments assigned to dealing with foreign business firms, from socialist enterprises in Eastern Europe, as well as business executives (largely from Europe, but occasionally laced with businessmen from other continents). The purposes include the broadening of perspectives in respect to geographical, sectoral and political environments (that is, developing insight into the distinctive problems associated with the first, second, third, and fourth worlds; public and private sectors; capitalist and socialist enterprises). A second objective is to improve interpersonal skills, particularly among people from these various environments. An important part of the process takes place via informal contact among the participants. The college is currently making plans so as to be better able to respond to the specific educational needs of international business and to constitute itself as an international centre for meetings of public and private managers from all over the world. Although the college runs degree courses (MBA and PhD), it has developed sufficient flexibility to mount a diversity of programmes.

---

* It was renamed 'International Management Programme' in late Spring 1978.

Notes

[1] 'Recommended courses in international business for graduate business students', *The Journal of Business,* October 1977, pp.438–47.
[2] Ibid., p.446.
[3] Ibid., p.446.
[4] *Business and International Education,* a report submitted by the Task Force on Business and International Education to the Government/Academic Interface Committee, International Education Project, American Council on Education, Washington, D.C. 1976; see also Chapter 8 in this volume.
[5] Ibid., p.11.
[6] Supra.
[7] Ibid., p.14.

3 Does the International Manager Exist?

ALISTAIR MANT

Each generation has to re-learn the wisdom of its parents and we cannot, it seems, accelerate the process. Knowledge can be crammed but wisdom announces itself in strange and unpredictable ways, usually after years of apparently fruitless struggle. These musings are prompted by considering the notion of the 'international manager' and his education. The more we consider him, the more he becomes a mythical beast — a new and insubstantial invention of our fevered twentieth-century minds. Before we bother ourselves about him, we need to be much clearer about the humble manager. Who he is? What does he think? How does he spend his time? Does the manager of the future have to learn new things or recollect things we have all but succeeded in forgetting? Probably the latter. Of course, it depends what we mean by 'international manager'. There is a world of difference between the careerist in the big multinational (the usual meaning) and the entrepreneurial business proprietor trying to flog his produce to the Bulgarians. We can play at 'internationalism' between Hiltons, or embassies; but the true internationalist can be a patriot too.

In considering the international manager it is possible that we may now be in the grip of a rather unhelpful polarity — on the one hand, a parochial, cautious, chauvinistic philistine-manager, with a mother-in-law in the next village and a weakness for real ale; and on the other, a sleek, multilingual-jargon hatchet-man with a broken marriage, 2.3 maladjusted children in his wake, and a credit card wallet like a gambler's deck. Patriotism does not really get a look-in with either stereotype. For the first, it is rather too much of a good thing, and for the second, it does not really matter at all or, worse, it has become a bad object.

It is not, or should not be, a matter of either/or, but a sensible blend of patriot *and* international man; a homebody with a healthy respect for his own *cultural* roots and those of others. Patriotism, along with such important but unmeasurable qualities as integrity, character, courage etc., is due for a revival. For the truth is that effective managers need leadership skills and those skills depend in the end on the capacity of an individual to seem to be *admirable* to his subordinates, colleagues and customers — and that means, among other things, having some roots.

In this respect, all managers can be regarded as the same. It may not be that we need a special type with special motivations for the international arena, but simply that only persons of high intelligence and strong character can stay the course in any managerial role in the future. Our confusion is that we have promoted to high rank so many people of mediocre intelligence and dubious character in the past. While accepting Elliott Jaques' view that there is always an absolute shortage of top-calibre people in the population, nonetheless, there must be thousands of able people, in intelligence and character, who go unrewarded because their mediocre seniors have not the wit to see these qualities for what they are. In fact, some people languish for years below their level of competence precisely because they do possess these qualities — the last thing a weak, amoral or stupid boss wants snapping at his heels is a strong, bright youngster with his values more or less intact.

Research findings

In 1977 [1] the author completed a study for the Department of Industry in the UK. This was an attempt to understand why managers from foreign-based multinationals obtained so much more productivity from British workers than indigenous firms. The tentative conclusion was that the managers exported from other countries to Britain were much more likely than their British counterparts to approach the managerial task *institutionally*. What is meant by this? They did not regard management as the application of the most cunning motivational techniques to the *people,* but as the application of technical skill to *task* within a sound and detailed constitutional framework. They had not, it seems, been *taught* this; it was the normal assumption of Swedish and Japanese industry. At the time a simple model was devised, an oversimple one no doubt, to illustrate the difference in approach.

The behavioural approach

On the one hand, the manager can proceed as if the task system is given and his main field of activity is in motivating people. There is nothing wrong with this so far as it goes, but it gives work relationships an *inter-personal* dyadic character; thus:

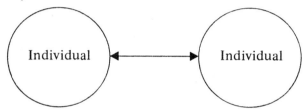

In the dyadic work relationship, the idea of 'master' and 'man' surfaces readily from the murky depths of the Industrial Revolution as conflicts arising at work tend to be seen as personal rather than in terms of the joint task.

The constitutional approach

On the other hand, in a triadic work relationship, it is as if both boss and subordinate are servants (though of a different kind) to an over-arching master — the task system; thus

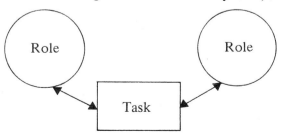

This was the implicit assumption of the foreign-based multinationals studied. They were not unmindful of people, but they assumed that there ought to be a watertight *policy framework* for that, so that managers and workers can get on with *work* without having to worry too much about being nice to each other. If the policy framework is sound, and detailed enough, we do not have to 'motivate' people.

In fact, the great charm of the British worker is that he is instantly suspicious when approached by a manager toting a motivational technique. The more we have approached the managerial task *behaviourally* — as though it is all about oiling inter-personal relationships — the more we have offended the worker in his role as *citizen* and the worse we have made our problems.

Thoughts on the research

The foreign worker will probably become more like the suspicious British worker wherever he finds himself managed by rootless, 'international' managers schooled in 'motivation'. Furthermore, the successful manager of the future is going to be, in fact, rather old-fashioned, not only task-oriented but also rather concerned with the constitutional arrangements of the firm. What is a constitution other than a written representation of the

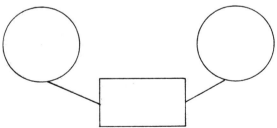

model? In other words, something which serves to clarify roles and *boundaries* between roles. Of course, talk of constitutional matters sounds to the brighter-eyed and bushier-tailed internationalist like a lot of fuddy-duddy red tape.

Indeed, the very idea of a *boundary* sounds hopelessly out of date to some people. They can be approached in two ways; either treat them as non-existent and trust that a smile and a warm handshake will carry all before them (the O————————O model), after the fashion of Joseph Heller's great character, Milo Minderbinder; or, and this is a more European and less American approach, acknowledge their existence as part of the real world, clarify their nature and location, and deal with them in a more limited, but maybe more authentic, way.

The difference may be observed in cocktail parties on either side of the Atlantic. The European is more reserved, maybe because he has several hundred years of European history to remind him that people's interests do not always coincide; there may not be enough room for everybody and the thwarted or neurotic human being can turn very nasty indeed. It may be a more pessimistic world view, but it is also less claustrophobic, especially for subordinates.

The point is that people who understand these things and are capable of applying them in their everyday lives tend not to have problems with foreigners. Management is about crossing boundaries, accepting responsibility to delve into the unknown on the basis of some agreed authority. Crossing national borders is perhaps the most obvious example of boundary management, but the people who do it well probably also have *role* relationships with their wives within the institution of marriage, *role* relationships with colleagues in other departments or with their subordinates within the institution of the firm, and so on.

There is, inevitably, a complication. Such admirable people of high intelligence and strong character are inclined to jib at naked economic exploitation of developing countries, corrupt practices, destruction of the environment, and so on. Some part of the problem of developing 'international' managers is probably, in fact, a displaced problem: how to get people, even for high rewards, to suspend their values in their work roles to become, as it were, morally stateless? It would be foolish to deny that much of what has been done by big multinationals in some countries is as unlovely, though subtler, than nineteenth-century colonialism.

Each manager has to decide which of his many member-ships, or roles, has first call on his psychic energies. Many of

the new international managers have placed corporate membership first (in the interests of career) and family and community
membership a long way down the list. The manager of the
future will be both a patriot and a skilled crosser of boundaries, rather than a stateless soul. Probably this means taking
people with an inbuilt grasp of the

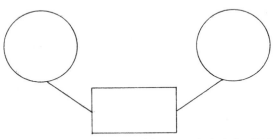

model idea (psychologists would argue it is inbuilt by around
seven years of age) and helping them see how the idea fits in,
or might do, with corporate life.

Learning implications

To this end, the author has concentrated in recent years on
an entirely new area of management training for both international and common-or-garden managers, in an attempt to
help them to see the link between the constitutional histories
of their homelands and the problems they are grappling with
at work. For example, for most Englishmen Disraeli and the
nineteenth-century Reform Acts are only vaguely remembered
from school history, but a source of pride just the same
because Britain alone in Europe extended the franchise just
in time to avoid revolution. However, few businessmen see
the link between those events and what is happening now
under the guise of 'industrial democracy' in industry. If, in
the role of citizen, we have come to expect certain rights
and privileges, we shall be bound to notice their absence in
the role of employee.

Most German executives are fascinated to discover that
the story is almost the opposite in Germany. Citizens' rights
are still less taken for granted there, but employee rights
were beginning to be established in 1848, partly as a result

of the British constitutional writers. It is possible to rummage in the history of any country for the links that illuminate the constitutional aspects of management today; it is doubtful whether these ideas can be 'learned' in adulthood unless they are reinforced by existing knowledge and values. It is an attractive approach to management education because it is simple, it draws on the students' knowledge, and can be fun. It even appeals to corporate sponsors who believe in 'broadening' their employees.

It is a sensible approach to the international manager because it teaches humility, a respect for history (others as well as our own), and a healthy regard for the usefulness of boundaries. It also teaches that the way people behave is largely a function of their institutions — a useful antidote to most people's stereotypes about the 'national characters' of other nations or the 'bloodymindedness' of workers and their representatives. As the great historian Trevelyan pointed out, the English in 1800 were about the worst governed, most corrupt nation in Europe. By 1870 they had become, magically, the sober and virtuous Victorians. Their genes had not changed — what happened was that every institution worthy of note in the country had been reshaped, and the behaviour followed in due course. It is easy to forget now how close Britain came to revolution in the first half of the nineteenth century; how quickly the 'rabble' that razed one-third of the city of Bristol to the ground became, a generation later, the law-abiding, tolerant Britons we know and love.

Many management educators now accept that the attempt to improve management performance by pumping in knowledge has not really worked. Managers seem to know, or have ready access to, most of what they need to know. But they are too rarely energised to useful action; their perceptions of their roles do not lead them to take risks, to feel entitled or authorised to cross the more dangerous-looking boundaries. By tapping in to the manager's grasp of his cultural roots he is taught little new, but he is helped to transfer to his work role things he knows perfectly well already wearing other hats — as community member, parent, churchgoer, chairman of the PTA, the bloke who sits in the corner of the pub, etc.

It sounds like the opposite of the stateless, switched-on international manager with the credit cards – and it is. The point is that the true entrepreneur believes in his work or can so mould his work that belief is possible.

This approach is an essential adjunct to action learning, organisational role analysis, project methods, and other work-specific management education approaches. At the end of the day, people function well if they are attached to their roles, rather than simply committed to them by impersonally enforced arrangements and pressures. Your work has to be 'you' just as it is when you play with your children, apply the strictest quality standards in DIY activity, or prune the roses. Too many managers are *not* attached to their managerial roles in this way for the perfectly sound reason that they cannot see a way to fuse their *values,* their preferred identity as an Englishman, an American, or whatever, with what they think they have to do at work.

We have to help managers to work on the link, drawing on what they know already from a lifetime's experience as citizens. If we cannot do this, then action learning and all the other methods will always fall short of their potential. If we can, the outcome of the suggested 'historical' approach may be a better *international* manager, with a grasp of constitutional principles, boundaries, roles, the authority of the product and a great deal more integrity (in the literal sense – more together). Really it means a better *manager* – the international bit follows naturally.

Notes

[1] See A. Mant, 'Authority and task in manufacturing operations of multinational firms', in M. Fores and I. Glover (eds), *Manufacturing and Management,* HMSO, London.

4 Changing Career Structures in International Companies

DAVID BARRON

At a time when the nature and role of international business is changing rapidly there is an increasing need to rethink the way in which the careers of those who are involved in the world of international management are planned, progressed and developed.

Until the early 1960s the international trading companies, and the other organisations which provided an international career structure, operated in a reasonably stable environment. Long-term career patterns were established; progress through the career structure was regular, reasonably assured, but generally slow; and emphasis was placed as much on service and seniority within the organisation as any objective assessment of the contribution the individual had made, or could make, to the organisation's success. Career structures derived largely from the traditional patterns developed to meet the demands of the overseas services of the colonial powers, and of the trading companies which followed, or led, them. Movement was slow because travel was slow. A tour in India lasted for five years more as a result of a combination of climatic demands, rudimentary travel facilities, and available medical services, than as a result of a detailed analysis of the needs of the business. Expatriate life for the individual tended to be concentrated on one geographic area only. He and his family grew strong local roots, built long-lasting personal and social links with the area concerned, and developed the depth of understanding of language, religion, culture, tradition and politics which became the hallmark and strength, not only of many colonial services, but also of the early international trading companies.

From the early 1960s the physical environment surrounding

international life and travel began to change. The value placed by the host country on the contribution it expected of the expatriate businessman or manager came into question, and the changing demands of business itself began to require a considerably higher degree of personal mobility and of organisational flexibility.

These external changes were taking place without immediately affecting the context of the career structures, which generally stayed constant or changed more slowly than the environment which they had originally been set up to serve. It is only in the 1970s, when the clear dichotomy between career structure and business demands has raised searching problems, that detailed attention has been paid within international organisations to revising the entire career package — recruitment, training, promotion, life-style, emoluments, support services, flexibility.

The 'career organisation' concept

It is noticeable that it is the international organisations which continue to employ a comparatively high level of 'career staff' rather than many of those, apart from the strongly paternalistic, whose activities are limited to a single geographic sphere. A high percentage join the organisation directly from school or university, undertake a form of basic training or 'cadetship' specifically designed to fit them for the particular nature of the work which the organisation demands, and then spend the bulk of their working careers on assignment within its operations either in the 'home base' country or as an expatriate. An examination of the boards of the international companies show this trend quite clearly.

The continuing attraction of overseas life, with its significantly greater financial rewards and standard of living, and the opportunity for early broad management responsibility, appeal to those high calibre entrants who once they have experienced the nature of international business, find it increasingly difficult to leave for alternative employment. A combination of a clear preference for the level of life-style to which they, and their families, rapidly become accustomed, and the highly individualistic nature of the work of most international operations, is sufficient to hold them to a single employer. Indeed, there is still a noticeable family tradition in international organisations where examples of three generations of a family working for the same company are far from rare. The maintenance of this level of continuing career experience and expectation demands a level of commitment on the part of both the employer and the employee which is far above that normally required in other organisations. So the career structures offered by such organisations must take into account not only initial educational and professional values demanded by job specifications, but must also cater for the *continuing* development of complex groupings of professional and managerial skills within individuals.

The expatriate, the home base and the overseas national employee

The international company in the 1980s has to offer a career structure which identifies *separately* the needs of those employees whose work demands mobility, from those with a settled and stable work pattern — whether this is in the company's home base or in its overseas operations. Although the needs may be separate at any point, over a period the individual may be required to operate flexibility in any of these roles, and the career structure must be flexible enough to respond. Although there should be no strong dividing line between employee groups, the expatriate typically enjoys higher levels of compensation reflecting the physical and social demands of his work. Thus there is a tendency for him to be seen as a member of an elite group. Those working in the static environment of either the home base, or the overseas operations, have tended to have a career structure limited by the business objectives — or level of business achievement — of 'their' part of the organisation.

The expatriate career base is now lessening in extent and possible future developments will be touched on later. It nevertheless remains a keystone in the management of international operations. The future role of the expatriate, however it develops will be to provide high-level expertise wherever and whenever the organisation requires it.

The people in the home base typically make up the central controlling body of the total organisation. Normally based in the country of incorporation, this can range from a small corporate headquarters for a widely devolved regional management to a major central operation controlling and supporting a lean, mobile, and overseas group. The home base career structure is often composed of grouped specialist structures which develop high levels of individual professional skill, e.g. corporate planning, financial planning and control, investment analysis, legal support, project management, corporate personnel, advisory functions.

The tendency increasingly is for a blurring of the roles of expatriate and home-based specialists. The former are moving more towards a centrally-based team of visiting firemen: the latter are spending more time on short second-ments in the field to lend weight to local activities. This blurring is likely to continue until unified corporate management and specialist groups emerge which can then be deployed quickly and flexibly to meet current local needs.

The career opportunities for those employed locally overseas vary considerably. In a developed country, local staff will be available at a level of skill and experience, and in a breadth of disciplines, to satisfy as many of the functional and management requirements of business as policy requires: the expatriate may be restricted to liaison or diplomatic roles. In less developed countries, where locally available skills and experience are limited, career opportunities can only be developed slowly through lengthy training and planned experience in that country. The effort and cost required to sustain such programmes are increasing in response not only to the needs of the company but to pressure from governments overseas to see control of expatriate companies in the hands of their own national employees. The role of the locally employed group is being strengthened because of these moves, and whether it is the case of a Briton employed in the UK by a US transnational, or an African employee of a UK Company in Africa, the influence on local operations and on the long-term overseas policies of the mother company will increase.

There is still a limitation on deployment of local skills: apart from their home countries, they can be regularly transferred on moves to the home base, but they are often found unacceptable in third country operations.

In the last few years the importance of an additional group has arisen, that is the 'third-country nationals' — temporary immigrants to a country needed to satisfy the operating demands of the company which cannot currently be met either by expatriate staff on grounds of availability or cost, or by the local staff of the country concerned. The response to the career needs of this group is often downgraded to ensuring that they are capable of satisfying specific job requirements. This is a reaction as much to political pressure from the host country's government as to cost pressure from the company itself.

Changing career patterns

The career pattern of the 'mobile' expatriate is still changing. Until recently it was not only possible but desirable, from the point of view of a total career structure, to maintain junior expatriates in the field performing technician and junior administrative roles in the company's operations outside its home base. While providing the infrastructure for overseas operations, they were acquiring experience to allow them to move into more senior roles later in their careers. However, there are now two pressures to reduce this level of expatriate support.

The first is the rapidly escalating cost of keeping any expatriate in the field. The cost differential between a junior technician and a senior executive overseas is now quite small; both require similar levels of expatriate support in such things as housing for themselves and their families, local allowances, education facilities, leave allowances, medical services, support for local social facilities. The only differential is specific grade and salary level which makes up a small proportion of the total cost. The pressure is building to maintain in the field only those expatriates who can bring clear added-value to the organisation's operation. Typically this means either professional expertise at a high level or broad and experienced expatriate management skills. How the next generation of expatriate staff is to acquire this level of expertise without having had the opportunity of earlier work overseas is a puzzle that has not yet had a clear answer.

The second and simultaneous pressure to reduce the numbers of expatriates is the increasing demand for 'localisation' of jobs in the majority of host countries, particularly those countries who are themselves developing. There is considerable pressure to extend the nature of the host country's local training and development programmes to encompass as broad as possible spectrum of local staff and then plan to replace expatriate labour by local staff at an enhanced rate. This increases dramatically in level and scope the future role of the national overseas.

Future patterns of international career structures

These influences together have a significant effect on the parent company's career structure for expatriate staff. The main effects are:

1   The use of home-country specialists on short-term assignments to deal with specific problems and projects in the host country, thereby cutting down the overall number of expatriate jobs available.

2   The reduction in junior jobs available overseas from which future senior specialists and managers can be developed.

3   The shortening of overseas tours for expatriate staff to months rather than years. At this point, short 'single-status' visits become acceptable from the home base, thereby reducing the cost to the organisation of long-term expatriate family support.

These changes produce a new range of problems for those concerned with managing international career structures. There is a blurring of the previously clear distinctions between the home base, expatriates and overseas nationals. With a reduced training and proving ground available for junior expatriate staff overseas, and with considerably more emphasis on the development of overseas staff — often at an earlier age and from reduced starting values — some effects on the career structure are seen as follows:

1   A need for higher recruitment values generally for the home base and for the expatriate. The time previously available for extended training must be shortened, to allow the expatriate to develop to the point where he can produce the required added-value overseas as early as possible.

2   A greater emphasis on the acquisition of internationally recognised professional qualifications by anyone due to be deployed overseas in order to gain ready acceptance in the host country.

3   A greater emphasis on measuring the contribution which the individual is making towards the success of the organisation so that the 'added-value' concept can be maintained. The natural result of this is a move towards target setting and objective controls in international organisations with less, if any, emphasis being placed on service and seniority.

4   The shortening of tours overseas is reducing the amount of cultural contact between the expatriate and the host country. The post-colonial phase is now past and the expatriate manager is seen more as a visiting fireman in support of a locally-based operation and is only acceptable because of the professional expertise which he brings. The development of this acceptable level of expertise therefore becomes a high level task for those controlling the overall career structure.

5   Additional mobility demands of the expatriate extra fluency in a wide variety of international, social, political, diplomatic and cultural circumstances. These have to be analysed and evaluated and training patterns developed.

6   The continuing process of change is demanding an expansion of retraining and mid-career re-orientation programmes. This trend will be one of the more significant influences on future career patterns worldwide.

Control

All the factors listed above require an increasingly sensitive degree of control both locally in host countries and by the corporate personnel function in the home base to ensure that there is an open and efficient means of establishing tasks, setting objectives and reporting on performance. Effective and humane decisions on posting, training, retraining and deployment need to be made quickly and positively to reflect the needs of the business in the short and long term.

A natural extension of the move towards openness in reporting is the ability of the individual to control his own career path to a much greater extent than has traditionally been the case amongst many expatriate organisations. This trend has to be handled with care because in the carrying out of the sensitive three-dimensional human jigsaw puzzle which controlling a large scale international organisation has become, it is impossible to meet in the short term the needs of every individual piece of that puzzle. Nevertheless, it must be seen as a guiding principle that unless the individual has an opportunity to discuss openly his wishes and expectations, the organisation has very little chance of coming up with a satisfactory set of career decisions.

5 Putting the European Community in the Curriculum

JOHN DREW

Direct elections to the European Parliament, enlargement of the Community to include Greece, Portugal and Spain and the development of the European monetary system and the growing intra-EEC trade (see Table 5.1) are current major European issues. Managers need to be aware of them as they have significant implications for European business. Senior industrialists have pronounced on the need to create a European awareness in their managers, but few actions have followed on their words. [1] Many recent courses in the UK on European business have failed or run only with small numbers and have thus posed a dilemma for both teachers and institutions. Should they persevere in their efforts or wait for a clearer indication of demand?

Table 5.1
Intra-EEC trade

1	United Kingdom exports to EEC as a percentage of total UK exports:

1960	1970	1978
22	29	38

2   In early 1978 the nine countries of the European Community exported for the first time more to one another than they did to the rest of the world. Intra-European Community trade is now over 50 per cent of total EEC trade (source: Department of Trade).

3   92 per cent of British industrialists are in favour of Britain's membership of the European Community (source: *Daily Telegraph* poll of 217 large manufacturing companies, 12 September 1977).

While accepting the judgement of the market place, the role of the management teacher as innovator cannot be ignored. If there is likely to be a future demand, he needs to be properly prepared for it. Managers increasingly want to learn more about business and the European Community as they see it becoming more significant to their companies, but as the investment in developing knowledge of the European business area is a substantial one, many teachers will need more than a sense of potential demand before they respond to it. There is a risk that demand for courses on European business could outstrip the very limited supply of those currently prepared to provide them.

This chapter deals with four aspects of business in the European Community:

1 Which subjects should be covered?
2 Teaching methods
3 Who needs to learn about European business?
4 How should teachers of management prepare themselves?

Managers and teachers of management must decide for themselves the importance of the European Community and put a corresponding level of effort into learning about it and influencing its development in areas of concern to business.

Which subjects should be covered?

There appear to be three areas of interest to managers:

1 The Community institutions and Community policies affecting business.
2 The business environment and management culture in the nine.
3 European export marketing and investment.

The Community institutions and policies

The institutions. Managers need to learn about the decision-making process. They will want to follow the development of a policy from its original conception until it becomes Community law. The key relationship is that of the Commission which proposes Community legislation and the Council of Ministers which decides on the proposals. The European Parliament needs to be covered as industry lobbying of European MPs will become commonplace. Other institutions mentioned in Table 5.2 are less important to business, although knowledge of how institutions interact provides the necessary basis for obtaining informed answers about policies and how they affect a business.

Internal policies of the Community. Nearly all policies affect business in one way or another but a few are of more immediate relevance. Competition policy is important because it has teeth. The Commission can impose fines of up to 10 per cent of a company's annual turnover and fines of over $1 million have been imposed on companies for infringement of Articles 85 and 86 of the Treaty of Rome.

Industrial policy is becoming more relevant as Community solutions are sought to the current problems of the crisis industries — textiles, footwear, steel and shipbuilding. It may have some importance too in developing growth strategies, although member states still guard jealously their national research into new technologies.

The common commercial policy and the customs union which form the basis of the Common Market need to be covered. Business does not always appreciate that Community external trade relations are now negotiated from Brussels, not from the capitals of the nine. The tariff wall of the common customs tariff can be raised or lowered and thus have considerable effect on the relations of the community with third countries.

Social policy is of renewed interest since member states come to accept that they cannot solve unemployment merely by exporting it. A Community solution is likely to last longer than individual country solutions. Eurobargaining and the role of European trade unions is also an area of growing interest. Policies relevant to business are listed in Table 5.2.

External policies of The Community. These affect business in particular because the Community is the world's largest trading bloc. The trade and commercial relations framework

Table 5.2
The Community institutions and policies affecting business

---

1 The institutions:
   the decision-making process;
   the Commission and the Council of Ministers;
   the European Parliament and direct elections;
   directorates-general of the Commission;
   directives and regulations;
   other institutions — Court of Justice, the European
   Council, Economic and Social Committee and the
   European Investment Bank.
2 Internal policies of the Community:
   competition policy;
   industrial and sectoral policies;
   trade and commercial policies;
   unions and social policy;
   other policies — energy, economic and monetary,
   regional, agricultural, transport, consumer, environmental, political cooperation, randD, financial and
   fiscal.
3 External policies of the Community:
   The Community and the United States;
   — Japan;
   — multinationals;
   — the developing countries and Lome;
   — enlargement;
   — Eastern Europe, China and other parts of the world.
4 Influencing policies and monitoring Community developments:
   trends in European trade and the reaction of business;
   export strategies and the Community;
   investment strategies and the Community;
   where to influence decision making;
   learning more about the Community;
   monitoring Community developments.

---

which the Community develops with the rest of the world
needs to be taken into account in the strategical development
of a company's overseas operations.

Influencing policies and monitoring Community develop-ments. Managers are interested to learn about the pressure points in the Community: who they can influence, at what level and in which institution. The role of the UK Office of the Commission, the Department of Trade and the British Overseas Trade Board and the UK representation in Brussels shuld also be considered.

The most important information companies require is 'pipeline information' – they need to know about relevant legislation being developed in the Community and the time scale for its likely passage into law. Companies also want to know how they should monitor Community developments. At what level in the company this should be done? To what extent can they rely on trade associations or consultants to do this for them? How large should a company be before it can justify having an office in Brussels? Can a company man in Brussels be justified at all?

Business environment and management cultures in the nine

How does the business environment in Germany differ from that in Italy? What are the differences in approach to business of the Dutch and the Belgians? Do you discuss business with a Frenchman before or after lunch? It is obviously impossible to teach about the business environment and cultures of all the countries of the nine, although there are specialist institu-tions which are able to cover most of them. It is worth concentrating on France and Germany. They are the largest of our major European trading partners. They also represent quite well the Mediterranean and Anglo-Saxon ways of doing business, the northern and southern tiers of the Community.

The comparative study approach helps to develop sensitivity towards doing business in a different culture and language. This sensitivity is taught with difficulty, yet it is an important skill. British managers, with notable exceptions, are not the most sensitive in dealing with foreigners, in part perhaps due to our island heritage and in part to our colonial past.

There are two possible approaches. The first is behavioural. There has been much sound academic research into problems of acculturation. The second is the environmental approach which has, in the author's experience, proved so far to be more successful. The business environment of a country should be taught whenever possible by a native of the country. He must be an experienced teacher. It is difficult to generalise about countries and cultures and too often an inexperienced speaker will be unable effectively to conceptualise his experience. For a Walloon Belgian to explain the Flemish position or a German to generalise about attitudes to the Second World War requires skills as well as careful preparation. Through a continuing process of trial and error a list has been drawn up, see Table 5.3, of the business environment subjects which most interested UK managers on the middle management executive programme at the London Business School during the last five years. In each case, the teaching stopped short of lists of useful telephone numbers, addresses and sources of information, but this was provided in written form for those who required it.

Managers were not very interested in hearing or reading about details of the French tax system or German labour law. While highly relevant at a certain moment in the investment decision-making process, the volume of information imparted tends to stifle interest. This is the problem with so many commercial guides to business practice published by banks and professional organisations.

European export marketing and investment

This is currently the easiest of the three areas for teachers. International business is an established subject area and there are good teachers able to develop European business teaching along international business teaching lines. It is argued that the Community should be regarded as a home market of 260 million consumers, yet to suggest that selling in Scunthorpe is the same as selling in Sienna is to carry the home market analogy too far. It is not only languages and business cultures which differ. Although tariff barriers have been removed there are still considerable problems in exporting and investing from one Community country to another (see Table 5.4). Customs posts still exist to collect different rates of VAT, for

Table 5.3
National and international environment

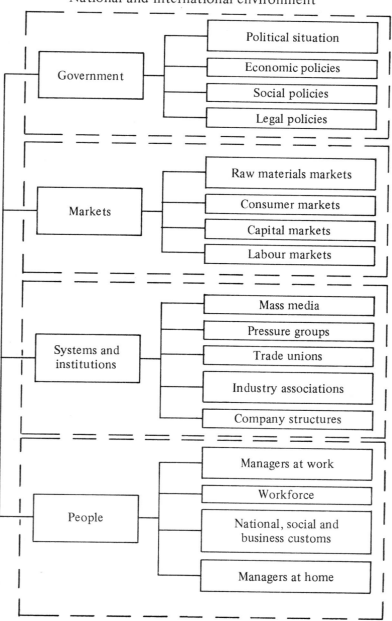

78

Table 5.4
Investment considerations

Political stability
Economic outlook
Attitude to foreign
  investment
Foreign companies
  expanding
Nationalisation
Government controls
Corporate forms
Price controls
Patent and trade mark
  protection
Remitability of funds
Taxes
Incentives

Capital sources
Labour
Trade policy
Social considerations
Personnel
Company structure
Search procedures
Current and future regional
  legislation
Exchange rates
Wage rates
Time
Distance
Competition

A simple method of evaluating investment opportunities: take the 4–6 most important points for your company from the checklist and weight them so that the total adds up to 10 as in the first column below. Then grade each factor for each country out of 10 and multiply across.

	Weight W	Country A	Country B	A x W	B x W
Political	5	9	2	45	10
Taxes	2	2	6	4	12
Personnel	1	4	9	4	9
Economic	2	3	5	6	10
	10	18	23	59	41

Country A preferred to country B

health or security reasons or even just to gather statistics. There are non-tariff barriers of different kinds which are being abolished only slowly. European markets in many ways require the same sort of business skills to penetrate as other more distant markets. The dimension which differs is the existence of the Community in terms of regional legislation and in political terms.

These are the three areas of European teaching which teachers of management need to consider seriously. There are other specialist needs. Accountants will need to know the meaning of French and German accounts, but only a few of them. Industrial relations experts will need to know about labour law in the nine countries. Managers will not normally need to have detailed knowledge of how their own function is structured in the other countries of the Community. Nor will teachers necessarily need to acquire this knowledge unless they are specialists wishing to teach specialists.

The functional manager and the teacher will need to know the legislation emanating from Brussels relevant to their company subject area, whether accounting legislation, banking, industrial relations, VAT, taxation, consumer or environmental policies.

Teaching methods

Community business in many ways is just another management subject and there is no reason why this chapter should discuss pedagogy. This is particularly the case with European export marketing and investment. There is, however, a need to lower expectations about what can be taught in a case study specific to the Common Market. Because a case is set in Community countries does not mean that it will necessarily be relevant to doing business in those countries. The dimension which is different is Community legislation. This cannot easily be taught through cases. It is undoubtedly important to have European case studies, for the appearance if not for the reality. In fact, much criticism of case studies for not being sufficiently European is based on the fallacy that there is a deal of difference between doing business in different parts of the world. Of course there are different cultural, legal and environmental dimensions, but management principles illustrated by cases are universal. Management is one of the few neutral subjects. It can be discussed sensibly by those whose political ideology differs from one end of the political spectrum to the other.

Cases on Concorde or on the problems of noise in the French environment may seem to be good European cases, but in fact have little more to offer than similar cases in, for example, a North American setting. A manager once pointed out that the sound of a pneumatic drill disturbs the peace just as much in Detroit as it does in Toulouse.

Teaching about institutions and policies presents a different set of problems. The subject is a large one and requires a considerable investment of time. The investment is continuing as events are moving fast in the Community and constant monitoring is necessary. Many of those who know the Community well are currently working in or with the Community institutions often as civil servants. They are not necessarily good business lecturers. The dilemma is whether to prefer a good management teacher who knows a little about the Community to an expert who may not teach well.

More imaginative teaching methods need to be developed. The official reading material available from the Community is competent, but uninspiring. It has to be written with the susceptibilities of nine different governments in mind.

Few books on the Community of interest to business have been written. Anything written tends to date quickly. Films present similar problems to books. There is a series of doing business films produced by *The Financial Times* for example. The one on France was relevant only for a comparatively short period of time and it is doubtful whether exporters would find it of great value now.

A most effective teaching method is to keep loose-leaf books of press cuttings, clippings, notes, statistics and articles and to photocopy a selection of recent ones for a particular course. This package can be used as a teaching note or handed out to participants to read either before, after or often during a class session. To break up the monotony of describing the functionings of an institution by a few minutes reading affords welcome relief to course participants and teacher alike.

Teaching business environments and management cultures is straightforward for nationals of the countries concerned, but inviting foreign nationals to the UK to teach is expensive. The wide gap usually found between the knowledge of participants and that of the teacher makes the sessions particularly rewarding. Although material is largely descriptive it is clearly perceived to be relevant. The lecturer's knowledge of English is even more important than his knowledge of the subject. A problem may occur if there is a member of the audience of the same nationality as the lecturer. Many environmental and cultural judgements will be personal, however professional the lecturer, and if the teacher and class member differ on their interpretations the result may be less rewarding than disruptive as the disputes are often over matters of opinion rather than fact. This type of teaching is more to do with appreciation of environmental and cultural differences than with hard factual knowledge. A native of the country is usually better as a teacher than an expatriate or a UK citizen who has lived abroad. Because someone lived in the Arab world ten years ago and understands to some extent the cultures and language, it does not necessarily mean that he can help business to operate in that part of the world today. Area studies knowledge dates very quickly.

The BBC finds this so even with language. Expatriates broadcast to their own countries in their own languages, but having left the country for a few years their knowledge of idiom and type dates as language is a living thing and changes over time.

Ideally we need to invite lecturers to this country from their country of origin to talk about their business environment. An alternative, and one which business schools will have to consider seriously, is to have regular visiting European Community faculty. Perhaps the next three appointments in your institution should be EEC nationals or the next appointment in your company management development department should be a foreigner irrespective of the fact that one would sense it would cost more.

The best form of learning about the European Community and business is undoubtedly by visiting Community countries and institutions. The author's own institution has sponsored the visits of over 1,000 managers to the continent on various programmes during the last six years. This has enabled managers to be exposed to a variety of teaching styles and to learn about community institutions and policies first hand while at the same time to be exposed to different business cultures. This has been achieved at great relative cost in terms of time but also in terms of money but the effort has been judged worthwhile.

There is nothing new to this type of teaching — learning by travelling. It began in Europe at least as early as the Grand Tour in a formal way and current efforts are only modest business versions of the same concept. Like the Grand Tour, not many people can go on them and like the Grand Tour they make significant and lasting impressions on many who make them. Ford Corporation have done the same thing at senior foremen level and sent first-line managers for example, to Germany to look at similar production lines.

The London Business School visits were secured educationally by basing them on management institutions in different countries. Traditional management teaching has provided part of the menu but also visits to companies, to the European Community institutions and project work of one kind and another have been included.

Who needs to know about European Community business?

Not only those involved in the European strategies of their organisations. It goes without saying that senior managers need to have a European awareness. It probably goes without saying that in the UK we will decide that it is middle managers who ought to be developed. Although the longest jobs that managers hold down in their lives are usually at board level or the equivalent (which they reach some time during their forties on average), it is often considered, especially in the UK, that training is something which is completed before reaching senior management level. Senior managers have therefore in many cases finished with their formal education except for the occasional day seminar in their mid-forties, even though they will be contributing to management decisions at senior level for the next 15-20 years.

Top managers, who need to broaden before they reach senior positions, need to learn about European Community business if they do not know about it already, just as do high-flying middle managers. Creating a European awareness in managers is not however just for those who may live and work in other Community countries. More of us will be dealing more of the time with managers from the Community and Community legislation will affect our work even if we remain in the UK for our working lives. Sensitivity to different cultures is something that needs to be inculcated right through the company as an increasing stream of foreigners at all levels visit UK companies.

A new approach to international business and European business in particular is required as the world becomes smaller and the implications are wide for those in companies or in management institutions who will have to define more care-fully just what training is required.

How should teachers of management prepare themselves?

Area studies ideally should be taught by those who have lived and worked in the management area. Institutions will need to encourage those with practical experience of working in and with Community countries to train as teachers. This will present problems of integrating non-traditional teachers into an academic system. Some teachers of management will need to invest time in learning about the European Community as it affects business, but probably not about business in the different Community countries themselves. Table 5.5 suggests how a management teacher might go about this basic invest-ment. The functional teacher may need to monitor Community activities in his specialist function and this will require rather more time and remain a continuing commitment.

The next few years will probably see European develop-ment on a scale far greater than envisaged at present. There are signs that continental-based institutions are developing European business studies at a faster pace than we are in the UK. It would be a pity if this area was not developed because of the inability of the management education profession. There is still an opportunity to lead management thinking and to develop more European-based courses and teaching. The ATM conference of 1979 recognised this. The opportunities still exist but they will not do so for much longer. Management education in general, so well and interestingly developed at all levels in the United Kingdom, may become increasingly less relevant to Europeans and non-Europeans if we continue to teach from our island base.

Table 5.5

Investing in the European Community: reading and visits

1   The European pages of *The Financial Times.*
2   The European Community pages of *The Economist.*
3   *Bulletin of the European Community:* there are eleven issues a year, plus supplements and an index. Contains a comprehensive description and index of legislation and sufficient references to follow up specialist interests. Costs very little and takes up only a small amount of shelf space.
4   Visit the UK office of the Commission at 20 Kensington Palace Gardens or in Cardiff or Edinburgh. The comprehensive library gives a quick view of publications in specialist areas.
5   Visit the Commission in Brussels. Briefings can be arranged for groups through the UK office of the Commission.

Note

[1]   Notably the EFMD Pocock Report, 1977.

6 Where British Training Lags Behind the Rest of Europe

J. LOWE

When Britain became a member of the EEC in 1973 the impact on managerial practice was neither immediate nor obvious. British multinationals continued to function on a global scale, whilst small to medium-sized companies were initially disinterested, or deterred by harmonisation legislation affecting their operations. As John Stopford's 1976 study showed, [1] British multinationals' annual increase in direct investment in the six was already running at an average of 37 per cent in the years preceding and following Britain's entry into the EEC (1970–74). Their pattern was well-established prior to membership. In addition, a 1977 survey of 100 UK public companies [2] indicated the extent to which smaller firms have taken the opportunity over the intervening six years to diversify, developing export markets and establishing foreign subsidiaries: 92 per cent of firms surveyed recorded an average 36 per cent increase in 'foreign sales as a percentage of total sales'. In some instances, where companies recorded more than a 70 per cent increase in foreign sales over the five-year period, these interests now outweigh home operation. The author of this chapter ascribes this 'considerable shift of emphasis outside the UK' to 'the pressure to protect markets abroad by local production, and to establish a physical presence in key markets, notably those of the Continent'. Undoubtedly, lack of scope in the British economy has been a strong contributory factor, but coupled with access to new markets in Europe, it has meant a radical change in operating patterns for companies which ten years ago would not have considered Europe.

In particular, EEC membership has brought with it a change in the parameters of managerial thinking, and what could be termed psychological access to Europe. There is an increase in information and awareness about how European competitors operate and how this affects UK markets. One small engineering concern is now making use of EEC provision to place employees on work secondment in Germany for three to six months to understand better the process of market penetration. Others have realised, with the psychological barrier lowered, that it is not necessary to be an international giant to gain access to European markets. An East Anglian horticulturalist claimed recently that from a zero base in 1973 he had now built up an annual turnover in excess of £4 million exporting bulbs to Holland. It is at this small companies' end of the scale that the most significant movement towards Europe can be detected.

Demand for British managers in Europe has also grown steadily during this period, as any rapid review of vacancies advertised in this country indicates. There has been no systematic analysis of take-up of these vacancies elsewhere in Europe, but there have been a number of 'intention surveys'. It has long been known that willingness to work abroad is closely linked to a pattern of previous mobility. Robock and Simmonds in their examination of the multinational management of human resources, [3] give as one of the few 'fairly reliable characteristics' of the successful manager abroad, 'previous cross-cultural experience'. The director of Lyon Business School in France recently noticed a marked difference in the take-up rate of foreign work opportunities amongst his business students. On closer examination, willingness to work abroad was shown to be linked to experience of foreign travel before the age of 14. If this finding has any more general validity, then it will be increasingly significant that the generation that has grown up since World War II can and does move freely around Europe, being one of the first generations in over a century not to have its travel constrained by warfare.

This greater mobility, coupled with depressed prospects in UK management, may underlie a British Institute of Management research finding [4] that 59 per cent of respondents under 29 were 'very keen' or 'quite keen' to work abroad. Confirming this, the Opinion Research Centre recently established that over 50 per cent of managers of all ages that they interviewed were prepared to work abroad;[5] 13 per cent were actively considering moving in the next three years, and 8 per cent had made definite preliminary moves in this direction. It is this group that will form the base of mobile, internationally-minded managers for the UK's future growth.

Changing organisational requirements

Coinciding with these changing horizons of British managers and the europeanisation of the number of British companies, there is evidence that multinationals are evolving new managerial patterns to match their steady international growth. At an international management conference recently, three leading British multinational companies assessed their total numbers of career expatriate managers who could expect to spend the greater part of their working lives outside their own country at less than 25 in global workforces in excess of 150,000. One company has a single British *career* expatriate in India, where it employs 11,000 people. The pattern of a limited number of home national managers choosing to make a life career as expatriates is being replaced by one of larger numbers of managers undertaking a single foreign assignment of two to four years at an early stage in their managerial progress, as part of a career development programme. In the view of the companies concerned, this change reflects both the increasing aspirations of young managers wanting to gain experience abroad whilst not committing their total careers there, and the unwillingness of more senior managers to impose on their families the effects of prolonged periods abroad. It is also coupled with increased reliance, often enforced by local regulations, on local nationals to fill key positions that would previously have been occupied by senior career expatriates, as the example of India, cited earlier, illustrates.

In part this is a recognition of the need for close local understanding in order to operate effectively, but is also reflects a realisation that management by home-national career expatriates, however accomplished, limits the scope of any multinational. As a Business International Report pointed out in 1972, [6] an American company relying as far as local regulations would permit on an expatriate managerial force 'limits its possibility of accumulating good managers to just 6 per cent of the world population'. The scope for a British company employing the same technique would be proportionately smaller. As it is, a policy of promoting young managers to short placements abroad at a level subordinate to more senior local managers, gives experience to many of them at an early stage of their career whilst allowing responsibility for the foreign affiliate to remain in the hands of local foreign nationals. Home nationals become part of a management development programme that is also open to third-country nationals, rather than representing imposed headquarters authority. Just how complicated this promotional ladder can become on occasions is illustrated in the chain described by one company whereby a young Englishman was given a two-year posting to Holland: the Dutchman he replaced moved on to India; the Indian went to Sydney and the Australian to London.

Ultimately this can lead to complete internationalisation of company control at board level. So far the number of companies involving a variety of nationalities at this level is few and the process a slow one. Massey-Ferguson for example, who took the decision to internationalise their board in 1959, estimate that it will take them until at least 1980 to complete the process even within the very limited scope permitted by national legislation concerning foreign shareholding. In 1974 Kenneth Simmonds and Richard Connell set out to discover whether the boards of British multinationals included a significant number of non-British managers. [7] Of 1,126 directors of 86 companies, only 5 per cent were foreign nationals, reducing to less than 4 per cent when joint directorships of companies such as Shell or Unilever were taken into account. Elsewhere, however, companies such as RTZ were making substantial progress towards internationalisation, indicating yet another area where British colonial past is still overshadowing company present. If we do begin to develop patterns similar to those prevailing outside the UK, the implications could be significant for British managers and management trainers, as they become more likely than ever to face a short period working abroad as part of a team rather than in a position of colonial-style authority.

At the same time, as we have seen, managers within smaller national or international concerns are apt to be faced with the effects of company diversifications into Europe on a scale unknown five to ten years ago, whilst those not directly seeking European markets have had to come to terms with the international dynamics of their industry bringing competition to their doorstep. With these changes has grown the demand for broadly-based multicultural executives who can adapt rapidly and function effectively in an international environment. Leo Tindemans, the former Belgian Prime Minister, recently used the phrase 'the polyvalent manager' to describe this type of executive, predicting it as a pattern for the future. [8] In British terms a 'polyvalent manager' might be:

1   One never leaving the UK, but forced increasingly to consider foreign market penetration, or the effects of EEC legislation on his activities.
2   The young executive facing a single foreign secondment early in his employment as part of a career development programme.
3   The UK-based executive who will be expected to undertake brief foreign assignments.
4   The UK-based executive, never leaving this country, but operating substantially with foreign clients, suppliers and subsidiary employees.
5   The manager gaining experience working abroad for a foreign company. Ease of mobility still favours the young in this position, but as internationalisation increases, no doubt other managers will move on to positions abroad.

In adapting to a management role within Europe, the polyvalent manager will not only have to face the specific constraints of operating internationally, he will also have to react to the pressures facing management throughout the EEC. He will need to be essentially adaptive and responsive to challenge, as 'the balancer between the multiple interests of various stakeholders in the business — workers, customers, investors and the public', [9] and an expert in Common Market legislation. In purely UK national terms therefore, there must be scope for the role of management development and training as a catalyst in the necessary process of international adaptation.

New training needs

Attempts to train or prepare this type of manager however face immediate limitations in this country. There is a distinct shortage of suitably qualified British managers familiar enough with other countries' business practice, legislation and socio-cultural expectations, to operate effectively elsewhere in Europe. Nor is there the language capability to be able to deal on equal terms with French or Italian businessmen. The disadvantages when compared with a multilingual multicultural Dutch or Swedish manager are obvious. The Swedish firm of SKF, for example, even uses English as its language of operation in Swedish headquarters, including board meetings. The historical inheritance of colonial attitudes, English dominance and unchallenged raw material sources and markets is still reflected in our managerial training where European markets, legislation and languages play a minor or negligible part. Compare this with the training of a young French member of the executive 'cadre dynamique' who will almost certainly be a product of a business school (unlike his UK counterpart) where two foreign languages will have been compulsory, and a period of working elsewhere in the EEC may have been a course requirement. J. G. Maisonrouge, president of IBM Europe, recognised the value of his country's multicultural approach to the training of future managers as long ago as 1968 when he stressed that 'we always underestimate the role of cultural background in management. We are oriented towards our own national cultures, and it takes time and dedication to understand how others react'. [10]

More recently, the Pocock Report [11] concluded that in future 'it is the individual manager himself who will have to make the major effort, learning languages, seeking to understand other cultures and keeping himself constantly abreast of changes in the political social and economic environment'. For the polyvalent manager this can mean dealing with the international division of labour, matching local socio-political demands to economic needs, and balancing the requirements of the 'stakeholders' mentioned earlier, on a Europe-wide scale. The report suggests various ways in which management education and training can assist in this process:

1   Blend new elements into what is valid in existing pro-grammes and eliminate the irrelevant.
2   Understand better the process whereby managers *learn*, and assimilate new skills.
3   Provide a neutral meeting point for company 'stake-holders', politicians and trade unions.
4   Encourage the process of continual learning, whereby the individual manager can enjoy 'a phased programme of training and development opportunities, extending from recruitment well into his 50s'.

This provides a framework for meeting the basic needs of the necessarily adaptive 'polyvalent manager'. It does not however deal adequately with the specifically international dimension of such a manager's activities. Nor, unfortunately, does it suggest how precisely these objectives can be met in practical terms, two areas where our training already compares badly with that on offer elsewhere in Europe and Scandinavia. Is there anything therefore that we can learn from our neigh-bours that might assist the training of internationally-adaptive managers? Let us analyse briefly what happens elsewhere.

Continental training developments

In France the process of internationalisation begins for most aspiring managers during higher education. As already indi-cated, the majority of top managers are products of the highly competitive grandes ecoles, or their provincial counter-parts, the ecoles superieures de commerce, where in additional to conventional business subjects two foreign languages are compulsory throughout the study period. In some schools it is possible to complete an entire degree course in international aspects of business and management (rather than this forming a supplementary part of an otherwise 'national' programme as in the UK), and at Lyon no student may enter his second year until he has worked elsewhere in the EEC for at least three months, and may not leave the school without having studied the international aspects of at least one business specialism, such as marketing. He therefore enters employment as a multilingual trained manager, familiar with business conditions elsewhere in Europe and prepared to work easily in an international environment.

At postgraduate or post-experience level, the best known French international establishment is undoubtedly INSEAD, which provides a twelve-month trilingual business programme for a wide range of nationalities based on English, French, German and American teaching material. Professor Weinshall of Tel Aviv University has shown that links formed at INSEAD survive into future employment, offering an invaluable range of international contacts for rising executives. Whitley, Thomas and Cabot in their survey [12] describe the school as 'a super grande ecole, for a highly selective group (which) seems to assure them of highly privileged positions in business'. Of those coming to INSEAD, 36.5 per cent belong to the 'patronat' or business-owning stratum, indicating the elitist nature of the school. Attempts are being made however to match the specialist opportunities of INSEAD, in short, international training programmes of the French Foundation for Management Education (FNEGE), devised for those outside the privileged 'cadre dynamique' of the grandes ecoles. These are intended to update and provide an international dimension for those middle managers not eligible for higher degree or executive MBA programmes in the grandes ecoles.

A more original approach to international management development at post-experience level is illustrated by the Swedish 'TIO Programme'. This stands for 'Training for International Operations' as well as being a play on the Swedish word for 'ten'. It involves executives of ten leading multinationals in a six-week programme at the Stockholm School of Economics, designed to bring together headquarters staff, senior employees abroad (of any nationality) and cross-cultural managers who are neither of the nationality of the headquarters, nor of the country where they manage (e.g. a Greek working for a Swedish multinational in Africa). The objective of the programme is to familiarise foreign staff with the nature of headquarters operations and managerial style; to enable headquarters staff to discuss foreign operations with their own and other staff operating abroad; and to examine the difficulties of being an international manager in a single foreign location. Teaching is based on case studies written by Stockholm School of Economics staff after visits to the ten companies' foreign subsidiaries. It is also a basic prerequisite of the course that staff teaching the programme should be drawn from six nationalities, to provide a balance in training approaches and business-cultural assumptions.

In Germany, programmes similar to the TIO scheme but less ambitious in scope, are offered by the USW, the Universities' Seminar with Industry. This is a joint venture between industrialists and academics established in 1968 in response to industry's concern at the need to retrain executives after five to six years in top management. In the Metternich family's moated castle in Liblar outside Cologne, German managers are encouraged to mix with their foreign counterparts either within their company (Ford, Siemens, Shell) or within their area of specialisation. In turn, foreign managers may attend programmes designed to help them operate more effectively, such as 'Doing business with Germany' for Japanese executives. All courses rely on intensive programming during a 13-hour working day in small groups, with international staff drawn from industry and academic institutions as far apart as London, Lausanne and Amsterdam.

These programmes form a small but growing part of USW's work in a country where all rising executives are expected to agree an individual training programme with their company 'assessor', taking part in courses every six to twelve months. Twenty-seven private institutions are currently listed as offering this type of training, but since 'management' is by definition in German a term only applied to senior executives approaching board status, 'management training' becomes the preserve of independent fee-paying centres outside the university structure. Generally recognised in Germany as the most prestigious of these is the DIF and its Baden-Baden colloquium. This is open on a competitive basis to executives aged 35-45 with at least seven years' top management experience. Within these narrow criteria, 30-40 per cent of eligible applicants are rejected for each course. Successful candidates attend Baden-Baden for a three-week dialogue of ideas and information between top executives, under the leadership of prominent industrialists. An international dimension is provided by four compulsory follow-up weekends in London, Berlin, Paris and Stockholm, looking at local problems and opportunities (e.g. doing business with Communist Europe in Berlin) and studying the wider aspects of operating inside the EEC. These weekends may have a stronger social than business basis, but clearly within the UK we offer no similar top-level internationally-orientated training to senior executives, where it might be argued that the need is greater.

Lagging British adaptation

There *are* in existence a number of training programmes; the Shell programme at USW mentioned earlier has also been run by London and Manchester Business Schools and Ashridge. But in terms of institutions we have nothing to match the multilingual internationally-staffed post-experience centres such as CEI Geneva, IMEDE Lausanne, or INSEAD Paris. Yet the presence of British participants and staff in Geneva and Lausanne, Liblar and Stockholm indicates the interest and scope for developing British programmes for international managers. This may be a gap to be filled during our next five years of EEC membership.

This does not mean however that there have been no moves to accommodate to Europe since we joined the EEC. Significantly perhaps in a country where management education and training is still largely linked to academic institutions, the greatest advance towards internationalisation may be represented by the 25 or so 'transnational' business studies' programmes currently on offer in UK institutions. They have the following characteristics making them different from previous educational patterns:

1   At least one, in some instance two, foreign languages are compulsory in addition to all business subjects.
2   Students must spend a period of time elsewhere in the EEC before completing their degree learning by moving across national boundaries (hence transnational).
3   Links with partner institutions elswhere provide a base for students whilst abroad, and ensure that the system is reciprocal.
4   Wherever possible, students are encouraged to work in foreign companies, rather than studying for up to 12 months.

The rate at which such courses are now developing in disciplines other than management (law, engineering, politics) indicates that this is seen as a valid pattern for the future, and indeed the sophistication of present programmes in management or business studies is a long way advanced from the tentative 'exchange' programmes of five years ago. Students of Middlesex Polytechnic's BA in European business administration spend exactly half their course in London and half in France, working and studying for a total of four years in a mixed group of French and English. At present this is the only course to give both a BA and a 'diplome', but there are a number of other internationally-based programmes, such as those at Surrey, linked with Russia, Sweden, France and Germany, or the former Leeds postgraduate European management programme, that show the way forward.

The validity, educational basis and marketability of such qualifications formed the subject for a two-year research project, [13] completed in 1978. This indicated that such programmes offer an acceptable means for young potential managers to learn about European markets, companies, culture and languages, without the pressures of family or executive responsibility. Over 60 per cent of students interviewed gave the existence of the 'transnational' programme as the key influencing factor in choosing their degree course; on graduation 83 per cent were making substantial use of their international skills in the UK or Europe. More significantly, over 90 per cent dismissed as 'garbage' or 'absolute rubbish' the concept that what they learnt abroad could just as well be taught in theory in a UK lecture theatre. They had in other words, recognised the value of first-hand business and language experience if they were to operate successfully with or against foreign companies in future, a learning process that few English middle managers appear to have undergone.

Management in companies employing these students often said initially in interviews that their organisation gave little value to international skills. When discussing the individual student, however, 89 per cent said that their language and cultural skills were crucial, and 82 per cent were prepared to recruit from the same source in future 'all the time, again and again and always'. If this is any indication of UK companies' need for those who understand how European managers think, do business and communicate, then it is indeed regrettable that we cannot offer similar training to more senior practising managers.

It is worth stressing however that such courses which include European work and study elements are a breakthrough; the general level of international content in UK training is still low or non-existent compared with the basic pattern elsewhere in Europe. Nor is the role of languages sufficiently recognised. It is still exceptional for a British student to leave university well able to speak a foreign language, as opposed to appreciating the niceties of its medieval literature. Alternatively, when the significance of languages in European business is appreciated, there are not enough business linguists to staff innovative programmes adequately. So a system persists where, to quote a BOTB finding, less than 5 per cent of UK job adverts for export positions mention languages as a prerequisite. Yet, as the previous analysis in this chapter of changes in UK management practice indicate, there is need for international ability and language skill at a variety of levels: (a) for those functioning 'supranationally' within the framework of a multinational; (b) for those needing to operate on a basis of international comparison, to protect their market share, establish a bridgehead in Europe, or to negotiate with foreign sister companies; and (c) for those moving rapidly between a company's European affiliates.

Future directions

At the moment, however, continental European managers, already more successful financially and in other ways than their UK counterparts, are the ones receiving training in the international skills that British managers lack and need in order to compete. Perhaps then there are four things we can learn from foreign success and example about management development in this country:

1 Whilst still maintaining functional skills, UK training needs to concentrate also on developing the attributes of the polyvalent manager, responsive to the challenge of managing more effectively in a European environment.

2 At post-experience level there is scope for a British prestige international management training institute, backed by and involving senior industrialists, academics, trade unionists and government, staffed on a European-wide basis.

3 At pre-experience level, more needs to be done to diversify and provide an international dimension in business programmes, extending to languages and direct foreign experience.

4 More thought needs to be given to the development of appropriate 'business-language' programmes for experienced managers (*not* the same thing as teaching languages to businessmen).

If these leads are followed, we may go some way towards meeting the rising needs and expectations of younger managers in this country for whom EEC membership is an accepted fact of working life. As one graduate of the type of 'transnational' programme outlined earlier, now an executive in a multinational company put it: 'I don't appreciate the role of the UK as an offshore island. Great Britain is part of the EEC. It's about time British educational thinking got around to seeing itself as part of it.'

Notes

[1]   J. M. Stopford, 'Changing perspectives on investment by British manufacturing multinationals', in *Journal of International Business Studies,* Fall-Winter 1976.

[2]   G. Foster, 'The changing UK business profile', in *Management Today,* November 1977.

[3]   S. H. Robock and K. Simmonds, *International Business and Multinational Enterprises,* Irwin Dorsey International, London 1973.

[4]   Y. Guerier and N. Philpot, 'The British manager, careers and mobility', in *BIM Management Survey Report No. 39,* 1978.

[5]   Opinion Research Centre, 'A survey of the motivation of managers', London 1977.

[6]   Business International, 'Managing the Multinationals', George Allen & Unwin, 1972.

[7]   K. Simmonds and R. Connell, 'Breaking the boardroom barrier', in *Journal of Management Studies,* May 1974.

[8]   L. Tindemans in 'Management Education in the 80s', published proceedings of the AIESEC international conference, 1978.

[9]   B. Davies, 'Developing managers for the 80s', in *MBS Review,* vol. 11, no. 4, 1978.

[10]   J. G. Maisonrouge in a speech to the American Bankers' Association, 15 May 1968.

[11]   European Foundation for Management Development, 'The educational and training needs of European managers' (the Pocock Report), 1977.

[12]   R. Whitley, A. Thomas and J. Cabot, 'The role of the business schools in the social reproduction of business elites', MBS Research Paper.

[13]   J. Lowe, *The New Euromanagers,* Woodhead-Faulkner, June 1979.

7 The International Dimension of Management Education*

BROOKINGS INSTITUTION

The internationalisation of business

> American business management finds itself operating increasingly in an international and even global context. . . Worldwide, the burgeoning multinational corporations are subjects of controversy. . .
>
> For the most part, schools of business have not responded adequately to the changing patterns of global enterprise. The relatively few outstanding programmes and institutions need to be augmented and multiplied severalfold. . . . Scholarship and research in this area needs to be broadened and deepened. Most important of all, faculties and institutions facing the challenge of educating businessmen for a global future need new capabilities, strengths, and commitments. [1]

These words begin a recent report on internationalising management education. Since they were written, the urgency of the message has increased. The pace of change in the world economy is compelling businesses and governments to cope with events and prospects that too few students are being prepared to understand. The challenge is as great and pervasive as any that American business schools have faced. Business schools abroad, with their deeper sense of the international dimensions of business, are not waiting for American schools to show the way.

* Reproduced by kind permission of The Brookings Institution, Washington, D.C.

Managers, scholars, and students in the United States now confront change quite different from the kinds most familiar to them. Change on the world scene is no longer simply evolutionary and organic, building directly on yesterday's experience. It may also be structural and, to the observer, largely discontinuous. It involves shifts in the basic fabric of institutions, their relationships with one another, and their environments. It affects all the complex systems — political, social, economic, technological, human — that compose our modern world. Disarray, anxiety, and conflict often accompany the restructuring. The emergence of the multinational corporation (MNC) and its impact on the world exemplify just such a shift.

International business enterprises — and even very large ones — are nothing new, nor is their entanglement in political affairs within and between nation states, but in recent years the MNC has become a phenomenon of new magnitude, emerging with breathtaking speed. A development not yet in ebb, it has arisen from a confluence of ever-changing technology in the production, financing, and distribution of products; new forms of information gathering, processing, and transmission; the weakening of the postwar Pax Americana; and the hard fact of heterogeneity in the worldwide distribution of natural resources, human skills, social and political institutions, and rates of growth of consumption and saving.

The earlier transnational corporation that produced for domestic and export markets is being replaced or surrounded by diversified corporations or conglomerates with numerous subsidiaries that buy, produce and sell in many countries, often worldwide. Even domestic business is increasingly affected by international influences related to raw material sources, exchange rates, foreign economic policies, and domestically situated foreign competition. The latter intrusion — painfully familiar in other countries (except, notably, Japan) and to US firms, in textiles, automobiles and electronics — is only beginning. In short, a global rationalisation of economic activities is occuring on a scale and in dimensions hitherto unknown. It may not continue at the same pace, but there is no reason to expect a major turnabout soon. We must now accept and cope with a new kind of world economic and business environment. The implications for everyone are enormous. [2]

An immediate implication is that we have entered a period of adjustments and surprises, the kinds of realignment that follow major structural changes as aftershocks follow an earthquake. Confusion and often anxiety are present to a degree greater than usual, bringing with them a sharp increase in conflict over such broad issues as jobs, incomes and wealth, as well as markets, technology transfers, capital movements, prices, taxes, profits and differing standards as regards such things as bribery and corruption. The conflicting parties are interested 'stakeholders': employees, organised labour, competitors, suppliers, customers, taxpayers, owners, local governments and nation states themselves, both developed and developing. To the extent they are not embraced in these categories, they also include the managers in their fiduciary roles for other stakeholders.

The realignments, uncertainty and acrimony will be unusually sharp in the near term, meaning five to ten years, as new laws, new institutions, new attitudes and expectations, new procedures and new leaders emerge. Then, perhaps, the strife will decrease as the world adapts to its new economic organisation.

Mankind's old problems will persist, if in moderated form, but the economic institutions for dealing with some of them will have undergone a structural change having profound implications for the training of future managers. It is these educational and developmental implications, the changing international dimension of management education, that are the subject of this chapter. Informed and concerned individuals believe it is imperative that business schools and business organisations, especially the former, to which this is primarily addressed, reassess their responses to the transnational challenge.

The challenge to business education

To broaden management education so as to prepare students

for the internationalisation of business and management
requires action on two levels:

1   To develop broad understanding of multinational and
     transnational affairs in order to add a global dimension
     to teaching and research.
2   To build a nucleus of faculty strength to provide leader-
     ship in curriculum design and research on global issues.

The first level of need applies to all schools, including those
that do not now think of themselves as involved with transnational business. The second must become a goal for any
school aspiring to distinction in management education.

Faculty

Central to any change in a university is the faculty: its
readiness, its preparation and its commitment to action.
Faculty change is essential to strengthening and expanding
the transnational emphasis in business education. What is
required for faculty members to cope effectively with an
increasingly interlinked world? Each must become familiar
with the complexities of such a world. Each should seek a
useful exposure to at least one foreign culture and to the
ways in which transnational organisations and processes differ
from purely national and local ones. Specific ways of achieving
such exposure include:

1   Academic assignments with foreign institutions involving
     residence and work abroad.
2   Seminars designed to orient and teach faculty members
     not previously involved with transnational issues.
3   Participation in the activities of transnational organisa-
     tions through research, collection of teaching materials,
     consulting assignments and participation in their internal
     training programmes.
4   Invitations to foreign professors, businessmen and
     government officials to participate in helping inter-
     nationalise regular school programmes through shared
     responsibilities for teaching or research.

The possibilities for bringing new resources to the university campus have been increased by the growth in staff and stature of business programmes overseas, by governmental and business support for 'diplomat' and 'executive in residence' programmes, and by the new potential for a limited number of 'reverse sabbaticals' from industry to academe.

For faculty members well grounded in other areas and willing to consider new fields of application, transnational questions provide an exciting array of possibilities for research. Research, especially if it involves work across cultural lines, remains one of the most powerful means for faculty education. Indeed, projects for faculty members in transition might well be chosen for their contribution to the faculty member's development rather than for their value to an external audience. Encouragement and guidance in choosing transnational projects should focus on school needs, not simply on the availability of external funds.

Students

Business schools have an obligation to present the transnational challenge as clearly to students as to faculty members. The presentation should begin, ideally, before enrolment and cover many elements outside the curriculum. To increase students' awareness of the challenge and their receptiveness to courses with an international orientation, several means could be emphasised:

1 Giving greater prominence to the transnational dimensions of the manager's job in publications telling applicants about a school's goals and programmes.
2 Encouraging potential MBA students, through publications and counseling, to include relevant language and cross-cultural training in their undergraduate work.
3 Giving greater attention to the recruitment of foreign students and their involvement on campus so as to make their presence an active source of educational enrichment, as the presence of students with previous job experience is widely thought to be.
4 Offering more seminars, field trips and organised activities to reinforce and supplement classroom work.

5   Developing more opportunities for summer jobs and co-operative or part-time work assignments overseas, or in multinational enterprises at home.

6   Experimenting with programmes that permit study abroad as an option within a domestic degree programme.

Over the longer run, admissions standards will require sharpening to identify the kinds of ability and personality that contribute to success as managers and professionals on the transnational scene.

Curriculum

If the faculty provides the driving force and student orientation the supporting assistance, the curriculum provides a school's most visible expression of goals, philosophy and competence. It should reflect transnational aspects of business even in schools that consider themselves as serving only domestic clients. Today's business school graduate must understand how a global society affects his future whether or not he ever works with a multinational enterprise or sets foot abroad.

We do not presume to specify a model curriculum or a set of alternative designs. Instead, we limit ourselves to some general advice.

The first task for each school is to re-examine its curricular goals to determine the appropriate kind and level of commitment. To what extent should the curriculum simply give a global perspective to students who are likely to spend their careers with domestic firms? To what extent should the curriculum service students who can be expected to become involved in international trade, to seek jobs with multinational enterprises, or to work at some point in their lives in another country and culture? What does each category of student require, given his or her educational background and previous work and living experience? The choice of goals can sometimes be aided by looking at the goal structures and curriculum at other schools, but the availability of other models should not be allowed to substitute for clear thinking within each institution about its own possibilities and its own students' needs.

Constructing an adequate curriculum is not simply a matter of introducing topics or courses on the transnational enterprise. Coverage should be broader and more pervasive. Whatever is taught about the international firm in general must be buttressed first by adequate attention to the international aspects of particular fields such as marketing, finance and accounting. Students must learn enough about comparative managerial and economic systems, and about the surrounding political, social and even philosophical environments in which firms operate, to understand the problems that enterprises have in operating across national boundaries. Interpersonal skills must be expanded to accommodate the traditional functions of leadership, persuasion and effective group performance in a foreign as well as in one's home culture. Development of these skills must include greater emphasis on learning to cope with unfamiliar environments, on building negotiating skills and on being prepared to learn to work in another language.

As some elements are added to the curriculum, others must be condensed or omitted. Good coverage of comparative managerial, economic, and cultural systems, of the diverse environments in which business is conducted in a global context and of the additional personal skills required for success in international work takes time away from other subjects in the curriculum. Each school must decide the appropriate trade-offs and perhaps reassess its coverage of internal managerial functions within programmes, but it should leave its curriculum strong in the environmental aspects of business, in personal skill development and in developing one management function in depth. This would leave to employers the responsibility for developing other functional skills, perhaps with the help of the university's continuing education programme.

Although priority in curriculum development must go to degree programmes, schools with capabilities and commitments in postgraduate executive education should build the international dimension into those programmes as well. For special programmes and seminars the strategies may be quite varied, depending on faculty competence and the audiences the school serves. Some effort should go toward intensifying coverage of international topics in all seminars in which those topics are part of the total picture seminar participants must understand. Some effort may also go toward specialised programmes in particular aspects of transnational management.

Curriculum development strategies should fit the particular circumstances of each school. Some schools can proceed rapidly, others more slowly, depending on faculty competence, student and employer demand, and the availability of resources such as library materials or visiting experts. Some may best begin by trying to present one or two basic courses well; others may take immediate steps to build a pervasive emphasis throughout the curriculum.

School leadership

Schools that intend to meet the challenge of preparing students to operate in a global society must make a central leadership commitment to this goal. Planning activities must be modified to ensure attention to needs and opportunities in the international sphere as well as to those closer to home. Faculty and student reward systems must be examined to make sure that they encourage a growth of involvement with transnationally oriented activities. [3] Enthusiasm for becoming 'more international' should not lead to shortcuts or lapses in quality standards. New activities with a transnational dimension should be planned to enhance, not diminish, the quality of the school. Whatever efforts are made to seek external support, the internationalisation of business and business education is so fundamental a phenomenon that schools must be prepared to meet much of the need and opportunity by reallocation of their present resources. [4]

The need to reach out

At a time when departments of humanities and social sciences in many universities are reaching out for new roles and missions, the growing need for attention to multinational business provides a basis for collaboration with business schools. At the professional level, new links could be forged between programmes in business and programmes in law, government, public management and international affairs. Some specific possibilities:

1   The exploration of joint programmes with humanities and social science departments to assure solid grounding in the cultural, political, social and economic dimensions of world business as part of undergraduate preparation for MBA programmes in international business, or to expand the range of elective work within the MBA programme itself.

2   Experiments in team teaching, both for business students and for other audiences, to bring together teachers knowledgeable about multinational enterprises with teachers who can present viewpoints from outside the enterprise and outside the home culture.

3   The exploration by business schools and schools of law and international affairs of new possibilities for student exchange in selected courses, and for innovative joint degree programmes.

4   Greater effort to develop research projects that would join faculty and doctoral students in business schools with their counterparts in other departments to study the global aspects of complex business-environment questions.

5   The design of postgraduate programmes to help students going abroad to master the essentials of an unfamiliar language and culture.

Partners and consortia — here and abroad

The development effort we are calling for is a massive one in which, for the good of business education in general, normal competitive and proprietary instincts should be moderated, much as they were when schools collaborated in introducing quantitative methods and competer-based materials into the curriculum. Several possibilities exist for the exchange of perspectives on needs and goals, for the development and dissemination of curriculum materials, for the exchange and development of faculty, for development of job opportunities for students, for the exchange of students between programmes, and for joint pursuit of research.

Consortia within cities or regions. These are especially important for the cultivation of employer interest, for the spread of curriculum ideas and faculty competence among schools, and for sharing access to skilled faculty members that a single school might be unable to afford.

National partnerships and consortia. These allow joint curriculum development, faculty exchange, joint research, and some kinds of longer-term student exchange among schools serving local or regional markets in different parts of the country. To the extent that they share common objectives and maintain similar quality standards, the partnerships may be more attractive to establish and easier to maintain than local collaborations among schools of widely differing objectives and quality standards.

Overseas partnerships. The essence of introducing a global dimension to teaching is to learn to live internationally as well. Schools that have set up consortia with foreign schools for research, faculty exchange, programme development or student exchange have found them extremely useful in driving home an understanding of what multinational operations mean. The benefits, particularly now that many foreign schools can enter such partnerships on an equal basis, can be substantial. [5]

Government and business

Although a good deal of useful contact and interchange can occur through the initiatives of AACSB and other organisations, each school working in the international sphere assumes a responsibility to encourage business and government collaboration in strengthening the transnational aspects of business education. These include:

1 Seeking out those business and government leaders whose perceptions of the future can provide guidance in the difficult task of reassessing goals and redesigning programmes.
2 Impressing upon business firms and government agencies the necessity for assuring that recruiters come to the campus with job specifications that take cognisance of

the international dimension of management, for providing worthwhile summer jobs and internships, and for providing access to information that will help in research and in the development of good teaching materials.

3 As programmes and experimental projects justify, seeking help in financing this important transition. When the resources of most business schools are badly strained, internationalisation has implications for travel and communication budgets alone that would be difficult to accommodate by reducing other expenses.

4 Getting help, particularly from multinational enterprises, in encouraging good foreign students to study in the United States, and good foreign academics and executives to visit our schools.

Corporate responsibilities

The task of preparing managers qualified to deal with the globalisation of business is as much the responsibility of the corporations as it is of the schools of business. Some corporations already have relevant selection and internal training programmes for the development of managerial personnel. Many send promising young executives to management programmes offered by universities. Often foreign nationals are sent to such programmes for an exposure to American management procedures. To fulfil their responsibilities corporations will need to:

1 Expand and encourage efforts to develop personnel qualified to deal with the changing international scene.

2 Inform schools of business of their personnel needs and the qualifications they seek.

3 Support special programmes and conferences to develop management skills for international situations.

4 Encourage their officers to support and participate in seminars and conferences devoted to a consideration of national policies, both political and economic, as they affect economic welfare. A reconciliation of conflicts in this area will depend on statesmanlike managers who

are sensitive to national aspirations and needs as well as
to corporate interests.

5 Make qualified executives available for advisory or even
instructional roles in schools of business.

6 Offer internships that expose participants to the realities
of international business.

Conclusions

The Brookings conference on the international dimension of
management education was designed to explore ways of
improving the preparation of managers for the new responsibilities arising from the rapidly growing internationalisation
of business. Although no formal consensus was sought, there
appeared to be general agreement on the recommendations
set out in this chapter, including the central one that management education and development programmes must respond
more effectively to the need for broadly prepared, flexible
and socially responsible managers.

Developing such managers is a shared responsibility. Business
schools have the task of broadening their curricula and for
preparing qualified candidates to function in a multinational
world, whether or not they work for a multinational firm.
Corporations have a responsibility to develop further, through
experience and social programmes, the skills and perspectives
needed in their enterprises, thus both relieving the schools
of certain burdens and reinforcing what the schools do.

In brief, the conference agreed that:

1 The internationalisation of business has so expanded
international influences even on domestic business that
all students of management should have a greater
knowledge of these influences and how they affect
business and management.

2 Schools seeking distinction in management on a global
scale should staff themselves and organise their programmes to prepare qualified candidates for positions in
MNCs and related enterprises.

3 Faculty members in several ways can acquire the know-

ledge, experience and skills needed to deal with the globalisation of business and to develop potential managers for international firms. Curriculum reforms and student interest must be encouraged. Diplomatic and executive experience enlisted from abroad can assist the effort.

4 Corporations, especially the multinationals, have a large responsibility for developing their recruits into qualified managers. To this end, in-service training and staff participation in special conferences and seminars are essential. The MNCs should cooperate in strengthening such programmes and other efforts to develop statesmanlike approaches to the multinational problems that lie ahead.

The multinational corporation and its managers are entering uncharted seas. They will need wisdom and statesmanship to steer a safe course through the private and public contests ahead, the nationalistic political conflicts and the social controversies this new institution will engender. Few other challenges in management, and thus in management education, offer greater opportunity for service.

Notes

[1] 'Internationalizing Management Education', a conference report by the Advisory Committee on Business and International Education of the US National Commission for UNESCO, Washington, D.C., 1973.
[2] Dean William R. Dill adds: "At the same time that new economic and technological incentives have appeared for global integration, business and governments alike — worldwide — are facing skepticism about and hostility toward bigness. The drives of business for integration, for transnational efficiencies, and for stability in relations with governments seem more and more in conflict with the reassertion of community and national identities and with the pressures toward democratization and decentralization".
[3] Professor Stefan H. Robock adds: 'If schools are really

committed to meeting the international challenge, their faculty reward system should reflect this commitment. The criteria for granting tenure should include a requirement that the candidate have developed a competence in the international dimension of his or her field. Similarly, the criteria for faculty recruitment should include a requirement that the candidate have, or be prepared to develop, familiarity with the international dimension of his or her professional field'.

[4] Dr Bohdan Hawrylyshyn adds: 'There is an additional need for deans to be internationalised through special seminars, travel, foreign sabbaticals, or by having schools obtain some foreigners to serve as deans'.

[5] Dr Cyril C. Ling adds: 'The involvement of institutions of traditional minority-group enrolment could be an additional enriching aspect of consortium arrangements'.

8 Faculty Learning must Precede Curriculum Change

L. C. NEHRT

The need

This chapter is concerned with a series of seminars which took place in the USA during the summer of 1978. They were attended by 245 business school professors and had as their primary object that of preparing these faculty members to internationalise some of the core (required) courses in the business school curriculum. Before discussing the organisation and content of these seminars, it may be useful to review the various developments which led up to the seminars.

One would prefer to think that business schools practice what they preach. We teach that the business firm should continually scan the environment so as to adapt the strategies of the firm to the environment in which the firm must operate. If business schools were to do this, they would have realised more than a decade ago that the business environment which their graduates would enter had changed dramatically. By the mid-1960s it was clear that the large international business firms (be they transnationals, multinationals, or simple internationals) were becoming a very important force in the inter-national economy as well as in their individual national economies. But this is only a small portion of the total number of businessmen involved in the international aspects of business. One must also include all aspects of exporting and importing of goods and services, in addition to the various international licensing agreements, international leasing agreements, short-term investing or borrowing in other currencies, and a wide variety of other activities. Thus, when one speaks of educating or training people for international business, one refers to all those individuals whose job can be better performed if they are familiar with the economics, politics and culture of various foreign countries, and if they have an understanding of the international aspects of politics, economics, finance and transportation.

This includes a wide variety of people who work in various capacities in different types of firms, yet never travel abroad. Their business is affected by competition from imports, or utilises imported parts or services; they correspond with foreign firms; they meet and deal with visiting foreign businessmen or government officials; their work entails an understanding of the foreign sales or foreign operations of their company; they must make decisions which affect, indirectly, the foreign sales or operations of their company; they must fully understand the environment in which their firm's foreign operations are located in order to communicate, in the complete sense of the term, with the company's overseas personnel. Thus, it is seen that the need for international education for the business world is not restricted to those businessmen who live overseas, nor just to those who are directly involved in managing the international operations of the firm. International business and its indirect effects have become a pervasive factor in the business scene. It is difficult to point to a firm of any size which is not involved in or affected by some aspect of international business.

However, very few business schools were responding to this need. American business textbooks continued to be written as though the world stopped at the boundaries of the US, and many European business schools used the American texts. The teaching of international business courses per se began to make inroads in business school curricula in the US in the early 1960s, and by the early 1970s was widespread, but in many schools only a small percentage of students was taking any of these courses.

The requirement

Finally, in 1974, at the urging of the Academy of International Business, the American Assembly of Collegiate Schools of

Business (AACSB) changed its accreditation standards so as to require that the curricula of business schools reflect the 'global' as well as the domestic aspects of business. However, the AACSB did not issue an interpretation of this new standard: it was left to each school to determine the way in which it would attempt to meet that standard.

Basically, there are three ways by which a school can satisfy this standard. The school may require that every student take a specific course in international business, such as 'Introduction to International Business'. Or, each student must take an international business course related to his field of study (e.g. a finance major must take a course in international finance etc.). Finally, a number of core courses which all students are already required to take would be internationalised.

Some schools began to follow one of these standards; other schools selected another. Yet other schools assumed a 'wait and see' attitude, until such time as the AACSB might issue an interpretation, or until an AACSB visitation team applied pressure for compliance.

The ACE study

In 1976 the American Council on Education, in Washington, D.C., received a grant from the EXXON Education Foundation, to carry out a study of the ways by which higher education might better prepare university graduates for the needs of business. This author was asked to chair the national task force, made up one-third each of government officials, international businessmen and academics. [1] The task force realised that the large number of individuals working in the business world came from a wide variety of educational backgrounds. A minority of them study in business schools; they also enter business firms with degrees in arts and sciences, or from engineering or one of the various other professional schools. Hence the concern of that task force was with all higher education, and not restricted to business schools.

The following comments, however, reflect only the results of a survey which was made of the deans of the schools of business in the USA. A questionnaire was sent to the deans of all 178 accredited business schools and of the 316 non-accredited institutions. There was a 76 per cent response from the deans of the accredited schools and a 65 per cent response from the other group. It was found that, as at spring 1976, 76 per cent of the responding accredited schools and 69 per cent of the non-accredited schools had taken steps to comply with the new AACSB standard on internationalisation of the curriculum. As none of the three internationalisation strategies can be followed unless the faculty are appropriately trained and motivated, the deans were asked their opinions as to the desirability of instituting summer workshops in international business for faculty members. The response was that 86 per cent of the deans of the accredited schools and 87 per cent from the non-accredited institutions indicated that they felt that such workshops were either desirable or highly desirable.

As a result of the above, one of the high priority recommendations of the American Council of Education task force was for the AACSB, jointly with the Academy of International Business, to lay out a three-year programme of such summer workshops and to seek funds from business firms, foundations and government to finance the major costs of these workshops.

Organisation and goal of the 1978 seminar-workshops

In late 1977 the General Electric Company agreed to give the AACSB $150,000 to finance a series of workshops during the summer of 1977. A task force, under the chairmanship of Dean Donald Carroll, Wharton School, was appointed to administer the grant and organise the programme.

It was decided that, for this first summer, the goal of the programme would be to assist schools in the internationalisation of the core courses of the curriculum. The rational for this approach was four-fold. First, many schools would not attempt to require that all students take at least one specialised course in international business because this may add to the total number of required courses. Secondly, there are not enough faculty members who are specialised in international business, available on the market, to permit hundreds of schools to implement this strategy at the same time. Third, many schools do not have the budget to hire the additional faculty members who are needed and on the market. Lastly, even where a school chooses to require a course in international business, logic calls for the core courses to be internationalised in any case, rather than continue to be taught from a provincial viewpoint.

The task force selected four core courses to be the subject of the workshops: accounting, business policy, finance and marketing. It was also decided that approximately 245 professors could be accommodated (with a portion of the costs to be paid by the participants' school), that all 245 would go to Washington, D.C. for a three-day seminar, and that a five-day workshop would be held in each of the seven AACSB regions (for the approximately 35 participants selected in each region). The president of the AACSB sent a letter to the dean of every business school asking him (or her) to nominate one or two faculty members for this programme. There were approximately 450 nominations, from which the task force selected the 245 participants.

Washington, D.C. seminar

The Washington seminar, organised by Professor Phillip Grub (George Washington University), was held on 22–24 May 1978. A series of speakers gave the participants a behind-the-scenes view of the process of decision-making by the US government in the area of international trade policy, exposed them to the interrelationships between MNCs and the various governmental and international organisations, and give them the opportunity to question important government officials in the area of international economic policy and policies affecting MNCs.

Regional workshops – general

The task force appointed a committee, chaired by this author, to organise and staff the regional workshops. A host institution was selected for each of the seven regions. These were: Massachusetts Institute of Technology (MIT); University of Pennsylvania; Georgia State University (Atlanta); University of Chicago; Wichita State University (Kansas); University of Texas, Dallas; and University of California, Los Angeles (UCLA). A faculty coordinator was appointed at each host institution. The workshops were scheduled for July 1978.

The committee decided that each regional workshop would be organised as follows: two days for a general background in international business, to be attended by all 35 participants; one day for visits to local international businesses, banks or trade centres; and two days for specialised workshops. The rationale for the two days of general background in international business was that the deans had been asked to nominate faculty members who had no background in international business and it was felt that by offering them a condensed 'Introduction to International Business' course, they would all be up to a certain level of understanding before getting into the specialised workshops. In general, local faculty members (at each regional seminar) were utilised to teach the parts of this introductory portion. Also each regional coordinator was given considerable freedom to organise those first two days (and the intermediate 'free' day) as he wished.

Specialised workshops

Each participant had previously specified his area of interest (the core course which he would be expected to internationalise) and had been assigned to that specialised workshop. Of the approximately 35 participants in each region, the number in each of the four specialised workshops varied from 5 to 13.

To select the specialised workshop leaders, the coordinating committee had scanned the universe of international business professors and had come up with a list of 54 names, to teach 28 workshops (4 workshops in each of the 7 regions). The committee was looking for workshop leaders who were teaching both the core course and the international course in that field, i.e. corporate finance plus international finance. Thus the workshop leader would not only know the international field intimately, but would also be fully aware of the time pressures and student capabilities in the core course. It was also obviously necessary that the workshop leader be available for the dates already set for the workshops.

At the last minute the committee decided that, rather than spend two full days for the specialised workshops, the last half-day should be a plenary session where each of the four workshop leaders would summarise the results of his workshop. Thus the person who attended the marketing workshop could benefit from a discussion of the approach taken and the conclusions arrived at in the other three workshops. This was to accommodate the realisation that many of the faculty members had been selected by their deans with the idea that they would return to their schools and lead the movement for the general internationalisation of the curriculum — not just the one course. In addition, much of the discussion during the last half-day centred around the politics of the intro-duction of the internationalisation concept into any given business school.

The general approach in each of the specialised workshops was as follows: the first half-day was devoted to a review of the international field (e.g. of international marketing), with the remainder of the time being allocated to the specifics of exactly how the core course (principles of marketing or marketing management) could be internationalised.

Taking corporate finance as an example, it was generally concluded that the inclusion of one section on international finance (most of the latest texts have one chapter, usually the last in the book, on international finance) was totally inadequate and was usually skipped by the professor. Profes-sors usually avoid that 'international' chapter because they do not feel competent to deal with it — to answer questions which might arise in class discussion, but they usually use the excuse that there is not enough time in the semester to squeeze in that chapter.

Therefore it appeared that the preferable approach would be that of identifying those topical areas which are part of every corporate finance text, which have a clear and necessary international dimension and which are now taught (because that is the way the textbooks are written) from a purely domestic viewpoint. The topical areas thus identified were:

1. Cash management.
2. Financial control systems.
3. Capital structure.
4. Short-term financing.
5. Long-term financing.
6. Capital budgeting.
7. Taxes.
8. Parent-subsidiary financing.
9. Profit remission and retained earnings policy.
10. Mergers and acquisitions.

It was foreseen that the next generation of textbooks in corporate finance might attempt to add an international 'capsule' at the end of each of the above sections. This would be the easy way out for the authors, but would be unfortunate from the point of view of internationalising the course because, again, most faculty members would simply skip that capsule. What is needed is that each of the above ten chapters be rewritten with an international perspective throughout. It became clear that finance today, by the nature of the environment, is international, and that 'domestic' finance — the way it is usually taught — is a subsection of the field of finance and does not even touch on some of the very important principles.

However, the necessary textbooks do not yet exist. What can be done today? Again, using finance as an example, several readings which covered the pertinent international aspects were identified for each of the above ten topical areas, and the workshop discussion centred around ways by which such readings could be made available to the students, and by which their content could be worked into the general discussion of that topical area.

Evaluation of the seminar-workshops

A detailed questionnaire was administered to each participant at the end of the workshops. On the basis of the responses, plus discussions between the regional chairmen and the workshop leaders, it was felt that future seminars should be organised somewhat differently.

First, although the Washington, D.C. seminar was interesting, it was very costly, particularly considering the 4,800 km. which the faculty members had to travel each way, from the west coast. It was not really a necessary part of the exercise and could be eliminated, saving both cost and time. Secondly, it was found that many of the participants who were selected by the deans did, in fact, have a strong background in international business, and for them the initial two days of the regional workshops were boring. Even for the others it was felt that two days were longer than necessary, *if* the participants were assigned background reading (a basic introductory text) prior to arriving at the workshops. Thirdly, the business visits had mixed results and were not a necessary part of the exercise.

Thus, perhaps the preferable design for future years would be to eliminate the Washington, D.C. seminar and to hold three-day seminars in the regions: one day of background in international business, one and one-half days of specialised workshops, and a half-day for summary. This would permit the workshops to be held on a Friday, Saturday and Sunday. They could then be held during the academic year and not interfere with summer school or summer vacation plans.

Problems of implementation

It became clear from the discussions in the workshops that, even though the AACSB has a standard, and even though the environment clearly demands that the curriculum be internationalised, the major hurdle is that of faculty apathy. The one faculty member who attends a workshop on internationalising his marketing course will very likely internationalise his own course, but how does he get his other colleagues to do it? Curriculum committees are reluctant to change requirements. Also, they and the department chairpersons have limited leverage to encourage faculty members to change the way in which they teach their courses.

The real problem of implementing the internationalisation of the core courses is not solved by sending faculty members to attend workshops of this sort, short of sending *all* the faculty members (including fresh instructors) who teach the course. The real problem is political and behavioural, and each school will have to find its own way of solving this problem of resistance to change.

Note

[1] The resultant study was entitled *Business and International Education,* American Council on Education, 1976. See also Chapter 2, which gives more detail on this study.

9 Educating Foreign Managers for African Responsibilities*

AMON J. NSEKELA

African states, people and foreign managers

The immediate question for you, as for me, is: 'What do I have to say about this topic?' True, I am an African, but so are 250 million other people on the Continent of Africa. True I am international in the relevant sense, but a high commissioner is hardly a manager. However, on reflection I do see four areas of experience which may have a bearing on our topic.

First, I am an African who has observed and been in contact with foreign managers and firms in Africa. This is not a racial point but one of location or viewpoint. A firm and its manager (like any institution and any of us) looks rather different to the beholder than its self image. Secondly, I am, by experience, primarily a public servant in both the civil and the state enterprise sectors. In that capacity I have seen and experienced the problems of ensuring that pursuit of enterprise and managerial concerns was consistent with national and public service goals. Doubtless you have had the same experience but, again, from the opposite – or hopefully a complementary – viewpoint. Thirdly, I have been directly involved in negotiating and controlling especially when I was Principal Secretary to the Treasury and chairman and managing director of the National Bank of Commerce in Tanzania. I do know something about what business negotiations and business regulations are and what is conducive (or corrosive) to their

---

* This chapter is the text of the speech given by His Excellency Amon J. Nsekela at the Cambridge Conference in April 1979.

success. Fourthly, I have been a manager, or to be exact, chairman and managing director of the National Bank of Commerce which was and still is a large, growing, profitable enterprise with extensive dealings with international firms and managers. The NBC also concerned itself with training and education. Indeed, it was that concern which, inter alia, led to my proposal to establish what is now our Institute of Finance Management in Dar es Salaam. The NBC too had to see how it could fit enterprise requirements and targets into a framework set by government regulations and national goals. I too have debated and discussed with civil servants from the business enterprise end of the table.

All that notwithstanding, I do not propose to discuss pedagogy as such, nor even the structure and timing of training, much as I may be tempted to do so. What seems to me more useful is:

1   To set out what I perceive as the goals which trans-national corporations (TNCs), and therefore the international managers' senior managerial representatives, have in Africa.
2   To indicate how I see these goals as interacting with African and African states' goals, giving special attention to areas of present or potential conflict and how these may be reduced.
3   To reflect briefly on possible future scenarios concerning the international managers and their firms' relations with us in Africa.

Perceptions, knowledge and training

The fact that I am here today marks a shift in major enterprises' perceptions of Africa. Last autumn the International Association of Planning Societies and the European Planning Federation asked me to speak on 'The Expanding African Continent', in the context of the management of strategic enterprise. After initial bafflement, I realised that the expansion was in their perception of Africa: as a geographical zone which could be of significance, as a group of states which had to be

understood and responded to like other states and not to be
treated like school children; as the home of human beings
who were no more passive or indifferent to how they were
treated than human beings in Europe; as an area in which states
and people increasingly had not simply goals of their own but
also the will, the knowledge and the power to pursue them.
They perceived, and I think you will perceive, that unless
Africa and Africans are better understood and related to
significant shocks and surprises, debacles could be envisaged
and whatever else expanded in Africa it would not be mutually
profitable and stable roles for the TNCs and their enterprises
in Africa.

Education and communication

Now, how does this relate to the education and training of
managers? I suggest in at least four ways: lack of knowledge
of Africa and lack of knowledge of African states and peoples
are endemic and expensive. Communication is poor, attitudes
are often as inconsistent with attaining your goals as they are
infuriating to many Africans. Presumably, education and
training do raise levels of knowledge, bolster ability to
communicate and further a self-critical examination of
attitudes. Let me illustrate this, initially at least, with examples
of what I should suppose you (as well as I) would wish to see
avoided.

A firm – a European/Tanzanian joint venture – set up to
process cashew nuts in Dar es Salaam. It presently came to
the government to complain that our nuts were the wrong
size for its machines, although those in Mozambique were (so
it asserted) right. Well, our nuts had not changed size to spite
the firm and there would have been no problem in sampling
before building! Mozambique and Tanzania are indeed both
in Africa, but it is not true that they are identical nor that
after you have seen one cashew nut you have seen them all.
The same firm presently came to complain of the wages it
had to pay under an industrial agreement with our trade
union (and we have only one in Tanzania). Our nuts were
middle level for a large firm but as it asserted, and proved,
they were four times what it paid in, still colonial, Mozam-

bique. The lack of knowledge necessary to attempt to convince Tanzania of appropriate wages in this way is breathtaking; but there is one further point. One of my officials calculated the total wage and salary cost per ton of saleable kernels for the two plants; it was 10 per cent lower in Tanzania. As he rather bluntly put it at the next meeting with the manager, 'Do you know your own costs per ton? Are you so sure slave wages pay you?'

Another very large transnational, with whom our general relations in a joint venture role were quite good and whose information disclosure and consultation on financial management was a source of satisfaction to us, and of a degree of trust not irrelevant to their profits, had an industrial dispute. Its management, at least its top international managers, rallied round the manager charged with discriminatory hiring, abusive conduct to workers, waste of funds and fought the case with vehemence and, indeed, venom. At a perfectly amiable meeting on financial prospects an official of the Treasury asked whether the man was really so innocent. The answer was that the manager believed half the charges (approaching 100) were false or gravely exaggerated and half, including some of the most serious, were basically true. When asked why the support, the answer was it was the principle of the thing not the innocence or competence of the manager.

Knowledge and attitude

It is indeed the principle but, I fancy, the other way around. Hierarchical authoritarianism and 'we managers, right or wrong, are right' attitude — especially by foreign managers — are not acceptable to Africans (nor, I may suggest, any other labour force). To act as if they were acceptable, betrays a lack of knowledge informing your enterprises' point of view which verges on criminal negligence. Equally, Tanzania's policy on worker/manager relations was well known, or should have been, from print and practice. The firm was simply begging for a needless confrontation. The naive confiding in the official, suggests both a remarkable 'we — they' outlook with any 'senior' person 'we', and a lack of knowledge of the degree to which our officials were sensitive on matters relating to workers' interests, the awareness of their responsibility to the party and government for the implementations of our national goals and their willingness to act on what they knew and felt even when inconvenient. Another, but smaller, transnational corporation was discussing a joint venture with us and in the course of the discussions proposed a revaluation of net worth by 'updating' fixed assets according to a somewhat complex formula which it stated in the vaguest of terms. The firm declined to spell out the formula or its effects on major fixed asset items. The result, which was not surprising, was that our side, having some commercial management sense, declined to discuss the 'net worth' figure. After hours of scribbling, one of our officials looked up and enquired whether the formula was as follows. . . ., and the main value charges so and so much. The managers gasped and indicated that they would not care to contradict him. What is the use of playing 'tic, tac, toe' instead of providing adequate facts for a dialogue?

Similarly, a major transnational — again one with which we did a large amount of business on mutually beneficial terms, at least I suppose so as they kept coming back with new ventures, and bids — always presented draft agreements with a number of serious 'booby traps'. I do not mean too high asking prices or proposed profit shares; within limits, those are inevitable and reasonable. Negotiators do leave themselves room to manoeuvre. Rather, by that I mean terms and conditions which no reasonable manager could accept and that they knew we would not accept if we discovered them. After one mistake, we did find them; then one of our top economic and legal talents went through every clause on a 'mine detection' exercise as well as a mere normal 'bargaining for a business deal basis'. When the booby traps were challenged the transnational corporation's managers would presently agree to changes, sometimes with a laugh. Frankly, that is a form of hide and seek game that I, and most African managers and public servants, do not appreciate.

'Do unto others as you would have others do unto you'

This is perhaps not a communication but an attitude problem. It comes out in utterances like: 'We must make allowances;

they are just down from the trees'. 'It is useless to expect a decent day's work'. 'This bloody fool workers' participation. What do workers know about anything anyhow?' I, and many senior officials, have heard all of these and scores of other such mumblings and perhaps only slightly less obnoxious, in the 1970s. My point is not one of decent attitudes to human beings. It is not even that this type of comment, flowing from a set of attitudes which are hard to conceal, leads to strained relations with African governments. It is that it is counterproductive for you and your enterprises.

The person responsible for the first statement was promoting several contracts. Who knows whether the uniform negative advice of the official he condescended to talk to so freely was totally on some real analytical weaknesses or on some other equally real doubt that the attitude was one consistent with good faith dealings? The second was from a firm whose labour costs per unit of work were 20 per cent above, and whose ability to complete work on time was 3 to 18 months behind, other units in that sector. One wonders whether its attitudes were not self-fulfilling and the cause of half its troubles. The last firm had very serious problems with its workers. It asserted, perhaps correctly, that some workers threw scrap metal into machinery and others were wilfully deaf when instructed to remedy defects promptly. Output began to fall, costs to rise and pressure from the trade union on the government to be intense and, as a result, the joint venture and management contract was ended. Did it pay?

The brighter side

Now let me turn to opposite examples. One manager said of me to one of my officials, 'He knows what he wants and how to bargain, but he's too tough'. Fine. I was not fishing, nor have I ever fished for compliments; that comment revealed an attitude toward negotiations and Tanzanian negotiators which poses few problems. Another firm said of its workers that, up to supervisor level, their productivity was better than in the parent European plant — and so was the profit record. The general manager of a major transnational corporation, discussing workers' councils with an official, remarked that workers' councils were very time consuming, sometimes irritating, but had resulted in the best labour relations he had experienced in half a dozen postings and in a labour productivity above target levels. Again we never supposed that workers' participation was cost or strain-free. The attitude expressed seemed a perfectly reasonable one, including his comments that some Tanzanians sought to abuse the system of workers' councils.

There were, and there are, managers and enterprises — sometimes clearly as enterprise policy, sometimes as a matter of the manager's own 'style' — which regularly saw senior officials to discuss programmes and prospects, not because they had immediate requests or problems but in order to create a body of mutual understanding and trust for times when, and if, specific issues arose. There were, and there are, firms and managers who were and are very proud of having trained and retrained local Africans to the point where only two or three expatriates remained out of say, twenty or thirty senior managers, as well as cases where the numbers were the reverse. There were, and there are, enterprises and managers whose written and oral submissions (including projections) to the Prices Commission made and make their work of safe-guarding reasonable return on assets, consumer welfare (or cost structures for commercial users) and limiting inflation relatively straightforward and any ensuing debate informed and to the point. For whatever reason they, rather than the firms which file incomplete data and suspiciously inaccurate projections, have fairly substantial and rising profits and a relationship with the state characterised by good will as well as, of course, occasional tensions not emanating from mutual distrust and acrimony which can be no easier personally, nor more useful institutionally to you than to us.

Enterprise and managerial goals

I shall treat your goals, as international managers, as those of your enterprises. I know this is oversimplifying the matter but it is broadly correct. As managers you must be concerned with furthering the interests and reaching the targets of your enterprises. The same is true of me as a high commissioner in relation to my government. Of course, you and I have personal concerns; of course we both participate in setting goals; of course, at times, we disagree. The fact remains that we cannot, and should not, pursue goals basically at variance with those of our enterprises or states.

Evidently not all firms have the same particular goals, nor are those for one African country necessarily the same as those for another, even within the same enterprise. However there are a number of goals fairly widely expressed and acted upon. These include:

1   Trade expansion both to provide markets for exports and to ensure dependable and predictable (or low cost) sources of particular African goods.

2   Sales of knowledge and technology through management, technical, turnkey and licensing contracts as well as the more traditional sales of banking and insurance expertise.

3   Stable relationships (business or political) which allow for forward planning, not necessarily because the relationships are unchanging but because changes are negotiated and phased, as opposed to unilateral and overnight.

4   Ability and intention by the African parties to agreements to carry out their side of the bargain (including making payments) as well as a genuine commitment by African states and enterprises to carrying out agreements once they have been made.

5   Opportunities for commercial and business relations beyond simple current account trade, including for example, varying forms of investment, lending and joint ventures.

6   A setting in which the business transactions involved in the preceding goals can be completed at a profit which can either be reinvested fruitfully in Africa or remitted to the companies' home countries.

7   African decision-taking processes and decisions which are either strongly influenced by western states and

firms or are, at least, not perceived as hostile to them nor strongly influenced by European or Asian socialist states.

8   Avoiding African development patterns creating problems for the self-reliance policies of the capitalist industrialised economies, such as the EEC's Common Agricultural Policy, by seeking to produce and export in the relevant fields and, similarly, encouraging African economies acting in a way which might minimise the adjustment problems of the economies of the industrialised states. (For example, the situation leading to the enforcement by the economies of the industrialised countries of the so-called Multifibre Arrangement in Textiles and Garments).

9   Following human rights policies acceptable to the decision-takers or pressure groups of the countries where you are citizens.

And what about African goals?

The goals of the African states, of their decision-takers and of individual Africans, are, of course, *not* identical either; still less are they identical with yours. To pretend otherwise is to create a smokescreen obscuring possible joint or negotiable interest areas and potential to achieve contractual relations for mutual benefit. African goals and African interests, by definition, place Africans, African institutions and African states first. African goals and African interests place African development first and external business-partner profits next; African control over decisions in and directly affecting Africa and Africans first and responsiveness to external interests next; as well as giving priority to the negotiated resolution of divergences resulting from African policies which cause problems to you and from your policies which cause problems to us. These are the African priorities.

Does this mean that relationships must be red in tooth and claw, that contracts must be more likely to be broken than performed, that uncertainty and massive surprises must be the norm? No. By no means. How would an African – this African – perceive your view of interests vis-à-vis Africa?

1　African states and firms seek to build up exports and to secure dependable and predictable sources of supply for the imports they need. There are disagreements on particular issues of which imports and exports, at what prices and through what channels? But these are the normal stuff of the state and enterprise business negotiations and not a basic conflict of interest.

2　We do not deny our need to buy knowledge, nor that business firms who have built it up will charge for such sales on a profit-making basis. Again one set of differences is simply on price and quality terms of particular contracts. Other issues relate to the appropriateness of what is sold to us (and the truth of the sales pitches for it) and our having the right to buy selectively (without unwanted tie-in terms packaging items that we do not need and items we wish to produce ourselves). But these are not an inevitable part of knowledge sales and need not prevent their growth (even if on a gradually changing and more selective basis).

3　Pure uncertainty is not something which helps Africans, African states or Africa. The poor and the weak find it harder to shield themselves from the impact of strategic surprise than do the rich and strong. There is a real problem however: the maintenance of a status quo biased against us for historical reasons is not an acceptable interpretation of stability to Africans. Like you, we see relationships, contracts and the like, as needing to be adjusted to changing realities. It is attempts to freeze them, by you or by us, which ensures rather than prevents sudden, surprising and destabilizing changes.

4　So far as ability to carry out agreements goes, for instance paying on time in convertible currency, your interests and those of Africa are at one level the same. However, there is disagreement on means: the type of stabilisation and 'aid' programmes often proposed to African states to make them 'able' to 'carry out obligations' have such high costs in terms of growth, employment, consumption and inflation – all at once – that any government in Western Europe that accepted programmes half as draconic would be swept into the dustbin at the next election. At that level there is divergence: cooperation and negotiation on how, in the face of crises such as drought and world recession, we can meet our external obligations must take more serious account of our domestic African requirements. Until there is such two-way concern, what we perceive is an external attempt to impose the giving of absolute priority to our external over our internal obligations. That we can no more accept in relation to our states and firms than you do in relation to your firms and states.

5   African attitudes to desirable forms of business ventures with foreign firms vary. Most Africans foresee change in the institutional structuring of such ventures over time as desirable, indeed as inevitable. Most African decision-takers see some relationships over some period as mutually beneficial. Within those ranges the problems are again the standard stuff of business negotiations. Where proposals simply fall outside the range both sides would see as desirable, then they could not be negotiated among your own firms any more than between them and African states or enterprises. We are by no means the only people who find some forms of joint ventures or production units unacceptable.

6   We do not suppose that commercial firms are in the charity business, indeed, we are usually suspicious of those who claim they are. Therefore, we accept that foreign business enterprises will need to have the opportunities to make profits on their business in, or with, Africa if they are to continue doing such business.

7   Strong influence on African decision-taking processes by outsiders is not acceptable to the vast majority of Africans and African decision-takers. Attempts to exert such influence on African decision-takers will not be conducive, except in the very short run, to stability or harmony of interests. That, however, is consistent with the second half of your own goal: the absence of domination of Africa by external states or firms which you consider hostile to you.

8   African decision-takers do not deny the right of your states to undertake self-reliance programmes, such as the

domestic production of basic foods, or those based on mixed social and production concerns nor the need for your enterprise to respond to such programmes in location of production and marketing. We do, however, reject an unbalanced view that we must go out of our way to avoid interference with foreign state or enterprise policies, and have no claim to negotiated compensation when they damage us, whereas we are expected to secure your and/or your home governments' consent to actions, relating to self-reliance and mixed social-cum-production development, which might interfere with your economic relations with Africa. The rights and obligations need to move towards being rather more symmetrical and being realistic about whose actions can really do serious damage to whom. For example, Botswana's basic rural cash economy can be destroyed if the EEC does not continue its 'temporary' beef waiver provisions to allow Botswana to continue selling beef to the markets for which it built up its industry before their shift towards self-reliance in beef. But can you imagine any possible African self-reliance production measures, even on a continuing basis, having a comparable effect on the economy of any OECD member state? I wonder! Similarly the pressures of French garment manufacturers leading to blocking Tunisian garment sales to France (from Franco-Tunisian joint ventures) did harm to Tunisia out of all proportion to any Tunisian economic policy which affected the French economy or large French firms.

9   The human rights of Africans obviously concerns me. Equally it is evident to me that there are states in Africa whose disregard for human rights is appalling, to say the least. However, I am afraid this does not mean that the present form of external assertions of a right to define and promote human rights in Africa is an area of agreement. This kind of concern with human rights is selective in that the reaction and publicity given to one European's violated human rights in Africa is out of all proportion to that given when, say, 1,000 Africans are murdered in Africa by a white, racist, fascist and minority régime

such as apartheid-ridden South Africa, or by a white racist minority and illegal régime such as that in Ian Smith's Rhodesia, or even elsewhere by a black African régime, or when 1,000 Africans have their human rights violated in Europe. It is more selective in that human rights issues are not handled consistently. They are played down if the African state concerned is perceived as friendly and trumpeted as a cover story when the real disagreement turns on very different issues. Indeed they are triply selective in that those who, being naive at best, call for sharp cuts in personal consumption, external vetos on economic decisions, loss of growth in order to 'meet external obligations' and at least three major 'economic reform' programmes which have been or attempted to be imposed on African states during the past 18 months do fit that pattern — then cry out when dissidence and riots by the losers have to be suppressed. Equally selective is the concern of those who cry out if an intellectual is denied the right to speak or write but fail to comment on the denial of the rights of millions to land, to work, to education to decent wages, to access to public services and to effective participation in society. I do not say that we, in Africa, are perfect. Nor do I say that the human rights of all human beings are a concern only of some human beings. Human rights are and must be of universal concern. I do say, however, that the external record in Africa and the form and selectivity of present external human rights' concerns renders them more than a little suspect to me and to most of my fellow Africans. It is especially suspect from international managers. You have sought stability, low wages, low taxes. You have sought state support against 'assertive' unions and opposed workers' participation. You know, or ought to know, that the only easy way to deliver on that package is for a state to practise authoritarianism and repression of workers. If you really are concerned about human rights you have a good deal of rethinking to do before you become its prophets!

Two guidelines

I think I have shown that your interests in relation to those of African states, enterprises and Africans, properly studied, are far from wholly and inevitably antagonistic to each other. Finding the areas and means of promoting joint interests requires examination, discussion and negotiation; for that process let me offer what I hope are two helpful guidelines:

1   Business enterprises should not seek to operate in Africa in ways they could not at home, nor seek to call in their governments to support claims against us which if made against their fellow home-country enterprises or their governments, would be viewed as totally unacceptable. We are people and we are states; viewed that way it is imperative therefore, that acceptable conduct for enterprises operating in our states and their conduct towards us should not be basically different from that with which you carry out their operations in your home states.

2   Foreign states and enterprises, particularly western industrialised states and their TNC's should not behave towards us in ways radically less participatory or co-operative, and less based on negotiating to arrive at mutually agreed arrangements than they would with each other. To treat African states as passive and malleable masses subject to total external manipulation is to prevent the development of stable relationships and to ensure the recurrence of unpredictable, explosive and mutually damaging change. Those who do not respect us can hardly be surprised if we do not respect them or the 'agreements' they impose on us. Those who try to form relationships with African states solely in terms of their own interests without regard to mutual interest (and sometimes for truth) can hardly expect African states to abstain from unilaterally altering them with parallel disregard for external interests whenever the opportunity arises. 'As ye sow, so shall ye reap' is an ethical principal but it is also a practical operating truth in international political and economic relations.

Areas of conflict

So far so good. Let me now continue my argument in a little more detail in respect to five areas of actual or potential conflict which, on present evidence, are going to give rise to strategic surprises unwelcome to many of you. These are: Southern Africa; transnational corporations; corruption, contract and regulation; as well as patterns of production, trade and knowledge; and overall change in the international economic order.

Southern Africa

It seems to me that most large capitalist enterprises, and most of their home states, have been pursuing policies diametrically opposed to their own medium and long-term interests. South Africans will liberate South Africa — with help from whoever will provide it and against whoever seeks to support (militarily, politically or economically) the present régimes. The new states and their citizens will perceive their friends, their potential business partners and the compatibility (or other-wise) of their interests with those of particular non-African states and enterprises in the light of their own history and liberation struggle. Those who help shore up the present régimes should not be surprised if they find they are not preferred as partners, nor readily perceived as having potential common interests.

I do not believe that these rather brutal facts of life have yet fully penetrated the planning of most European firms or states. Let me illustrate this. If Namibia becomes independent with South Africa using a legal quibble to hold its only deepwater port — built for, integrated with, and governed as part of Namibia for sixty years and populated by Namibians — then any Namibian government with an interest in national self-preservation will at once set out to secure the building of a new port. That, as it happens, is quite feasible but would cost, say, $150 million. One may suppose that all offers to build such a port free or on concessional terms will be considered and that packages including fishing rights or berth facilities will not be rejected out of hand. Do the major

Western states really suppose it is in *their* interests to build a new port for Namibia — or to force Namibia to seek some other port builder such as the USSR — rather than to force South Africa to include Walvis Bay in the territory which comprises Namibia on Independence Day?

I now come to companies operating in Namibia. Companies have acted with equal lack of planning for their own long term interests. Consider those who 'contracted' with South Africa to create the Rossing uranium oxide complex and those who 'contracted' to buy its output. They did so after the mandate over South West Africa had been revoked and the South African occupation was illegal — a view of legal reality clearly affirmed by the International Court of Justice. Thus, the so-called investment and purchase contracts have no legal basis. South Africa, as an illegal occupier, could confer no rights to mine; the producing company, having no valid title to the oxide, could not confer any lawful ownership on purchasers.

Rossing clearly has made the liberation of Namibia take longer and cost more lives. It gave South Africa, and also several firms and their governments, reasons to resist or delay change. The whole saga is morally outrageous. There are some in Namibia, in South Africa, and elsewhere, who would say that the men who made the Rossing 'contracts' have blood on their hands!

My point, however, is not moral outrage. It is to point out that the parties to the contracts have damaged their own interests. Namibia will, indeed, wish to operate Rossing and to sell its output. To do so, it will need to purchase foreign knowledge on the technical and managerial side and to sell the yellow cake on the world markets. SWAPO has quite clearly stated that it will seek international managers, and use international markets. But why should anyone suppose, as some do, that she will see the old 'contracts' as anything other than evidence of conspiracies to commit grand larceny and to receive stolen property? Who should it be any surprise if she seeks new sources of knowledge and new selling arrangements and treats the former investors and purchasers as least not most, favoured candidates? If she does do so, will 'investing' in Rossing under the South African occupation have been a way to make or to lose money and contracting to buy that oxide a way to safeguard or to endanger medium-term supplies?

There are, and have been, other possible courses of action open to states and to companies. For example, after the illegal declaration of independence by the rebel forces in Rhodesia, Zambia and Tanzania required additional petroleum refining, storing and transport facilities. To create them required finance, management and technical skills not available domestically. The ENI group, Italian banks and Italian state entities did contract to provide those inputs and to do so within corporate structures subject to Zambian and/or Tanzanian control.

Yes, Italian interests were served. Exports were enhanced, profits were made and the chances for future business deals were increased. Of course there was not always complete identity of interest. Some of the negotiations on prices, interest rates and contract clauses were quite tough. But, in retrospect, I believe that the African and the Italian parties do see the business done as having been in all their interests and see the resulting relationships as ones providing for negotiation of continuing and new contracts which each party will find to be in its own interests. That is true because there has been a serious attempt to reach agreements which recognised that two, or more, parties with different needs and interests could, on a basis of mutual respect, negotiate contracts, companies and other forms of doing business which were advantageous to each. That is a very different perception of reality, of Africa and of prudent business planning from that of the men of Rossing, of the oil sanctions' busters or of the corporate group who are so notably Botha's friends in Johannesburg, Nkomo's in Lusaka, Smith's in Salisbury and, so they used to say, ours in Dar es Salaam.

Transnational corporations

And now let me say a word or two on transnational corporations. Transnational corporations are a fact of life. Since they account for about one-third of the first and third world output and about a half of these states' international trade, as well as being the major source of applied technology (both hard, like machines, and soft, like general management and marketing), there are no African states likely to decide to do no business at all with them. However, that is very different from saying that African states will not, like other states, perceive a need to limit, regulate and negotiate transnational corporations' activities, profits and prices and to use state action to build up the scope of African owned and controlled economic activity. Nor is it to say that African states will perceive all transnational corporations as equally suitable bodies with which to do business. The perceptions of AGIP in Tanzania and of the companies who fuel Smith and Amin in Rhodesia and in Uganda, for example, are very different indeed.

Let me therefore suggest a few headings for types of action by transnational corporations which could lessen conflict and unpleasant surprises without preventing business activities which would still be profitable for them. They are:

1   Disclosure of adequate information on activities relating to the African state, or African enterprises, even when this went well beyond the accounts of the subsidiary or affiliate actually located in the African state.

2   Recognising that no particular business arrangement is eternal and that changed contexts require the negotiating of new forms and conditions of doing business.

3   Greater flexibility in at least examining seriously non-traditional forms of business relationships depending less on 100 per cent (or 51 per cent) subsidiaries and more on joint ventures or term contracts with built-in 'fadeout' clauses and programmes for those activities which the African state or enterprise can develop the capacity to do for itself.

4   Negotiating agreements on the basis of arriving at a mutually understood and accepted set of commitments to be performed in substance as well as form, and not abusing superior knowledge in order to arrive at apparent 'agreement' based on the African party's not understanding the true nature of the contract.

5   Considering whether there does not come a point at

which dealings with violently repressive, evil states, such as Rhodesia, South Africa and Amin's Uganda, do not become as economically counterproductive in a broader context as they are morally open to challenge. The old English proverb: 'He who sups with the devil needs a long spoon', is true in more senses than one.

Certainly, each of these actions may reduce short-term profits. Their absence can lead to violent medium-term confrontations and still greater loss of potential medium and long-term profits. They are, in fact, not uniquely African nor particularly idealistic proposals. Major industrial capitalist economies seek to enforce them, with uneven but *not* negligible success, and transnational corporations tend to find it prudent and, indeed, necessary to abide by similar guidelines in doing business with each other.

Most African states and firms are still relatively weak and badly informed. We cannot enforce these guidelines consistently as yet. However, as is already evident, that too is subject to change! And when the change comes, the firms which have acted on the type of approach suggested, whether for moral or prudent business reasons, will find less sudden, unpredictable and unpleasant changes than those which have thought: 'Each for himself and the devil take the hindmost' — a good operating rule of thumb.

Corruption, contract and regulation

On the face of it TNCs, and we, agree that corruption is a bad thing. In practice, however this mutual interest becomes less clear. TNCs do offer bribes and 'fringe benefits' to officials, which come to the same thing; and TNCs do complain that they cannot get business done without bribes and fees to 'fixers'. Quite bluntly I believe that in many African countries TNC managers are too quick to offer bribes; too quick to assume that nothing will happen without them; too quick to employ agents and contact men whose 'commissions' are a 'washed' form of bribery; too slow to refuse to pay; too slow to report demands for bribes to officials or politicians known to oppose them; too slow to take a firm stand that bribery is bad for government and for business as well as bad for confidence and stability. TNC managers have done much to spread this disease; by their rather condescending view that it was already endemic they have, in some African states, given rise to epidemics.

If there are any here who say that there are states in which 'no bribes, no business' really is the case, then I am afraid I cannot give any advice; but in my old business days I could confidently say that Tanzania was certainly not such a state. Indeed suspicion of bribery delayed or blocked several otherwise acceptable contracts while I was at the Treasury and NBC. There may of course be such states; but if the misuse of public office for private gain is general, I wonder whether you as managers do not need to ask how stable, how able (or willing) to honour bought commitment that government (or its successors will be)? Business based on bribery is not, and cannot be stable or safe business.

There is a broader problem than bribery within the meaning of the relevant acts. That is the misuse of company loyalty to buy Africans away from their people, their states, their convictions and their culture. It is not always international – I do not deny the value or propriety of loyalty to one's employer. But when it is carried to the extreme that a man is loyal to his company first, to the international managerial corps second, to Western management culture third, to his family fourth and to his people and his nation a poor fifth, a dangerous abuse is present. It is possible this might be particularly true when the state in question is committed to a non-capitalist path of development.

Contract law raises two sets of problems. The first is that international managers and their enterprises attempt to apply *pacta sunt servanda* (treaties must be honoured) to contract even when circumstances have changed beyond the expectations of either signatory, or the original contract was an unequal one for reasons short of fraud, but inconsistent with a full faith and credence bargain.

Pacta sunt servanda in the first place, is a legal principle of treaties (i.e. public international law) and not of contracts (i.e. private international law). Moreover, equity (in the Anglo-American or the broader legal sense) privides that if events beyond the expectation of either party to a contract arise, then there is a legal case for altering it. At least one TNC sought and secured a contract modification on these grounds in Tanzania after the oil price increases of 1973-74 and two more received similar treatment on that basis following the 1967 sterling devaluation. Further, in your own domestic law, 'buyer' and 'consumer' and 'borrower' protection legislation exists allowing legal reopening of unequal contracts well short of fraud. We in Africa will follow the same equitable line as you, and the same unequal contract compulsory review line as your home states.

The second problem of contract law is unequal or unclear duties. Here let me spell out a few problems:

1   Contracts with fixed prices (other than short-term goods supply or purchase) are rare; on cost plus contracts, the African party normally ends with the whole risk.
2   Performance deposits or bonds – for completion, deadlines, suitability/workability – are usually so small as to be virtually no safeguard when failure to perform is more than marginal.
3   The indirect costs of not having the unit – for example, a power station whose failure as a result of faulty equipment installation caused major power cuts and output losses in Dar es Salaam – are never covered even when the direct are met (as they were promptly and without serious question in this case); but they are often the really major costs to us.
4   The duties of an international manager in a joint venture to his two shareholders are either not clear or vary widely. Some clearly do feel a comparable set of duties to each and when forced to choose in specific decisions do not always come down · on the international company shareholders' side. With others the local (state or private) shareholder – even when a majority one – is treated as a vexatious, outside nuisance. The latter approach does not augur well for the stability of joint ventures.

I know there are problems on the TNCs' side in each of the areas cited. I know that, except in the last case, standard contract law is consistent with the results we challenge. My points are simple: contract law is intended to serve the interests of both parties; at present in these areas it serves the interests of TNCs and not ours; there is an urgent need to see how it can be made more balanced if TNCs seriously want to see stability of contracts and respect for contract law sustained.

Regulation is often a nuisance to TNCs and, I might add, to officials and politicians doing the regulating. That is hardly unique to Africa. So long as there are states and enterprises, regulation will remain. States must be concerned with goals and interests different from those of enterprises. Therefore they must regulate the actions of enterprises. Enterprises, no matter how large or globally diversified, need overall social and economic contexts and services which only states can provide. Unless they pay taxes and accept regulations, states cannot provide the services or contexts.

I think, and hope you think, my last statements were obvious. But if they are obvious the nature of the outcry of the international manager and enterprise about regulation and taxation is often wrong-headed. Surely the appropriate debate is on particular forms or levels of taxation, of security of employment or wages legislation, on multiple data requests with different forms instead of one report to be copied and distributed to users by a single state recipient. Some managers do argue in those terms, and in my experience often get marginal changes though sometimes such changes are not so marginal. Much depends on whether the managers can make their case; others challenge the whole idea as if all regulation were anathema and all state intervention illegitimate. Such managers are very likely to get a flea in their ear because their attitude shrieks so loudly as to drown whatever limited particular case they may have.

Production, trade and knowledge

I suggested earlier that I would also say something about patterns of production, trade and knowledge. These require that attention be paid to African requirements. These are that African patterns of production, of knowledge creation and use of trade become more complex and more productive and that they should be increasingly operated and owned by

Africans and African private or public enterprises. Africans are not unique in seeing these as critical issues. Dominant foreign ownership, external limitation — whether official or unofficial, explicit or implicit — on trading partners and narrow specialisation in a few simple, low productivity and low income economic activities do not meet with much public or state approval anywhere.

The difference in respect of Africa is twofold. First, because we have been weaker, we have not made these requirements known uniformly and forcefully, let alone effectively, in the past. Secondly, perhaps for precisely that reason, foreign states and firms have perceived such issues to be irrelevant to economic relations with, or activities in, Africa. The first of these factors is already declining and if the second persists there will be increasingly numerous and bitter confrontations. These requirements have nothing to do with socialism or capitalism. For example, Nigeria and Kenya have insisted on action on these fronts among the capitalist-orientated African states quite as frequently and on as broad a front as have Algeria and Tanzania among African states seeking to achieve a transition to socialism. The differences have been in form, and perhaps effectiveness, and not in the quest for more diversified and more productive economies with a growing share of African participation ownership and control.

Conflict is particularly likely to arise in respect of knowledge and technology sales, training and marketing. Let me list a few areas where conflict is likely on this score:

1 'Blackbox' transfers in which TNCs' machines, management and knowledge happen to use our unskilled workers in our countries will be questioned increasingly often and severely.

2 Transfers of knowledge/technology will need to become more like those among the firms in the TNCs' home countries — i.e. they should include full power and ability to use the technology, service and maintain the equipments and, more slowly and selectively, create machine building, adaptation and design capacity.

3 Training must go beyond semi-skilled and clerical levels

to engineering, accounting and other professional/ technical levels including senior management. The issue is not whether an initial team or a subsequent handful of international personnel are acceptable, but that continued use of large numbers of international workers denies us knowledge, ability to operate our own economies, and employment.

4   Joint venture or local subsidiary marketing organised to benefit the external partner, or owner, only will not be acceptable much longer. For example, one joint venture (now ex-joint venture) under international management bid up the price of its raw input incurring large losses. Its external partner took 15 per cent selling commission and used the extra output (paid for at standard world prices less the marketing fee) to maintain its European market share. Several joint ventures and subsidiaries in another processed product line declined to sell in their home market and reduced their Tanzanian production even though at home market import prices it was highly competitive. Under pressure, they have, I am happy to say, reversed the decision, albeit their future behaviour will, I fear, evidently be subject to close scrutiny. I am aware that in both cases group profit was increased, but one of the prices of operating in Africa, especially in joint ventures, it that to pursue group profit without regard to the impact on the units in Africa and African economies leads to trouble as soon as the African government realises what is happening. A decent regard for the concerns of partners and host states is not something which can be jettisoned while flying southward across the Mediterranean.

International economic order — and disorder

Finally, let me look briefly at the international economic order, or global macro-economic issues. The broad topic is, of course, beyond the control of any one enterprise but as the main actors in global production and trade you would be most imprudent to deny that it is a proper concern of the international manager and the firm he represents.

I wish to say three things. The present new international economic disorder, for that is what we have achieved over the past eight or nine years, is damaging to all of us: states and firms; Africans and Europeans. It is certainly prone to maximising strategic shocks. Very small low income, fragile economies like that of Tanzania, find the new disorder particularly costly.

Stability, politically or economically, requires an economic setting consistent with survival and at least the hope of progress. Expansion of mutually beneficial economic relations requires that both parties be able to expand their incomes and be able to make payments as and when due. For many African states, the present international economic setting does not meet these requirements.

The means are neither very hard to state nor are they limited to aid. They include not only concessional financial transfers but also bridging finance to allow phased adjustment to external shocks which these states, including my own, find very hard indeed to meet. For example between mid-1973 and mid-1974, international price changes of grain and oil reduced the real purchasing power of Tanzania's total output by at least one-tenth. When the starting point was about $125 per capita in present prices and the possibility of substituting domestic grain during a two-year drought, or energy sources, was nearly non-existent, it takes little imagination to see the nature of the problem.

Beyond, and ultimately more basic than financial transfers, is effective access to dependable markets for commodities, for processed goods and for manufactures. The least developed do not wish to be charity cases; they wish to be able to increase their incomes and pay their own way. Because we are small and will require substantial imports to achieve development, however defined, that requires market access. Today, we do not have it. The commodity prices are far more unstable than those of manufactures. Processed goods often face prohibitive tariffs. Simple manufactured goods suddenly have the doors slammed in their faces by unilaterally imposed 'agreements'.

All this hurts us most, but I submit it is not more in your interests than would be parallel national policies against, or at least malignly neglecting, economically and educationally weaker groups within your home states. The poor are limited buyers and poor payers; those without hope are likely to pay scant heed to appeals by the more prosperous to recognise a mutual interest in stability and in avoiding sudden, unplanned and unilateral change.

Prospects and reflections

You will notice that I have avoided making specific predictions. For that I have three reasons: first I am no great devotee of futurology as an exact science (or perhaps the modern version of astrology), nor of detailed forcasting models on as broad a front as that of the future interaction of Africa with large capitalist firms and their home states. Secondly, Africa is a continent not a country. I do not know all African states in detail and certainly do not claim to be their spokesman or be able to describe the not insignificant variations in goals and outlooks which exist among them. Nor do I suppose all your firms will perceive their interests in relation to Africa and African states identically or act to further them in the same ways. Thus, I would expect a good deal of variation in future relationships. Thirdly, on several of the problem areas that I have cited, I simply do not know how you and your fellow first world business and state decision-takers will act. Without that knowledge, I am in no position to construct scenarios. What I can say is that if the general trend of 1960-75 attitudes and actions were projected, then the speed of change on your side would be quite inadequate to prevent a series of very nasty surprises for you and for us. There is some evidence to suggest that in the past few years, your perceptions have begun to change faster and in ways increasing the chances of building mutually beneficial relationships; but there is also evidence in the opposite direction.

Why should I care?

You may well say to yourselves at this point, that since I

have no claim to be a disinterested analyst nor to place equal weight on your interests as that which I place on those of my fellow Tanzanians and fellow Africans, my tentative signposting and advice is rather suspect. In one sense you are quite right. I would be a very poor person for you to allow to take your decisions on relations with Africa, African states and African enterprises. But that, of course, is not what I am asking nor what you are in any danger of agreeing to do!

Serious building of relationships among parties who have different, whether necessarily conflicting or not, priorities and goals should start from a mutual and frank statement of each actor's goals and how he supposes they are, or can be made, compatible with, or complementary to, those of the other actors. Claims of total mutuality of interests are not convincing. They raise suspicion and serve to hide rather than reveal possible areas of genuine mutual or joint interest.

I am quite aware that business enterprises are not philanthropic foundations. They need to earn surpluses. Their surpluses are not one of my priorities as an African unless, and except to the extent that, they contribute to African development. If there are areas, and very often there are, in which some form of business relationship with a foreign enterprise can contribute to African development, then there is a mutual interest in seeing how the relationship can be structured to yield a surplus which the foreign enterprise finds acceptable and to provide the particular gains – in output or exports, knowledge or employment – the African side is seeking.

I have looked at what I perceive as your interests in relation to Africa and suggested how they are, at least in a number of cases and to a substantial degree, actually or potentially consistent with African interests, precisely because I am primarily concerned with Tanzanian and African goals, needs and aspirations.

I do not believe that escalating shocks and violent confrontation, whether military or economic, are inevitable or desirable. There are cases in which there are antagonistic contradictions of interest which will lead to violent change. One needs only to reflect on the past decade in Southern Africa and on the probable next decade to see major sombre examples. But I do not believe these cases need typify our relations. If they do become typical, it will be evidence of bad communication, faulty planning and incompetent management by you, by us, or probably by both of us.

How events will unfold depends in large measure on the education and training of international managers (and of African officials and managers, but that is a topic for an equally critical but rather different presentation). TNCs presumably do want to pursue the interests of their enterprises in Africa and to do so in ways which lead to dialogue and no diatribes; to profits and not prohibitions; and to stability and not shocks. This is not impossible if, and only if, the international managers and the TNCs they represent know Africa and Africans better, communicate more fully and openly, adopt attitudes which are less 'superior', less hierarchical and less insensitive. There are constraints and contexts for enterprises anywhere. One major role of managerial education and training is, I believe, to make them known to managers so that they do not damage their careers and enterprises by needless collisions or wanderings down dead-end roads. The problem is hardly unique to Africa. Especially in respect of communications and attitudes, Prince Charles recently, is reported to have said:

> People are not impossible to deal with. Unions are not impossible to deal with. . .
> Bloodymindedness, if it arises, must do so surely because of misunderstanding somewhere along the line.

However inaccurate you may feel it to be on particular points it suggests very similar challenges for education and training. This may be difficult, I see no reason to suppose it either impossible or not worth the time and funds required.

Therefore, I believe the training of managers is relevant to identifying potential mutual interests and negotiating to capitalise on them and also in identifying potential serious conflict and negotiating to avoid or reduce it before there is an explosive confrontation. There are many areas in which we can 'do business' to our mutual benefit. However, I must again underline that for these possibilities to be achieved requires a change in the general perception of, and approach to, Africa and Africans. We are not passive objects, nor are we children. Quite apart from moral considerations it does not, and increasingly will not, pay a firm to act in Africa in a way it knows would be seen as intolerable in an industrial capitalist state, nor for a state to act in relation to an African state with a degree of unilateralness and lack of concern for discussion and identification of an agreed position which it would not apply to a fellow industrial economy. It is precisely those Eurocentric perceptions of Africa and Africans which may well thwart the building of mutually beneficial relations, the doing of mutually profitable business. Interdependence is not a utopian slogan nor is it merely a moral principle. It is a fact of life for all states, for all business enterprises and for all international managers. To ignore or to fail to explore its reality is to guarantee frequent surprises which could have been avoided.

10 Management Education in Poor Countries

MALCOLM HARPER

The ultimate goal of good management is to improve the human condition. Since that condition is in considerably greater need of improvement in the poorer parts of the world than in so called 'industrialised' economies, people and institutions which try to improve management ability should presumably turn some of their attention away from the countries where they are currently situated towards the generally hotter, more agricultural, and less wealthy countries which are called 'developing'.

Continuing public awareness of, or at least exposure to, horrifying statistics of inequity between nations has been accompanied by reducing aid flows measured as a proportion of the income of the rich countries, and by increased reluctance to lower tariff barriers against imports from the poor. This situation may be caused by concern for our own problems, by disillusionment with the results of earlier attempts to help, or by the belief that to be poor is not necessarily to be unhappy, and growing disenchantment with our affluent life style may have led to some reluctance to assist others to reach the same questionable goals.

It is important, however, to be aware that the life of the common man or woman in a poor country in no way resembles that of Dryden's noble savage. Indeed it is questionable whether a traditional tribal society, untouched by 'progress', was ever as idyllic as some would have it; life in the bustees of Calcutta, the kampongs of Jakarta or the favelas of Sao Paulo is wretched, bitter, hard and disappointing.

A truly primitive existence, whether pleasant or not, at least has the virtue of consistency; everything is scarce, nobody is very much better off than anyone else and the situation is more or less in balance, albeit at a low level. Underdevelopment of the modern kind can be characterised as a chronic state of disequilibrium; in wealthy countries the number of jobs available may be less, or more, than the number of those who wish to fill them by a few percentage points; in a poor country up to half the labour force may be unemployed, or seriously underemployed, and the overall figures often conceal shortages of some types of labour and even greater surpluses of others. Education, of some sorts, may be in massive surplus, health care and transport facilities are wholly inadequate in relation to demand, and vast quantities of crops or products for which there is no market are produced while there is a desperate need for other things which could be produced with the same raw materials and resources.

There is something to be said for using an apparently euphemistic phrase such as 'less developed countries' rather than a more brutal and realistic word such as 'poor'; poverty implies a shortage of resources. There is indeed such a shortage in most developing countries, although not all, so that if the 'national cake' was fairly divided between all the people, and rationally allocated to all the goods or services which they need, there would still not be enough. Rich countries are constantly reminded of this fact at UNCTAD meetings, and they have responded with financial assistance of various sorts. Equipment, skilled labour and even money without strings has been given in large quantities over many years, and in addition a few countries have been fortunate enough to acquire increases in their available capital through unexpected price increases in commodities, oil, and other minerals.

Poverty, or shortage of resources, does not however completely explain the condition of underdevelopment. Whether one points to marginal capital output ratios or dramatic anecdotes of profligacy and waste, it is clear that the available resources are rarely used in the most effective way. Additional resources may serve only to exacerbate imbalance and increase the frustration of those who are now educated but cannot find work, or who now own factories but cannot obtain raw materials.

There is an interesting parallel between the failure of capital inputs alone to improve the lot of many countries, and the experience of agencies which attempt to promote and assist individual enterprises and in particular small ones. The owners, or potential owners, of businesses all claim, as do many countries, that finance is their only constraint; given the necessary funds for investment all will be well. Institutions and government, like bilateral and multilateral aid agencies, have responded to the clearly expressed need by providing money, often on heavily subsidised terms which amount to interest-free loans or outright gifts. The results have been disappointing for enterprises and nations. Money has not been repaid when it should, and the burden of repayment has only exacerbated hardship, and all too often the final result has been merely to add crippling indebtedness to all the other problems of the enterprise or country without any improvement in its welfare.

Dramatic and horrifying as are the stories of absolute poverty in many developing countries, they can usually be almost new vehicles are lying unused for the want of simple spare parts, massive agricultural processing plants operate at a quarter or less of capacity because of insufficient crops, vast sums of foreign exchange are spent on importing school furniture and chalk while competitive and competent local suppliers go out of business for lack of orders and warehouses are jammed with the equivalent of many years' consumption of a commodity so that money and space are unavailable for the purchase and storage of others in short supply.

Purposeless government agencies, vast surpluses of overpriced farm produce, irrelevant educational institutions and absurd prestigious projects can be found in industrialised economies, but it can be argued both that they employ the otherwise unemployable and that a rich society can afford profligate waste of this kind since it consumes only a small proportion of the wealth that is provided by the massive hard core of productive enterprise. Poor countries cannot afford such waste; an expensive and underused highway is unfortunate even in an economy which can afford to support the uneconomic farms and unemployed teachers by whose houses it runs, but it is offensive to the human condition when it straddles teeming shanty towns without any semblance of facilities or services, or marginal farm land which could be brought into production with a small investment in irrigation.

Management in a developing country

Mant and others have argued that to talk of 'management' can be dangerous, in that it implies the existence of a separate activity apart from doing things that actually have to be done to make an organisation work. There is some truth in this, but the best way to identify a discrete activity may be to look at situations where it might be thought to be lacking. Management has been defined as making the best use of available resources; this perfectly describes what so many poor countries, and enterprises within them, are patently not doing, and if we believe that 'management' has anything to offer society, and can be taught in business schools, the developing countries surely offer an unrivalled opportunity to prove the case?

It may, however, be suggested that management of public or private enterprises in an industrialised economy is so different from that in a developing country that institutions or individuals originating from and based in industrialised countries can have little to offer. The demands of government, the extended family and an individual manager's own ambition are far more diverse and likely to conflict with one another and the objectives of the firm, particularly if it is foreign owned. There are few supporting services or subcontractors, inside or outside the firm, communications, channels of distribution, sources of supply, statistics and similar services are far less developed, so that the individual manager must take responsibility for a far wider range of activities. Legislation, labour regulations, product standards and environmental protection measures are less formalised and less comprehensive, so that a manager has many more alternatives open to him and decisions are thus more difficult. The types of organisation to be managed may also be very different; the boundary between the public and the private sector is indistinct, and a cooperative, or an uneasy partnership between government and a foreign investor, present new and unfamiliar problems of reconciling conflicting objectives.

Management in a developing country is therefore more complex and more demanding than elsewhere, but the need for better management and more effective managers is a matter of life and death for millions rather than marginal improvement in already abundant life styles. Can management educators in industrialised countries make any contribution? The task of management does not appear to be basically different in kind; in wealthy countries, profit and growth, as well as personal wealth, are ceasing to be the only objectives of nations, corporations and individuals, and social obligations and the desire for leisure and personal development are complicating the management task. The objectives, and the urgency may differ, but the jobs of a manager in a rich and a poor country may be gradually becoming more like one another rather than more different. Since the needs are so great, and the tasks not wholly dissimilar, it would appear likely that management educators and institutions in wealthy countries can play some part in improving management in developing countries, so long as the recipients, and any intermediary aid agencies, can avoid using marginal institutions whose mediocrity may be concealed in the less competitive and more courteous environment of a developing country.

Developing countries can presumably be expected to progress, if this is the correct term, from the colonial situation when every enterprise of any significance was initiated and managed by foreigners, to total political and economic independence. Assistance with education and training should be intended to accelerate this progress, and there are a number of ways in which such assistance can be provided. Some of these are closer to the colonial pattern, although they are still widely used today by the United Kingdom, France, the United States and other industrialised countries while others approach more nearly to total independence. A number of such approaches are now considered, starting at the 'colonial' end of the spectrum.

Patterns of management education provision

A method which involves the educational institution in a

minimum of trouble and may also fill some embarrassingly empty classrooms, is to accept large numbers of developing country candidates for its existing programmes, and even slightly to modify standards of acceptance because of language or cultural difficulties. Students from developing countries make up over 50 per cent of some undergraduate business courses, and while the numbers of postgraduate courses are lower they are nevertheless substantial.

Even when the proportion of students from the third world is very high, there is usually little or no attempt to modify the content of the course; text books and case studies refer almost exclusively to enterprises in industrialised economies. Since so much of the material originates from the United States it may be suggested that the British or other European students are no better served than the Malays or Nigerians, but the courses appear to offer little of direct relevance to a manager who must operate in largely agricultural economy where the form and ownership of organisations and the whole nature of society is fluid, fast changing and quite different from an industrialised economy. Generalised statements of principles of organisation theory or marketing are virtually meaningless without reference to familiar examples, and the fact that they, and the unfamiliar examples, can be regurgitated in examinations is no evidence that the student will be a better manager on his return home.

Many such students do not of course return home, or if they do they are often totally alienated from their own society and concentrate their attention either on leaving the country as soon as possible or on subverting its institutions and attempting to replace them with similar and no more effective ones. Only a student of exceptional merit with some practical experience can select from a western-based management course those parts which are relevant to his own situation and then modify and apply them effectively. He is more likely to be successful if he is working with a Western-controlled company, or dealing closely with such companies. The majority of third world students studying management in the West may well lose more than they gain from the experience, and there is certainly no evidence that a period of study in a foreign country induces the ex-student to favour that country as a political ally or source of imports.

A number of institutions have been aware of the problems involved in encouraging large numbers of third world students to join management courses which have been designed for the British environment, and have designed special courses for such students, either from one country or developing countries in general. These are generally short non-degree courses, lasting up to three months, in specialised subjects such as investment appraisal, export marketing, or management training methods, but some diploma and postgraduate programmes have been offered. Teaching staff are recruited with developing country experience, some of the most successful of whom are incidentally ex-colonial administrators, and since the students are usually sponsored by organisations for which they have worked for some time they can contribute their own experience and thus ensure that the course is partially relevant to their needs. British institutions are sometimes inappropriately held up as examples of what should be done. They might be better used as neutral examples which all participants can criticise, advise, and use as a basis for developing solutions to their own problems.

Courses of this kind are expensive, if only in air tickets. In a subject such as management, as opposed to technical subjects requiring expensive hardware, it may be more cost effective to move a few teachers rather than many students and the methods and text books they suggest can be tested on the spot against the reality of the developing country's situation. Three months or a year spent in Europe or the United States is undoubtedly an educational experience itself for a manager from a developing country. The appeal of such a visit is such that attempts to promote regional training courses based on one developing country, using expatriate staff and drawing students from several other countries, are fraught with difficulty; for all its weaknesses, therefore, the 'travel intensive' course held in an industrial country but catering exclusively to third world students is likely to persist for many years.

Institutions attempting to improve management in developing countries must in the end aim to 'put themselves out of business', hence the ultimate goal must be to develop local management educational resources. This need has led to the establishment of links between institutions in industrial and developing countries, which involve interchange of staff, assistance with recruitment, and advice and assistance not only with teaching itself but with administration and the development of effective institutions. Such a relationship can be a fairly modest one, involving a small number of visits to and from fairly well established institutions, or it can at the other extreme involve the establishment of a satellite in the developing country, drawing most of its initial staff and its inspiration from the western partner. The Harvard Business School has been involved in a number of such ventures; they have inevitably had political overtones and in view of recent events it may be significant that one was in Nicaragua and another in Iran.

Relationships of this sort, whether between equals or parent and child, have a greater impact on local capability than individual attendance on a course, and they have the merit of concentrating on instructors and teaching institutions rather than on managers themselves, so that there can be a larger multiplier effect if the intervention functions as it should, and the inputs from abroad can be filtered through the local institution and thus avoid some aspects of alien irrelevance.

Experience with these linkages suggest however that their value is limited if only for practical reasons. The activity is inevitably viewed as peripheral to the main goals of the western institution which is unlikely to commit its best staff members to its foreign partner, and may even recruit people for longer contracts who although nominally on its staff do not in fact conform to its normal standards. Short term visits may be treated as a form of patronage, or pleasant interludes in kinder climates; and if the relationship is taken more seriously the recipient institution may be viewed as a creation of neocolonialism. Effective links have been developed, but they are usually between institutions of more or less equal standing; both sides can benefit from exchanges of staff and examiners but, as is so often the case, those institutions least in need of external assistance are usually those that benefit most from it.

While inter-institutional links as such may be of limited

value, they can provide a useful basis for individual staff members to commit themselves to a developing country for a number of years, secure in the knowledge that they will not be unemployed on their return home. Such a contract nevertheless inevitably involves a considerable sacrifice, since a guarantee of continued employment is by no means of the same value as personal participation in the struggle for advancement which characterises many business faculties; in addition a period in a developing country is often regarded as a void in an academic career rather than an important exposure to a different environment. Committed individuals who are willing to sacrifice their own career can and have made a significant contribution. They are, however, few in number and they face the problems of not staying long enough to be a part of the situation they are trying to improve, or becoming so acculturated that they cease to be initiators of change. Visits which are made in days or weeks rather than years are more common; these are rarely of much value since no effective communication can begin in so short a time.

Problems of programme content and process

The foregoing discussion of various ways in which management educators and institutions can help developing countries suggests that they are limited in scope and likely to be of little value, even negative, in their effects. It may be appropriate at this stage to attempt to define exactly what it is that western management educators have, and developing country ones do not. Only if this is identified can an appropriate transfer mechanism be suggested. The theories, concepts and techniques of effective management presumably form the basis of management education, and they have been written in innumerable text books many of which have been translated and eagerly sold or donated to third world management training institutions. If management could be improved by reading, reciting, paraphrasing and regurgitating principles of management, the deficiencies of third world managers, and of their western colleagues, would long ago have disappeared. The ability to *apply* these principles is clearly what is needed. The objective of foreign intervention is not to do this, but to enable others to do it; what missing link is there between the enunciation of principles and successful management itself?

The critical difference between effective and ineffective management training is not the subject matter; it is the *way* in which it is taught. The media are not wholly seperable from the message, but it is surely here that management trainers can make an effective contribution in a developing country?

Methods of teaching, or facilitating learning, can be transferred through all the mechanisms which have been discussed, such as courses in western schools of management, inter-institutional links, individual visits and so on. All suffer from the various disadvantages which have been outlined. There is however one method which has not been discussed, and which has many advantages from the point of view of cost effectiveness, wide coverage and local adaptability. It is generally agreed that participative learning methods are more effective than one-way lecture presentations for teaching management skills. Professor Revans may claim that action learning [1] lies completely outside and beyond the normal spectrum of learning methods, but it can be viewed as one extreme of a continuum, the other end of which is occupied by reading a book or listening to a lecture. The latter are solitary passive reception exercises, while action learning involves real management activity, with responsibility for results, which is different from management itself only in that it is usually carried out in another organisation within the context of a self-conscious learning activity with some external guidance. Either extreme, or any other method in between may be appropriate for a particular set of objectives and constraints, but far more can be done by experienced management educators through sharing their approaches than by teaching particular subjects in isolation.

It is possible to produce a book which says exactly what should be said in a lecture, and impossible to produce a book on *how* to manage an enterprise. The conduct of effective participative learning, which lies somewhere along the continumm between a lecture and actual management, can to some extent be structured, guided, assisted and enhanced, at a distance, by the use of imaginative books, manuals, audio or visual tapes, slides and other media. Many teachers, and not least those whose lack of management and teaching experience make them particularly reluctant to admit that they need assistance, are reluctant to use 'training packages' because they appear completely to take over the learning situation and to make the teacher superfluous or at best a mere operater of hardware. Completely packaged material of this sort may be legitimate for teaching people how to operate copying machines or to fill in forms, but management training material must, in order to be acceptable to the instructor and effective for the trainees, be flexible, adaptable and complementary to the skills and personality of the instructor rather than a substitute for them.

Substantial resources have been devoted over many years to case-study workshops in developing countries, where local instructors have written and taught case studies with guidance and assistance from foreigners with extensive experience in this area. A large volume of material has been produced but follow-up suggests that it is rarely used after the workshop even by the writer himself. It may be that writing case-studies without giving any assistance with the design of the course on which they are to be used is like making the components of a car before the car itself has been designed.

Participants in such workshops return to their universities, institutes of management, business schools or company training departments bearing one or more case-studies which they may have taught, or seen taught, to a highly selected group who were, at least for the period of the workshop, totally committed to 'the case method'. They returned to a less sympathetic environment, where instructors and students are preoccupied with examinations and certificates for which case-studies and participative learning methods seem a poor preparation. The workshop is often forgotten, and the case-study collection in its elaborate plastic binder retains pride of place on the office shelf but is rarely removed for use.

Case-studies alone are thus not enough, and totally programmed-learning material is too restrictive. The middle ground, however, provides a fascinating opportunity for management teachers who believe that they not only have useful ideas about what should be taught and how it should be taught, to share their ideas; and thus not only make some positive impact on those countries most severely in need of better management, but also improve their understanding of the learning processes they are trying to develop, by their attempt to share them with others.

The perfect candidate for such an approach is 'action learning' where the content, if it may be so described, emanates from the students and the organisations where they work. It may be significant that this approach to management development has been enthusiastically and successfully applied in large and small private and public enterprises in many developing countries; educators, and managers, who are sated with new models of the management process seem eager to learn about and apply a method which introduces no alien content but merely provides a structure within which practising managers can learn from their own and others' experience.

Management educators, and institutions with some aspiration to excellence, presumably believe that they make an impact on management and management education elsewhere through the influence of their ex-students or faculty, and through research and publications on various aspects of management itself. The production and dissemination of 'packages', for the want of a better word, which contain complete guidelines and suggested material for the conduct of the whole course or post-experience programme provide a further extremely powerful multiplier device. The authors, or originators, should not want or expect to see an exact replica of what they have created in one place being recreated in another by an instructor who slavishly follows instructions at every step. Such instructions are impossible to give, because effective learning depends on student participation which cannot be predicted, but the aim should in any case be to provide the local instructor with a source of themes, ideas, approaches and methods which he can use, discard, adapt or supplement as he thinks fit.

A musical analogy is perhaps not entirely inappropriate; a programmed course might be likened to a composition which attempts to impose every nuance of pace, phrasing and dynamics, leaving nothing to the initiative of the conductor or player. A traditional text book, on the other hand, provides only the bare melody; the local interpreter must orchestrate it, decide on its length, the variations and every aspect of how it is to be translated into a piece of music. Effective management learning material should be somewhere in between; the melody is supplemented by suggested structure of movements, with some idea of the time to be taken and a number of possible variations and decorations from which the local interpreter can choose. The goal is not only to enable the local instructor to perform more effectively by using the material, but to enable him to discard and replace it with his own ideas, based possibly in part on what was provided from outside.

The exercise of preparing such material, based either on existing management courses or on courses which are first designed for particular groups on the basis of research into performance deficiencies and training needs, involves extensive testing to ensure both that the suggested learning methods achieve their objectives, and that the guidelines for the instructor are sufficiently clear and comprehensive without stifling individual initiatives. The originator may realise when he sees it used by someone else that a favourite learning strategy is of little value, he may learn fundamentally new and improved approaches from the people who are testing his material and he will in any case gain a far deeper understanding of his own teaching methods, as well as the satisfaction of making a significant contribution where it is desperately needed. Material, or 'packages', of this sort may not be an enormously attractive commercial publishing proposition; the market is the instructors, not the students, and since one 'package' can be used several times, with many different groups of students, a text book with a potential sale of one per student is obviously likely to achieve a far greater volume. The origination task, including initial research, writing, creation of enhancement material, field validation and revalidation, will take longer, and cost more, than the preparation of a text book covering the same ground. A substantial element of institutional and personal good will, supplemented perhaps by international or national funding, may therefore be necessary to support the preparation and production of such material.

The need for effective training in all aspects of management in the third world is however so great that support is usually forthcoming for material which can make some contribution. In addition to the instructors and trainees for whom it is intended, the ultimate beneficiaries may be management students in industrialised countries; those instructors who attempt to assist developing countries by showing approaches to learning in the way that has been described may find that they return to their own classrooms, and their own students, with an enhanced understanding of the learning process they are trying to facilitate and of the potential contribution of effective management to society as a whole.

Note

[1] Reg Revans, *Action Learning,* Blond & Briggs, London 1979.

11 Manpower and Control Issues

R. M. MARCH

Introduction

The establishment and development of overseas subsidiaries poses problems of control and staffing that are variants of similar problems that arise when a firm decentralises into multiple divisions or becomes conglomerate in nature. Headquarters has to determine a general policy that will lie somewhere on the scale between the extremes of maintaining total central control over strategic, tactical and operational decisions, and allowing complete autonomy for the subsidiary or divisional chief executive officer (CEO). Moreover, headquarters must choose who is to manage the unit: a local executive, someone from the centre or from another of the subsidiaries. Executives from the centre may be better trained and more experienced, but they may also be more costly to maintain abroad. Local executives may have greater situational or cultural familiarity and require lower incomes, but may also be less skilled, less experienced and less effective communicators.

Choices of policies for control and staffing are closely related. Together they go far in determining the parent-subsidiary relationship as well as the efficiency of the subsidiary. In the international business literature three aspects of these choices have been given particular attention: the difficulties that expatriate CEOs have had in adapting to foreign environments; the merits of local CEOs rather than expatriates and the development of locals as executives; and the determinants, both cultural and organisational, of headquarters' needs for control and communication.

Adaptive problems of expatriate CEOs

Expatriate executives face difficulties in adapting to a foreign environment. Arpan and others, in their study of 'blunders' in international business, [1] attribute many to the lack of cultural insight on the part of expatriate CEOs. A business consultant has estimated that 20 per cent of US executives posted to subsidiaries in the UK fail to adapt and return home well before due. [2] The failure rate is even higher in Australia for US executives. Lee states [3] that 'the root cause of most international business problems' lies in the expatriate managers' use of the self-reference criterion (SRC) – 'the unconscious reference to one's own cultural values'. March has suggested in one paper [4] that 'managers in any new environment (be it a foreign market or merely a new industry in one's own country) have to undergo new learning in order to develop strategies that are appropriate to the new circumstances', and in another [5] he has argued that the failure of many foreign subsidiaries in Japan is attributable in part to the expatriates' 'distance' and 'insulation' from the Japanese market and the society.

Zeira, in a study of 70 MNCs in Europe, the Americas, Middle East and Africa, [6] concluded that many expatriates did not want to adapt. Rather, it was better for their long-term career prospects to continue 'managerial patterns that proved successful at HQ', and they therefore ignored the different expectations or patterns of their host country, peers or subordinates. Phatak speculates [7] that 'the greater the difference in cultures, the more likely is a manager abroad prone to suffer failures and frustrations'.

The difficulties of adapting to foreign environments have been described by many authors (Aitken [8], Almaney [9], Alpander [10], Baker and Ivancevich [11], Fayerweather [12], Heenan [13], Ivancevich [14], Kapoor and McKay [15], Miller [16], Teague [17], Wallin [18], Ziera [19]). Practical ways of reducing the difficulties have been developed, both as described elsewhere in this book and by such institutions as the Centre for International Briefing at Farnham Castle, which for many years initially serviced businessmen going to overseas postings, but which now briefs anyone moving into a new culture. Brooke and Remmers [20] report that some firms recognise the special problems of overseas postings by guaranteeing 'an executive going abroad for the first time a similar post back home if he has to return prematurely'. Teague reports an alternative approach, used by some US MNCs, of not putting their best people into the most difficult foreign posts.

While some of the failure to learn about and understand the new culture may be attributed to Lee's self-reference criterion, Zeira's analysis suggests that the parent company may operate as a more powerful reference group than the local subsidiary. Edstrom and Galbraith [21] suggest that this results from a deliberate control strategy of 'local discretion, indirect and impersonal control, and overall integration', which is fostered by assigning for short terms, managers who 'do not learn the language or become integrated into the local subsidiary'. Add to this Teague's observation that 'inferior' managers may go into the most difficult posts. This is understandable if it means they are managers who are not intellectually equipped to adapt to and create new business strategies for complex and alien environments.

The indications are that expatriates going abroad will make the best contribution and experience the fewest personal problems if they are properly briefed beforehand; if they are thoroughly committed to the subsidiary and its personnel; and, to the extent that the foreign environment is complex and the subsidiary is experiencing problems, if they represent the best managers available. Nevertheless, it seems clear that many MNCs have manpower policies quite different from this ideal picture. For one thing, as Neghandi and Baliga [22] have pointed out, US CEOs are assigned for shorter terms than English or European counterparts. This practice is rooted in some very distinctive cross-cultural value differences, according to Nowotny. [23] Europeans prefer stability rather than mobility, and job rotation is not widely used by the Europeans as a training technique. Hence, at home or abroad, we can expect Europeans to be more committed to their immediate company, with no short-run interest in moving to another appointment. Interestingly, however, European companies only began to internationalise in the late 1960s and early 1970s, [24] so the full effects of their differing policies may not yet be fully apparent. As for UK owned subsidiaries, many of those in former British colonies date from colonial days when managers were appointed for indefinite but long terms. [25] Presumably, in the light of emerging legislation in these countries British managers today are now being appointed for shorter periods.

The development of locals as executives

The employment of local national executives in foreign subsidiaries has long been a matter of priority, for economic and motivational reasons. It has always been costly to maintain HQ nationals overseas and most MNCs try to groom young locals to take over most if not all senior positions as rapidly as possible. This has also been necessary in order to retain the services of outstanding young people, who would otherwise become dissatisfied and seek other employment.

It is also often desirable for MNCs to demonstrate publicly to their host country that they are providing worthwhile opportunities for locals. Thus in 1973 the US Chamber of Commerce in Australia undertook a survey of local US owned subsidiaries in response to widespread public criticism. They reported that 46 per cent of CEOs in US subsidiaries were Australian. Pohlman and others [26] found that in 31 per cent of a sample of US MNC subsidiaries 90 per cent of the executives were locals.

Spurred by these reasons as much as by local regulations enforcing change, many firms have been promoting local nationals in the management heirarchy, even to the top-most levels. Watson [27] has quantified the steady growth in the employment of locals as CEOs of US companies in Brazil. The figure increased from 46 per cent in 1950 to 64 per cent in 1970, while CEOs of American nationality dropped from 51 to 25 per cent. At the same time, third country nationals were more often employed. More recently Neghandi and Baliga reported [28] that US companies employ a higher proportion of locals as executives than do European companies, and that both are substantially ahead of Japanese companies. Pascale, in a cross-cultural study of corporate communication and decision-making, [29] reported that every CEO in 13 Japanese-owned corporations in the US were Japanese, while only 23 per cent of 108 'managers' in those corporations were non-Japanese. [30]

HQ control and communication requirements

The particular characteristics of control and communication relationships between parent and subsidiary seen to be due to a wide variety of factors including: the firm's management philosophy; the stage of its development as an MNC; the sizes of the parent and subsidiary; ownership pattern; distance from parent; degree of understanding; whether or not in production, and age of subsidiary.

Observers like Nowotny attribute much of the differences in control to differences in basic approach or philosophy. Efforts to measure such differences led Neghandi and Baliga [31] to conclude that the notion of efficiency as expressed in 'plant productivity, cost of goods produced, and similar financial indices' and summarised in 'annual bottom-line performance', was the cardinal US principle. This led US companies to tighten control over the subsidiary by what amounted to literal programming by the parent 'to produce, sell and make profits at certain levels'. They also added that UK CEOs overseas 'lack self-esteem' and feel 'just a cog in a wheel'. In contrast, Europeans and Japanese measure success or failure, in terms of 'system efficiency, i.e., the degree to which their organization was able to adapt to and cope with . . . the environment'. This suggests that the European and Japanese local manager has greater autonomy and a longer time-frame in managing the subsidiary.

Control is influenced to a degree by the formal requirements for the subsidiary to report to the parent. Brandt and Hulbert [32] identified cross-national differences that are consistent with the foregoing. In a study of 63 subsidiaries in Brazil, they found that 91 per cent of US companies made monthly 'financial reports' to the parent, whereas only 68 per cent of the European companies did so. Overall, they found US companies received and made significantly more reports and visits than did the Europeans.

A number of scholars have reported that the systematic organisational changes that firms experience as they evolve from domestic to international directly affect control relationships. For instance, when a firm sets up a marketing subsidiary, the extent of control depends on the degree of confidence placed in the subsidiary's CEO. [33] Initial moves into overseas manufacturing may be on a highly autonomous basis, but increasing complexity or declining global performance may lead to restrictions on that autonomy, as top management reviews deficiencies in policy, corporate objectives and control systems. [34] Management may come to see the 'gains to be realised by coordinating production on a world-wide scale', [35] and further restrict the mature subsidiary's areas of autonomy.

Other factors have been reported as affecting the control relationship. Size is one. Alsegg [36] in a study of 153 European subsidiaries of US firms, found that companies with a few large subsidiaries in a region tend to exercise less control than those with many small units. On a different level, Brooke and Remmers found that the smaller the parent company, the more the subsidiary's autonomy. The degree of understanding between parent and subsidiary is another factor. When there is imperfect communication, a confidence gap exists, and HQ may exercise close control over the subsidiary. [37] Sheer distance between subsidiary and parent is also involved. The greater the distance, the greater the autonomy, especially when the country is culturally unfamiliar or politically unstable (Alsegg).

Areas of enquiry

In this chapter, some of the issues raised above are examined in the context of a sample of MNC subsidiaries in five countries: Australia, Indonesia, the Philippines, Malaysia and Japan. Both parent companies and local chief executive officers are drawn from the USA, UK, Continental Europe, Japan and Australia. Thus comparisons among country of location, country of parent and nationality of local chief executive are possible.

The topics and issues considered are: (a) *concerning local chief executives* – environmental learning and adaptation, environmental knowledge, nature of appointment in country, and nationality; (b) *concerning subsidiary executives* – proportion who are local nationals; (c) *concerning control and communication* – reporting frequency, planning autonomy, and control and communication problems.

Research method

A full description of the research method and the standard data collection instrument appears in March, [38] March and Liau, [39] and March and Quah. [40] In summary, all firms in each country listed by foreign chambers of commerce were contacted. The lists were considered to be comprehensive in every country except Japan: published government surveys there indicate over 1,800 foreign-equity firms whereas the list used covered only 350 of them. Response to the stand-ardised self-administered questionnaire was around 20 per cent in each country, with a low of 15 per cent in Malaysia, and a high of 28 per cent in Australia. Most respondents were chief executives, and most were expatriates or third country nationals. The sub-samples vary considerably in size as shown in Table 11.1. Conclusions drawn about the smaller sub-samples within the overall total of 310 firms must necessarily be regarded as tentative.

Table 11.1
Sub-samples of firms taking part in questionnaire

Number of firms in:	N	Nationality of expatriate CEOs	N	Nation of parent company	N
Japan	68	US	55	USA	138
Australia	123	British	70	UK	84
Malaysia	32	European	17	Europe	32
Philippines	34	Japanese	15	Japan	10
Indonesia	53	Australian	13	Australia	13
Total	310		170		277

Analysis of results

Environmental learning and adaptation

Respondents in each country were asked a series of questions about their difficulties in 'finding their way about', 'learning about competitors . . . markets and distribution channels', 'learning about how the local people think, their customs and belief'. These questions were asked twice of all expatriates, once in respect of their first arrival in the country, and (except for the Japanese) once for the current situation.

Responses were made on a five-point scale, graded from 'very easy' (scoring +2) to 'very difficult' (scoring −2). A further question concerned the respondents' current 'understanding of the society, including business, government and social life'. Again, responses were made on a five-point scale, from 'excellent' (scoring +2) to 'below average' (scoring −2). A summary of the responses is shown in Table 11.2.

Initial learning. Table 11.2 shows that Japan is rated as initially the most difficult country to get to know and understand, followed by Indonesia. Interestingly, Malaysia is rated less initially difficult than Australia in respect of 'finding way around' and 'learning about competitors and market', although Australia and the Philippines were easier places to learn about 'how the locals think etc'. No doubt the relative smallness and centralisation of industry and population in Malaysia makes for a less complex environment. That the Philippines is rated easier to learn about is probably attributable to the widespread use of English (70 per cent versus 20 per cent in Malaysia). Indeed English is one of the three official languages in the Philippines.

Current difficulties and knowledge. When asked the same question as before, but this time for a current appraisal, respondents again rated the Philippines as the best known and least difficult country. Present difficulty in 'finding way around' is virtually as low as Australia, and present learning difficulties concerning competitors and markets are the lowest of the four countries, as are those concerning 'learning about the locals'. Moreover, current environmental knowledge is as high amongst expatriate respondents in the Philippines as it

Table 11.2
Chief executives' learning and adaptation
(Mean scores on questionnaire)

Japan	Australia	Malaysia	Philippines	Indonesia	
(a) Ease of finding way around					
−0.40	+0.85	+0.97	+0.56	−0.36	When first arrived
N.A.	+1.50	+1.20	+1.48	+0.91	At present
(b) Ease of learning about competitors, markets, distribution etc.					
−0.44	+0.28	+0.25	+0.13	−0.64	When first arrived
N.A.	+0.62	+0.48	+0.87	+0.26	At present
(c) Ease of learning about how local people think, their customs					
−0.89	+0.48	+0.00	+0.12	−0.43	When first arrived
N.A.	+0.59	+0.04	+0.70	+0.11	At present
(d) Understanding of society, business, government					
+0.76	+0.62	+0.24	+0.64	−0.04	At present

is amongst expatriates in Australia (although Japan is higher than either on this). Indonesia continues to be the country with the highest difficulty ratings. The higher ratings of current environmental knowledge in Australia and the Philippines, together with the low levels of current difficulty, suggest that understanding and adaptation difficulties are negatively related to the extent of English language fluency in a given country. There are also, however, considerable differences amongst countries in the average time the respondents have been there: Australia 12 years; Philippines 9.9 years; Japan 8.3 years; Malaysia 5.7 years and Indonesia 2.8

years. Thus, in part the difficulties articulated in Indonesia remain those for the newcomer, as well as of language.

The same data as above were classified by nationality of those respondents who were expatriate. Continental Europeans show the most consistent initial difficulties, although the Japanese seem to experience even more difficulty in getting to know about the locals. Two other differences are of some interest: US nationals claim fewest difficulties in learning about the competitors etc., while Australians have fewest difficulties in getting to know the locals.

As for the current situation Americans claim to be the best informed national group. Europeans' current knowledge etc., is close to that of the British, except for ease of finding way around. The main surprise, however, is the very poor showing of the Japanese, who admit to substantial difficulties in learning about competitors, the locals, and the current business environment. It is hard to escape the conclusion that the Japanese manager overseas is isolated from the foreign environment.

Other research (March, [41] March and Liau, [42] March and Quah [43]) has investigated some hypotheses concerning ease of learning and current knowledge *within* specific countries. While most relationships were statistically weak there was some support for the following:

> In Japan and Malaysia, British managers showed higher initial ease of learning than overall, while Europeans showed lower ease of learning in Japan.
> In the Philippines, however, it is Americans who show higher initial ease of learning and the British who show lower.
> In every country, but especially Japan and Indonesia, language ability and years lived in the country were positively correlated with current environmental knowledge.

These earlier results are consistent with the data shown here.

Nature of the appointment. Table 11.3 shows that all those in Japanese companies and Japanese managers have spent the

176

longest average time with their company, followed by the British, American, with Europeans and Australians last. However, with respect to the years spent in a given country, it is the Japanese who have spent the shortest time there, with the Australians having only a slightly greater mean time in the country. UK companies' local chief executives have spent the longest time in a country, followed by US companies. Yet it is European, followed by American nationals who have spent most time in a foreign country.*

Table 11.3
Profile of local chief executive officers (averages)

Nation of parent company	Years with company	Years in country
US	12.6	9.3
UK	15.7	10.9
Europe	9.9	5.2
Japan	17.0	2.7
Australia	10.5	2.9

Nationality of CEO	Years with company	Years in country
American	12.5	7.6
British	14.0	6.8
European	11.7	8.4
Japanese	15.1	2.7
Australian[1]	11.0	3.5

[1] Excludes Australian CEOs in Australia.

* The average year of establishment for company of different parent nations in our sample were: US companies, 1950; UK, 1944; Europeans, 1962; Australian, 1965; Japanese, 1967. These figures help explain why Australian and Japanese CEOs have spent so much less time in the overseas post than the Americans, British or Europeans.

MNCs are often accused of providing insufficient opportunities for advancement to senior positions by host country nationals. Table 11.4 shows that US companies have substantially more local and third country nationals as their foreign CEOs than any of the others. Of local CEOs in US firms 50 per cent are not American, [44] whereas the figure for UK, European and Australian companies is only about 25 per cent. All Japanese company CEOs are Japanese nationals. [45]

Table 11.4

Nationality of CEO, classified by nation of parent company (percentage)

	US	UK	Europe	Australia	Japan
Host country nationals	14	7	0	0	0
Parent country nationals	50	73	72	75	100
Third country nationals	36	20	28	25	0

Employment of Local nationals as executives

Respondents in each country were asked to state how many 'executives', including themselves, there were in the company, and how many of them were locals. Data, broken down by country of location and nation of parent company, appear in Table 11.5.

Table 11.5 (A) indicates that firms in Japan and Indonesia employ the lowest average proportions of local nationals as executives; the other three countries' proportions are higher and differ only slightly from one another. Although it is perhaps surprising to see Malaysia higher than Australia, this may be attributable to the high incidence of immigrants in Australia. Immigrant status was not checked in the questionnaire.

When classified by the nation of parent company (Table 11.5) (B)) the results are consistent with earlier findings on CEOs. US companies have the highest average proportion,

93 per cent of local national executives, [46] just ahead of UK companies, while the Japanese figure is only 31 per cent. [47]

Table 11.5
Employees and local national executives

(A)

Country	Mean number per firm		Local nationals as % total executives
	Employees	Executives	
Malaysia	385	23.5	92
Philippines	386	18.0	90
Australia	584	26.0	88
Japan	369	7.9	80
Indonesia	416	12.7	67

(B)

Nation of parent company	Mean number per firm		Local nationals as % total executives
	Employees	Executives	
US	493	19.0	93
UK	598	23.9	91
Europe	170	8.1	85
Australia	130	8.8	75
Japan	522	21.5	31

Control and communication

Reporting frequency. Table 11.6 shows the frequency with which companies of different national parentage report profit and loss, budget expenditure and sales expenses. US companies, as expected, have the greatest frequency of reporting. Japanese companies are next in frequency, just a little below US, followed by Australian and British. Continental European companies report with far less frequency than any of the others. In all cases reports on budget expenditure are much less frequent than the others. Differences in reporting frequency also occur between countries of location but they are not easily interpretable.

Table 11.6
Percentage of companies required to report to
parent monthly (or more frequently),
classified by nation of parent

| Nation of company country | Monthly Reports on: | | |
	Profit and loss statements	Budget expenditure	Sales expenses
US	93	79	88
Japan	90	70	89
UK	72	59	88
Australia	69	69	92
Europe	39	28	69

Planning autonomy. Respondents were asked two questions concerning their extent of independence or autonomy from the parent in broad planning and goal-setting areas. One question, open-ended, inquired into the CEOs degree of freedom to 'plan all aspects of (the subsidiary) operation'. Responses were subsequently classified, coded and ranked from 'no autonomy' (score 0) to 'virtual/total autonomy' (score 4). No significant differences in parent company practice were indicated. The scores ranged from 1.4 to 1.6, suggesting that autonomy on these issues is decidedly constrained.

The second question inquired into how local objectives were set, and the extent to which the parent company was involved. Pre-coded responses ranged from 'wholly set by parent company' (scored 0) to 'wholly set by local executives' (scored 4). Here too the differences were small. UK companies showed slightly more local autonomy than the others with a score of 3.5 compared to the lowest score of 3.2 for Australian companies. Subsidiaries located in Indonesia were allowed slightly less freedom (3.15) than others. Although the differ-

ences are not significant, the rank order of results, with
Philippines being most autonomous (3.56), suggests that
difficulty of obtaining local knowledge (see Table 11.2) and
this measure of autonomy are related.

Table 11.7
Suggestions for improvement, classified by nation of
parent company (by percentage)

Suggestion	Nation of parent company*					
	US	UK	Europe	Australia	Japan	Total
Become more involved, make more visits; send better, more specialised personnel.	21	18	41	89	20	28
Give more autonomy.	18	22	8	–	40	18
Invest more, think long range, sacrifice short-run rewards.	18	22	8	–	20	18
Design, modify products for local market, diversify product range.	11	9	41	–	–	15
Understand the special feature of the country.	11	11	21	–	20	13
Better communications, co-ordination.	11	4	8	32	–	10

Table 11.7 *(continued)*

Suggestion	Nation of parent company*					
	US	UK	Europe	Australia	Japan	Total
Do not apply unsuitable systems, management concepts to this country.	13	2	8	—	—	8
Change ownership strategy; more local equity.	5	11	—	32	—	8
Permit us to export	3	—	—	—	—	1
Total of responses	58	44	19	4	5	130
Respondents answering	52	37	15	3	5	112
Respondents not answering	86	45	23	13	5	172
% Response	38	45	39	19	50	39

* Percentage figures add to more than 100 because some executives made more than one suggestion.

Control and communication problems. Respondents were asked the question: 'What changes, if any, should occur in the way your IHQ controls or views the . . . (subsidiary) operation, in order for it to become (even) more successful?' The answers are shown in Table 11.7.

The most common response was a call for greater involvement and support from headquarters, especially in understanding the country better, visiting more often, in sending more specialists or expatriates more able to adapt to the local environment. Nearly one-third of all those responding to the question made this suggestion. Those men located in the Philippines however, did not feel strongly about this issue, perhaps because, as earlier data shows, they felt more at ease there than did their counterparts elsewhere.

Set against this suggestion were the opposite ones of a desire for 'more autonomy' from the parent; 18 per cent of the respondents felt this way, particularly those in Malaysia, though no-one in Indonesia agreed. There was also considerable support for the idea that parent companies needed to invest more and take a longer-run view of the local operation.

Executives in European companies, however, differed sharply on both these latter suggestions. They seem able to take a longer-run view and be more autonomous than those of other parent nations. This view is consistent with the literature and our findings on report frequency. But if the European-owned subsidiary is less controlled, it is also less considered by IHQ, as indicated earlier. This conclusion is reinforced by the greater frequency with which European companies ask for products to be designed for the local market, or for the product range to be diversified — a comment amongst Europeans as amongst US or UK companies. The same disparity existed for both manufacturing and non-manufacturing activities. Indeed, the nature of the subsidiary's activity seemed to have little effect on the suggestions made generally.

Some other responses, small overall, were selectively related to particular countries. The plea for greater understanding was specific to Japan and Australia (the latter especially because of labour problems), the plea 'not to apply unsuitable systems or concepts' was specific to the Philippines, while the plea for more and more diverse products was most frequent in Indonesia.

Summary of findings

For ease of comprehension, the findings can be summarised under three headings: country of location, parent country comparison and CEO nationality comparison.

Country of location

Japan. Of the five countries, Japan presents the most difficult environment (business, culture, government etc.) for expatriates to learn about. Foreign firms there have (with those in Indonesia) the smallest ratio of local nationals as executives, and parent companies seem to find it most difficult to understand. However, expatriates claim high environmental knowledge.

Australia, Malaysia, Philippines. Expatriates have few difficulties in learning about the business environments in these countries. American chief executives seem particularly 'at home' in the Philippines, though parent companies find Australian union problems difficult to understand.

Indonesia. Like Japan, this is a difficult business and cultural environment to learn about. While initially it presents a little less difficulty than Japan, *current* knowledge by chief executives is lower than that for Japan. Moreover, foreign companies here suffer from inadequate communication and support from their parent companies, feel there are inadequacies in their product range, have the lowest level of autonomy over their affairs than those in any other country, and have (with Japan) the lowest proportion of local national executives.

Parent company comparison

US owned. US companies have the highest proportion of local and third country nation executives, together with the highest level of financial reporting to parent. Their chief executives seek greater local autonomy than do those of any other company group.

UK owned. Generally, these companies are second only to US owned in frequency levels for all variables, although they have slightly more local autonomy.

European owned. European companies are distinguished from all others by the high level of local autonomy, and low levels of required financial reporting. One apparent cost of this is an inadequacy in parent involvement in the local subsidiary, as witnessed in a lack of understanding of the local situation and of product support.

Japanese owned. Japanese companies are markedly different from others by virtue of their almost total reliance on Japanese executives abroad.

Australian owned. Australian companies are generally most similar to UK ones, except with respect to the employment of local nationals as executives, where they resemble the Japanese.

CEO nationality comparison

Americans. Americans claim to be the best informed national group on local business, society, markets, competitors, and experience the fewest initial learning difficulties. However, while they adapt very well in the Philippines, they have greater problems in Japan than any other expatriate group.

Britons. Britons adapt well in Malaysia and Japan, but relatively poorly in the Philippines.

Europeans. Perhaps because of the second-language role of English for them (also less international experience?), Europeans have the greatest initial environmental learning difficulties.

Japanese. The Japanese, more than any other nationality, are company-oriented men. They have worked more years with their company than any other nationality, but fewer years in the present country. These facts, plus their greater isolation from and ignorance of the local environment than other nationality, suggest an extremely high level of commitment to the parent company.

Discussion

MNCs generally assign expatriate staff to foreign subsidiaries for one or more of three reasons: locals with equivalent skills and experience are not available; or they need to be trained by expatriate staff in order to be able to replace them; or home country nationals have the communication skills and in-company knowledge necessary for smooth control and communication between parent and subsidiary. There is usually, however, a significant financial cost to this last reason as the expatriates almost invariably enjoy both higher salaries and higher standards of living. Hence, it is common to find MNCs with clear-cut policies for training HCNs to replace all expatriate personnel sooner or later, with the one frequent exception of the chief executive.

Cost, however, is not the entire problem. Expatriate personnel experience difficulties in learning about and adapting to the various relevant aspects of the foreign environment. These difficulties can arise from the complexity of the environment itself, from cross-national differences in values or orientations, from the time spent in the country, from facility with the local language, and indirectly from the type of relationship existing between parent and subsidiary. For instance, Japan and Indonesia seem particularly difficult environments to learn about. In both, only a fraction of the population speaks English and there is relatively little information available in English (in Japan, there is a wealth of market and other environmental information available in Japanese, but there is little such information in Indonesia). On the other hand, Australia and the Philippines, the two countries included in the research where English is widely or even universally used, environmental knowledge is much higher and learning difficulties minor.

Our findings give some grounds for concluding that national values and cultural habits affect the expatriate's orientation to and knowledge of the environment. In particular, the superior environmental knowledge of American chief executives is plausibly to be attributed to a greater national spirit of inquiry and more professional training in management. The greater degree of control exercised over many American CEOs may not always mean restrictive control that inhibits initiative but involvement by internationally minded and experienced executives at home who have a good grasp of and insight into local conditions. This seems a reasonable inference given the long international experience of US MNCs.

In great contrast to the Americans are the Japanese managers who, although only a small sub-sample in the present research, exhibit considerable isolation from their foreign environment and its inhabitants. This may be related to two characteristics noted by Yoshino. First, the Japanese management system is closed and exclusive, it is virtually impossible to enter it from overseas, and we may add, it is also the focus of a Japanese manager's social life as well. Second, foreign assignments are unattractive to Japanese managers, because they erode close relationships and seriously retard the education of children.

We found that European CEOs had, overall, the most difficulties in environmental learning, even though they had, on average, been in the foreign country longer than any other national group. This may be due in part to a greater conservatism and narrower training, and possibly to their need in most countries to communicate through English, a foreign language. Other possible determinants, however, may be the much smaller size of and more recent establishment of the European MNCs: an average of 170 employees as against US (479); UK and Japanese (496); and an average set-up year of 1962, as against US (1950), UK (1944), but Japanese (1967). Taken together, these factors may mean that a European manager does not have available to him, in his organisation, the same amount of or capacity for environmental learning that his British or American counterparts have.

It is not advisable, however, to consider separately the expatriate chief executive's knowledge from the knowledge that has been built up by his immediate subordinates over the years. Note that US companies, whose American managers have good environmental knowledge, employ the highest proportion of locals as executives, whereas the Japanese have the poorest environmental knowledge and the lowest proportion of HCNs as executives. The cross-cultural differences in ease of learning, therefore, do not permit us to draw strong conclusions about the impact of cultural difference on ability to learn and adapt to new environments. But it does at least seem clear that all managers can benefit from comprehensive briefing prior to posting overseas. It is curious that only the British have actually institutionalised the facilities for such training.[a]

With respect to communication and control, the sharpest contracts emerged between US and European companies. The former exhibited a high level of reporting, control and therefore parent-subsidiary communication, whereas the latter exhibited a high level of autonomous activity and relatively low parent-subsidiary reporting and communication. There are a number of possible explanations. US MNCs are relatively mature, having developed regional control and centralised reporting over the years as a response to growing transnational complexity. On the other hand, European MNCs are much more recently developed, their CEOs probably tend to be the original or pioneer subsidiary managers who are given ample latitude and trust to develop the new operation. If so, we can expect European MNCs to tend toward increased centralisation and reduced local autonomy as their worldwide operations become more complex and foreign manufacturing increases.

Another way to view the contrast is as representing two opposed management philosophies, each of which has its benefits and costs. The European approach emphasises the individual CEOs dignity and responsibility giving him adequate autonomy to develop the subsidiary in his own way. It would thus, in an important sense, become *his* company. In return, he commits himself for a long but indefinite period to reside in that country, and suffer perhaps from headquarters' benign neglect, failure to communicate, failure to provide skilled support, new products, and absence of interest in or commitment to the subsidiary. At the other extreme is the US model, where the CEO is more a career executive with commitment to the parent not the subsidiary, who will serve a relatively fixed tour of duty in the foreign country, operating under direct parent control with high levels of reporting and communication. The costs, however, may be

---

[a] *Editorial Note:* March is incorrect here: see Chapter 2 for US examples.

the uncritical and excessive demands by headquarters for regular operational information, and a failure to capitalise on all the opportunities in a given country, either because the expatriate CEO concentrates only on short-run profit-generating activities, or because headquarters adopts a short-run comparative approach to evaluating the performance and prospects of its subsidiaries.

In short, the manpower, control and communication practices and policies of MNCs seem influenced more by the stage of development of the MNC (and related factors like the size and age of a subsidiary, employment of nationals as executives), rather than by the activity of the firm or by national cultural habits and values, or by individual skills like languages and special regional knowledge.

Notes

[1]   J. S. Arpan, D. A. Ricks and D. J. Pattan, 'The meaning of mis-cues made by multinationals', in *Management International Review*, 14, 1974, pp. 3—11.

[2]   Robert Haupt, 'How Executives Can Handle Cultural Shock', in *Australian Financial Review*, 18 August 1974, pp. 2—3.

[3]   James A. Lee, 'Cultural Analysis in Overseas Operations', in *Harvard Business Review*, 44, March-April 1976, pp. 106—14.

[4]   R. M. March, 'Some Constraints on the Adaptive Behaviour of Foreign Consumer Goods Firms in Japan', in *European Journal of Marketing*, 11, 7, 1977, pp. 491—9.

[5]   R. M. March, 'Opportunities and Problems for the Foreign Business in Japan', Business Paper No. 7, University of Queensland, April 1977.

[6]   Yoram Zeira, 'Overlooked Personnel Problems of Multinational Corporations', in *Columbia Journal of World Business*, Summer 1975, p. 97.

[7]   A. W. Phatak, *Managing Multinational Corporations*, Praeger, New York 1974, p. 138.

[8]   Thomas Aitken, *The Multinational Man: The Role of the Manager Abroad*, Wiley, New York 1973.

[9] Adnan Almaney, 'Intercultural Communication and the MNC Executive', in *Columbia Journal of World Business,* Winter 1974, pp. 23–8.

[10] G. C. Alpander, 'Draft to Authoritarianism: The Changing Managerial Styles of the U.S. Executive Overseas', in *Journal of International Business Studies,* 4, Autumn 1973.

[11] J. C. Baker and J. M. Ivancevich, 'The Assignment of American Executives Abroad: Systematic, Haphazard or Chaotic?' in *California Management Review,* Spring 1971, pp. 39–44.

[12] John Fayerweather, *The Executive Overseas* Syracuse University Press, 1959.

[13] David A. Heenan, 'The Corporate Expatriate: Assignment to Ambiguity', in *Columbia Journal of World Business* May-June 1970, pp. 49–54.

[14] John M. Ivancevich, 'Selection of American Managers for Overseas Assignments', in *Personnel Journal,* March 1969, pp. 189–93.

[15] Ashok Kapoor and R. J. McKay, *Managing International Markets: A Survey of Training Practices and Emerging Trends,* Darwin Press, 1971.

[16] Edwin Miller, 'The International Selection Decision: A Study of Managerial Behaviour in the Selection Decision Process', in *Academy of Management Journal,* June 1973, p. 241.

[17] F. A. Teague, 'International Management Selection and Development', in *California Management Review,* Spring 1970, p. 2.

[18] Theodore O. Wallin, 'The International Executive's Baggage: Cultural Values of the American Frontier', in *MSU Business Topics,* Spring 1976, pp. 49–58.

[19] Yoram Zeira, op. cit.

[20] M. Z. Brooke and H. L. Remmers, *The Strategy of Multinational Enterprise,* Longman, 1970, p. 144.

[21] Anders Edstrom and J. R. Galbraith, 'Transfer of Managers as a Co-ordination and Control Strategy in Multinational Organizations', in *Administrative Science Quarterly,* 22, June 1977, pp. 248–63.

[22] A. R. Neghandi and B. R. Baliga, *Quest for Survival*

and Growth: A Study of American, European and Japanese Multinational Corporations, International Institute of Management, Berlin 1976.

[23] Otto H. Nowotny, 'American vs. European Management Philosophy', in *Harvard Business Review,* March-April 1964, pp. 101–8.

[24] L. G. Franko, 'Strategic Planning for Internationalization – The European Dilemma and Some Possible Solutions', in *Long Range Planning,* 5, 6, 1973, pp. 58–65.

[25] D. Channon, *The Strategy and Structure of British Enterprise,* Division of Research, Graduate School of Business Administration, Harvard University, Boston 1973.

[26] R. A. Pohlman, J. S. Ang and S. I. Ali, 'Policies of Multinational Firms: A Survey', in *Business Horizons,* 19, 6, December 1976.

[27] Charles E. Watson, 'The Brazilianisation of U.S. Subsidiaries', in *Personnel,* July-August 1972, pp. 53–60.

[28] A. R. Neghandi and B. R. Baliga, op. cit.

[29] R. T. Pascale, 'Communication and Decision Making Across Cultures: Japanese and American Comparisons', in *Administrative Science Quarterly,* 23, March 1978, pp. 91–101.

[30] M. Y. Yoshino, *Japan's Multinational Enterprises,* Harvard University Press, Cambridge, M. A. 1976. Commenting on managers in overseas branches of the Mitsui and Mitsubishi trading companies, Yoshino has observed that apart from a few token appointments, 'key positions were dominated by Japanese' (p. 122).

[31] A. R. Neghandi and B. R. Baliga, op. cit., pp. 6, 7 and 28.

[32] W. K. Brandt and J. M. Hulbert, 'Patterns of Communication in the Multinational Corporation: An Empirical Study', in *Journal of International Business Studies,* 1, Spring 1976, pp. 57–64.

[33] M. Z. Brooke and H. L. Remmers, op. cit., p. 29.

[34] E. P. Neufeld, *A Global Corporation: A History of the International Development of Massey-Ferguson Ltd,* University of Toronto Press, 1969, p. 213.

[35] J. M. Stopford and L. T. Wells, *Managing the Multinational Enterprise: Organization of the Firm and Ownership*

of the Subsidiaries, Basic Books, New York 1972, p. 25.
[36] R. J. Alsegg, *'Control Relationships Between American Corporations and their European Subsidiaries',* A.M.A. Research Study no. 107, 1971.
[37] M. Z. Brooke and H. L. Remmers, op. cit. p. 123.
[38] R. M. March, op. cit., 1977a.
[39] R. M. March and C. M. Liau, *'A Comparative Study of Multi-National Companies: Japan, Australia, Malaysia and the Philippines',* Business Paper No. 11, University of Queensland, October 1977.
[40] R. M. March and E. O. Quah, *'Managing Multinational Companies in Malaysia and Indonesia',* Business Paper No. 12, University of Queensland, March 1978.
[41] R. M. March, op. cit., 1977a.
[42] R. M. March and C. M. Liau, op. cit.
[43] R. M. March and E. O. Quah, op. cit.
[44] This is much the same finding as Watson for US subsidiaries in Brazil.
[45] This is essentially the same as Pascale's finding.
[46] This is substantially greater than the figure given by Pohlman et al., viz. only 31 per cent of US companies have a local national ratio of +0.9.
[47] This is remarkably similar to Pascale's figure of 0.23 for a sample of Japanese-owned companies in USA.

Further reading

David E. Berlew and D. T. Hall, 'The Socialization of Managers: effects of expectations on performance', in *Administrative Science Quarterly,* 10, 1966, pp. 207–223.
Bruce Buchanan, 'Building organizational commitment: the socialization of managers in work organizations', in *Administrative Science Quarterly,* 19, 1974, pp. 533–46.
Anders Edstrom and J. R. Galbraith, 'International transfer of managers: some important policy implications', in *Columbia Journal of World Business,* 11, 1976, pp. 100–12.
Richard N. Farmer, *International Management,* Dickenson Publishing Co., Belmont, California 1968.

R. M. March, 'Corporate and Marketing Management of Foreign-Managed, Foreign-Equity Companies in Japan', University of Queensland Business Paper, no. 14, 1978.

A. R. Neghandi, 'Cross-cultural Management Studies: Too many conclusions, not enough conceptualization', in *Management International Review,* 14, 1974, pp. 59—65.

A. R. Neghandi and S. B. Prasad, *The Frightening Angels: A Study Multinationals in Developing Nations,* The Kent State University Press, 1975.

C. Reynolds, 'Managing Human Resources on a Global Scale', in *Business Horizons,* 6, December 1976.

R. D. Robinson, *International Business Management,* Dryden Press, 1973.

A. B. Sim, 'Decentralized Management of Subsidiaries and their performance — a comparative study of American, British and Japanese subsidiaries in Malaysia', in *Management International Review,* 17, 1977, pp. 45—51.

US Chamber of Commerce in Australia, *The Impact of US Investment in Australia,* Sydney 1973.

Brian Toyne, 'Host Country Managers of Multinational Firms: An Evaluation of Variables Affecting their Managerial Thinking Patterns', in *Journal of International Business Studies,* 7, Spring 1976, pp. 39—55.

M. Wilkins, *The Maturing of Multinational Enterprise,* Harvard University Press, 1974.

12 Management Education for Orientals

S. GORDON REDDING

It seems that the Chinese in particular carry oriental culture into the western world, and there are few institutions of management education in Europe or North American which do not have at least a small contingent of students of Chinese origin. They come almost always from the vast body of Nanyang, or overseas, Chinese who live and work outside mainland China. Their social backgrounds vary greatly but they have in common a strong sense of Chinese tradition and usually Confucian values — and this includes a notable dedication to education. In the main they identify with Hong Kong, Singapore or Taiwan and always, eventually, with China itself.

In more recent years, the ranks of oriental students in the West have been swollen by groups of Malays, Indonesians, Filipinos, and occasionally by Thais and Koreans. The Japanese have tended to take their education at home, but at postgraduate level many go abroad to the West. On the one side, therefore, there are large numbers of students who come from oriental cultures to learn western systems of approach. On the other side there are many institutions of education in management in Asia itself, which teach the subject from western textbooks, using teachers who were educated abroad. To an important extent, it is a 'western' subject and no indigenous theories of management have been formulated in the East to contrast with it. That is not, however, to say that there are no indigenous *practices* of management to contrast with those of the West. There are, they are important and, except for Japan, they are hardly understood.

In either context, teaching management to orientals in Hong Kong or in London meets the same problem. Management is a subject designed to solve problems of cooperation in western socio-economic structures; it is founded on western assumptions about the scientific understanding of reality; the business norms which it serves are western, and the research on which almost all its models are based owes virtually nothing to Asia. The people to whom it is being taught, not being epistemologists, do not usually question the assumptions, or the norms, and are not usually in a position to question the research. Nor do they fully understand the business systems of their own cultures, having usually had little access to descriptions or experience of them. The transfer of understanding may well be superficial and, eventually, problematic.

Against this background, the following topics will be considered:

1   Contrasts between western and oriental views of reality.
2   Special characteristics of western management theory.
3   Implications for teaching.

Contrasts between western and oriental views of reality

In order to discuss this topic at all, it is necessary to resort to two fairly massive ideal types — the oriental and the western mind — and, in doing so, to enter here a very large caveat. There is no such thing as 'the oriental mind' in any rigorous sense, nor a western equivalent. There are very large variations within such a grouping and consistency within it is not to be expected. At the same time, even though they overlap, there are some fairly crucial differences between the two sets which bear examination; and which can be considered more precisely by examples from subgroups within each.

We need a way into the maze when confronted with such complex issues and it is proposed to use the word 'paradigm' to represent the structure in which things are understood, in other words the mental map which is more or less typical of a culture. Masterman [1] proposes three principal categories of such mental maps:

> *Metaparadigms* are those of a philosophical sort equated with a set of beliefs, an organising principle governing perception itself.
> *Sociological paradigms* are manifestations of the former seen sociologically as scientific achievements, political institutions, or accepted judicial decisions. (This author would add systems of organisation.)
> *Construct paradigms* are artefacts such as textbooks, tools, instruments, grammars and analogies.

All three are clearly related and the present hypothesis will be along the lines that underlying the systems of organisation (sociological paradigms) in the West are certian organising principles governing perception (metaparadigms) which are evident in the textbooks, models and teaching methods (construct paradigms) commonly used.

The main argument of this chapter may now be put as follows:

1 Western management theory, as evident in textbooks, is closely related to western management practice, e.g. Koontz and O'Donnell talk about planning, organising, control etc., and organisations actually do plan, and organise and they have systems of management control more or less along 'textbook' lines.*

2 Such management theory and practice is founded upon a set of organising principles within the process of perception itself, this set being characteristically western.

3 Other cultures see reality differently. Without long exposure they can only superficially or partially comprehend the sociological and construct paradigms of the West, and cannot share its metaparadigm.

4 They have equally valid world pictures of their own at all three levels.

---

* There is no wish to imply that there is necessarily a cause-and-effect link between theory and practice. Whether management theory is normative or descriptive is another argument.

5   The true nature of this problem is hardly ever acknow-
     ledged and the teaching implications of it have not been
     faced.

Areas of cultural difference

The problem in discussing the patterns of perception of a
culture is the impossibility of developing exhaustive or even
mutually exclusive categories. It is only possible to choose
aspects of the view of reality in the hope of conveying
differences in *flavour*. At the same time we are not entirely
without guidelines and in trying to understand patterns of
organisation and management, the crucial questions would
seem to be in the areas of: (a) the basic understanding of
cause-and-effect relationships between events, activities,
phenomena; (b) the assessment of probability; (c) the way
time is perceived; (d) the view of the individual and his role,
and (e) processes of control over human behaviour. Although
eclectic, these categories do provide insights into managerial
activity both in terms of structuring of activities and human
relations. They will be discussed cross-culturally under the
headings of causality, probability, time, self, and morality.

Causality. It is a common question why an active tradition
of scientific investigation failed to develop in China in the
way in which it did in the West? The most appealing explanations for it centre upon differences in cognitive processes of
a fundamental kind. Northrop has said 'There is very little
science in the East beyond the most obvious and elementary
information of the natural history type'. And, further, that
'a culture which admits only concepts by intuition is automatically prevented from developing science of the western
type beyond the most elementary, inductive, natural history
stage'. [2]
    This characterising of Chinese thought as proceeding via
'intuition' is in contrast with the western mode of proceeding
via the *rational* processes of (a) describing phenomena using
abstract labels and categories, such as 'heat', 'length' 'role',
'motivation'; (b) searching for *causal* connections between
events using the abstracts as a framework, and (c) attempting
to develop *universal* explanations. The Chinese mind, on the
other hand, is described by Nakamura as one which lays heavy

emphasis upon the *concrete* and the particular; and which has not developed abstract logical thought to the extent found in the West. Thus:

> The Chinese esteemed the data of direct perception, especially visual perception, and they were concerned with particular instances. This meant that they were little interested in universals which comprehend or transcend individual or particular instances. They thus seldom created a universal out of particulars.
> The esteem for the individual and the concrete, a lack of interest in universals, aborted the discovery of laws which order many particulars. [3]

It is necessary, then, to come to terms with a way of thinking which does not naturally use abstracts or link them with rational logical connections. Instead it perceives what Northrop described as the 'undifferentiated aesthetic continuum'. A way of characterising the differences is given by Maruyama [4] who distinguishes between what he terms the 'unidirectional causal paradigm' and the 'mutual causal paradigm', and who argues that the former is typical of western thinking and the latter of oriental thinking. A selection of the respective characteristics which he proposes is given in Table 12.1.

From these descriptions it is evident that processes of explanation and understanding are different at the most fundamental level (for further discussion of this point see Redding and Martyn-Jones. [5]). The Chinese student, if he has been initially educated in his own culture, and in his own language, will have begun to use a set of cognitive processes which give him a 'fix' on the world of a very distinctive kind. The simple conclusion of the practitioner dealing cross-culturally, that 'they think differently', contains more than a superficial truth. It is possible to see some rationale for the noticeable tendency of Chinese to excel in certain subjects, particularly the applied sciences, where 'the individual and the concrete' is paramount, and for their tendency not to move naturally into the abstract realms of philosophy and sociology; operations research yes, organisation theory no.

Table 12.1
Two ideal-type paradigms (after Maruyama)

	Unidirectional causal paradigm 'western'	Mutual causal paradigm 'oriental'
Science	Traditional 'cause-and-effect' model	Post-Shannon information theory
Cosmology	Predetermined universe	Self-generating and self-organising universe
Philosophy	Universalism	Network
Ethics	Competitive	Symbiotic
Religion	Monotheism	Polytheistic, harmonic
Logic	Deductive axiomatic	Complementary
Perception	Categorical	Contextual
Knowledge	Belief in one truth. If people are informed they will agree.	Polyocular. Must learn and consider different views
Analysis	Pre-set categories used for all situations	Changeable categories depending on the situation

Probability. The linear, sequential thinking of the West, with its logic and rationality has given rise to a whole science dealing with the 'calculation' of future events based on quantified probabilities. The current reaction against this (e.g. Ansoff and Hayes [6]) and the call for a 'looser' more 'intuitive' approach to managerial decision making is an interesting comment on its limitations, but its spread through both theory and practice has nonetheless been extensive.

The decision analysis unit at Brunel University has been conducting research into cross-cultural differences in perceived probability and has published the results of research which indicates a marked difference between Orientals and Westerners in this respect. [7] In simple terms, Chinese, Malay and Indonesian groups display a tendency not to think of the future in calculative terms. Percentage assessments of future probabilities are less sensitive (i.e. less accurate) than those of equivalent western samples.

Resort to explanation in terms of 'fatalism' seems at first simplistic, but when combined with non-linear thinking and (as we shall see) a different perception of time, a 'fatalistic' view of future events may well be a useful concept to use as explanation. A sense of not being entirely in control of events is part of the Chinese make-up, although obviously we are looking at something which is a matter of degree, rather than an absolute difference. Consider the form of the still predominant Confucian values which influence the Nanyang Chinese: 'Confucian injunction has been to cultivate one's moral life, develop one's nature, and let Nature take its course. The individual does not completely control his own destiny, but he is the master of his own ship in a sea that is not entirely devoid of uncertainties'. [8]

It is natural for the logical western mind to extrapolate, to think from past to future in terms of cause-and-effect. It is less natural for the Chinese mind to do so, and it is less comfortable in forecasting future events in what might be termed a 'scientific' way.

Time. There is very little research on the cross-cultural perception of time [9] and it is an area of subtle misunderstanding between cultures. Hall has described two major modes of time perception, which he names 'monochronic' and 'polychronic', and elaborates as follows:

> American time is what I have termed 'monochronic'; that is, Americans, when they are serious, usually prefer to do one thing at a time, and this requires some kind of scheduling, either implicit or explicit . . . Monochronic time emphasizes schedules, segmentation, promptness.

Polychronic time systems are characterized by several things happening at once, they stress involvement of people and completion of transactions rather than adherence to pre-set schedules. *P*-time is treated as much less tangible than *M*-time. *P*-time is apt to be considered a point, rather than a ribbon or a road, and that point is sacred ... Appointments just don't carry the same weight as they do in the United States. Things are constantly shifted around. Nothing seems solid or firm, particularly plans for the future, and there are always changes in the most important plans right up to the very last minute ... In contrast, within the Western world man finds little in life that is exempt from the iron hand of *M*-time. [10]

Perceptions of time found in Asia are very much within Hall's *P*-time category. The unending continuum of the West is replaced by a series of circular phases. An indigenous description of it is as follows:

Time in Asia does not have a beginning. While the West thinks in terms of the space-time continuum, and perhaps views history as a continuous process having a beginning and progressing toward an end, Asians see time as phases rather circular in form. One season follows the next, one life leads into another, one king's reign is followed by another's, one dynasty moves into the next, one calendar decade divided into twelve parts, each named after an animal, moves into the next. Hence while time and punctuality are of cardinal importance in the West, Asians do not take time seriously. [11]

The standard managerial activities of planning, scheduling, controlling and the plethora of techniques which surround them, such as PERT, stock control, production scheduling etc., are all predicated on a view of time which is linear and capable of fine subdivision. It is necessary to acknowledge the idea that when Orientals are learning such techniques, they learn at two levels. Underlying the mechanisms of the techniques themselves is another layer of understanding (or more likely misunderstanding) which is the character or quality of the time which serves as a frame.

Self. Individualism reaches probably its most extreme form in the United States, and is enshrined in the ideas of individual rights and liberties, the achievement ethic, and what often appears to be an obsession with the 'self'. Other western cultures follow close behind in seeing the individual as the key point of focus in the social structure, the person being seen as somehow separate from others, worthy of analysis in his own right, and in any case, responsible for his own status and achievements. In management theory dealing with human aspects of organisation, the concept of self-actualisation is still paramount and lies as an assumption behind many managerial systems.

The Chinese view of the self is very different. The person is seen as inextricably bound up with his social context. Man, in other words, includes his relationships and is not separable from them. Even the Chinese or Japanese word for man has a broader sense than in English [12] and takes in the state of transactions with fellow human beings. There is not, in the Chinese consciousness, an equivalent idea to the western 'self' with all its western ramifications.

If the self is not perceived in the same way, then self-actualisation will not be the same process. Maruyama has pointed to the ethnocentrism of Maslow's hierarchy and empirical support for such questioning is available from a replication in South East Asia of the Haire research on managerial beliefs and needs. [13] Although Asian managers display a distinct shift towards an 'autocratic' set of beliefs about managerial style, this is combined, paradoxically, with a greater expressed respect for subordinates than is found in the West. This may well be reflecting a heightened inter-personal sensitivity and thereby a greater tolerance and awareness of subordinates as hierarchical inferiors.

Morality. The use of the word 'morality' needs explaining as it will not be discussed in any absolute sense, but it may be valuable to consider the *mechanism* whereby a society impresses its morality onto its members and how it makes them more or less conform. This will lead to a view of how people are influenced in general. Here again we are up against systems contrasting on a large scale, and the use of broad general typologies.

The simplest distinction is that between 'shame' and 'guilt' cultures, an idea first popularised by Benedict in explaining the Japanese to Westerners, but one which also seems valid for Chinese and other oriental groups. Her definition is as follows:

> A society that inculcates absolute standards of morality and relies on man's developing a conscience is a guilt culture by definition . . . True shame cultures rely on external sanctions for good behaviour, not, as true guilt cultures do, on an internalized conviction of sin. Shame is a reaction to other peoples' criticism . . . Shame has the same place of authority in Japanese ethics that 'a clear conscience', 'being right with God', and the avoidance of sin have in Western ethics. [14]

There are many manifestations of such a mechanism in South-East Asia, and the most obvious, in the Chinese case, is 'face', an element in social relations which cannot be ignored in indigenous organisational behaviour. (Examples of related ideas in other Asian cultures are (a) the Filipino idea of 'hiya', only inadequately translated as 'shame', but without which a Filipino is considered socially incompetent; (b) the Japanese 'haji' of which Benedict writes; (c) the Malay sensitivities which focus attention on peer-group opinion.) The techniques of management control developed in the West often rest on unspoken assumptions about influences on behaviour and may well founder when those influences are not there.

The 'control' of people by leaders operates through processes which rest upon the individual's reaction to certain social or interpersonal pressures. If these are different then the activities involved in leadership will also need to be different. In shame cultures, the person aligns himself towards the verdict of others and thereby acts with them in mind. The individual socialised by guilt is to a greater extent accountable to himself, and the means of influencing his behaviour must take that into account. The overlap of these considerations with those discussed under the 'self' paradigm are inevitable, as the two paradigms are closely related.

To summarise what has been said so far, Table 12.2 contains a brief description of the contrasting paradigms and will be used as background for the discussion of teaching implications.

In parenthesis, it might perhaps be added that many of the characteristics of managerial activity in the Far East are arguably related to the above differences in perception. Japan is a separate case due to special causes, but Nanyang Chinese, Thai, Malay, Indonesian and Filipino managerial systems tend to display the following characteristics: (a) small-scale organisation, usually within the control of one paternalistic leader; (b) a lack of formal organisation structure; (c) a lack of bureaucratic procedures* in the Weberian sense; (d) a lack of formal planning systems, and (e) unsystematic control devices.

Special characteristics of western management theory

Management is usually studied within the overall framework of the social sciences and has stayed more or less within its tenets. Its process of understanding, at least as an ideal, was described by House and MacKenzie [16] as having four elements: (a) deductive-nomological reasoning; (b) crucial experiment; (c) experimenter control strategies, and (d) strong inference. The primacy of the deductive, nomological, explanation in social science is also clear in the majority of methodology textbooks — too numerous to cite, except perhaps for an exhilarating recent addition by Ford. [17]

Figure 12.1 shows a typical survey of the way in which management theory has developed. The approaches are seen as occurring in three consecutive phases. The 'traditional views' of scientific management, the bureaucratic model and administrative management theory, appear in the form of foundations laid down early and still relevant to modern thinking. There followed a period of 'modification' in which

---

* The much vaunted Chinese tradition of bureaucracy has recently been severely questioned as to its effectiveness, and criticised for extensive manipulation and corruption. [15]

204

Table 12.2
Western and oriental metaparadigms

	Western	Oriental (Chinese)
Causality	Attempts to understand logical connections between abstracted categories. Use of absolutes. Linear, sequential, explanations.	Situational, contextual perception without absolutes. Non-abstract, more sensual perception. Multi-causality.
Probability	Future is for calculation. Extrapolation based on logical cause-and-effect.	Fatalism. Calculation seen as naive.
Time	Monochronic. Scheduling, sequencing, promptness. Co-ordination possible.	Polychronic. Non-linear. Sense of repetition. Insensitive to timing.
Self	Individual isolated and important in own right. Self actualisation. Achievement ethic.	Individual inseparable from social context. Judgement based on relationships. Less pure self-consciousness.
Morality	Guilt. Action to avoid guilt due to infringing absolute moral principles.	Shame. Action to avoid shame due to infringing social norms which are situational.

approaches crystallised into two parallel schools, working without obvious coordination, and termed respectively the 'quantitative' and 'behavioural' sciences. These also are carried forward as contributors to the more recent 'systems' approach, seen within a contingency framework, and operating at the levels of either organisation design or management practice.

Considering first the earlier foundations, scientific management took a highly logical and rational approach to the study of work and attempted to build a causal model of efficiency in specific work contexts. Although it made too many simple assumptions about human factors, it adhered to the scientific methods of experiment established for the physical sciences, and these proved the principal source of its strength.

In parallel was the theoretical understanding of bureaucracy associated with Weber, and it is worth noting here the extent to which bureaucracy is the archetypal western form of organisation. As Child has pointed out:

> The one model of organization with which we are most familiar is bureaucracy. Bureaucracy not only has a long genesis reaching back to the administration of ancient civilizations, but it is in a more advanced form the type of structure commonly adopted by large organizations today. For several thousand years, bureaucracy has been widely accepted as the most efficient, equitable and least corruptable basis for administration ... it is only during the past few decades that bureaucracy has been attacked as an inefficient model of organization in the conditions of unprecedented change, complex technology and an ethos of personal individuality which prevail today. [18]

The principal characteristic of bureaucracy is its rationality, an act in Weber's ideal type being rational in so far as (a) it is oriented to a clearly formulated unambiguous goal, or to a set of values which are clearly formulated and logically consistent; (b) the means chosen are, according to the best available knowledge, adapted to the realisation of the goal. [19]

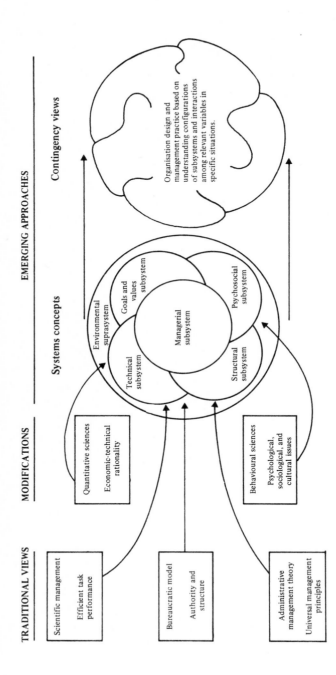

Figure 12.1   Evolution of organisation and management theory

Source: F. E. Kast and J. E. Rosenzweig, *Experiential Exercises in Management*, McGraw-Hill, New York 1976.

At a more practical level the same issue of rationality was dealt with by the administrative management theory school, in laying down what were seen as universal management principles. Logical sequences of activities were specified which, if practised, would provide complete 'management' of an organization. Such approaches are typified by an overwhelming concern for order, for tidiness, for the reigning-in of uncertainties and, above all, for a sense of complete control. This remains still the principal teaching approach and has shown a resilience which can only derive from the acceptability as a conceptual framework for students and practitioners of, e.g., planning, organising, leading and controlling.*

The quantitative approach to management theory took the application of mathematics and economics into the area of managerial decision making in a way which might be typified by the case of corporate planning. The application of logic to management is seen in one of its most extreme versions in Ansoff's model of decision flow in strategy formulation. [20] But the limits to rationality had been reached and the practical application of such a model has come into question, with the result that more recently Ansoff can write:

> Over the past 20 years, it has become increasingly clear through lessons of successes and failures, as well as through continuing research, that the Cartesian conception of the strategic problem suffers from two major deficiencies. First, in the language of management science, it is an 'improper optimization' — the excluded variables have major impact on the preferred solution. Second, strategic planning solves only a part of the total problem concerned with maintenance of a viable and effective relationship between the organization and the environment. [21]

---

* It is interesting to note that one of the longest established and largest volume selling textbooks, that of Koontz and O'Donnell, now in its sixth edition and first published in 1955, still uses the traditional framework, but has now added as a subtitle 'A Systems and Contingency Analysis of Managerial Functions'.

The behavioural approach to management theory rests on a large body of empirical research, the organisation being treated as far as possible (which is not very far) as a laboratory. The control of extraneous variables presents the major problem and more recently, conceptual developments have moved towards taking them into account, and building the more complex systems and contingency models, rather than in further attempts to control them. Whatever the outcome, the process of investigation, and later of explanation, has rested constantly on the building of scientific frameworks. These contain: (a) abstract constructs; (b) the operationalising of such constructs; (c) measurement of related phenomena; (d) the building of cause-and-effect models, and (e) attempts to derive universal 'laws' or prescriptions.

The special characteristics of management theory are obviously not perceived as 'special' by Westerners, because the 'monopolarised' mind conceives of no limit to the potential application of rationality. The scientific method is seen as so massively justified by its outcomes that it is heresy to deny its worth. What is in question, however, is not its power or the justifying of its extended application, but the assumption that *all* cultures can automatically understand and use it. It is in this area that the principal western–oriental teaching problems occur, and to which the argument can now turn.

Implications for teaching

In considering the implications for teaching, one is faced immediately with a thorny problem of whether to: (a) attempt to make an oriental into a western-type thinker; (b) convert western teaching into an oriental framework, or (c) build bridges between the two and allow the student to work out his own location on the continuum (which may in fact be a moveable position according to his context at any time). The last would appear to be of greater benefit to those being trained and has the advantage of leaving their options open. If it is chosen then the teaching processes will need to be effective in two respects: capitalising on oriental strengths, and transferring understanding.

First, it will be necessary to capitalise on the strengths of the oriental paradigm and to provide an opportunity for them to be brought out. This will provide the student concerned with a sound base from which to operate. There is a danger, of course, that such specialism will lead to narrowness and this must be deliberately counterbalanced. The areas in which strength would appear likely are:

1   Quantitative subjects and 'hard', bounded, disciplines such as operations research, computer applications, econometrics, economics, finance etc., in all of which oriental students appear to flourish. (GMAT scores for Chinese are higher than the international average for quantitative thinking, while verbal scores are lower than average.)

2   The intuitive understanding of complex situations which can be applied to case studies. Use of the freewheeling intuitive mind is necessary to counterbalance the rigidity of many planning exercises and the excesses of rationality. (The problem in this is that common debating ground is hard to establish as Orientals and Westerners will be operating from different perceptions).

3   Ability to use systems and contingency models at least at the level of the understanding of multi-causality. Here the Oriental can act as a useful foil to the mono-causally biased Westerner, although again a common language for debate is a problem.

In all these fields the aim is to tease out the oriental perception and add it to the class discussion. It must, however, be noted that the differences in perception make this a difficult process. It is not often realised by a western teacher that he may be asking a 'western' question. Nor is it always realised that a reply which does not fit with his structured expectations may derive from a totally different thought process, which in terms of its utility in dealing with real world problems, may be as valid as his own.

What is needed is a very open-ended, non-threatening and patient approach. This flourishes best when the discussion topic is practical and has a set of tangible elements like a case study. Here the oriental pragmatism and sense of the tangible can come into full play. Means of achieving these three ends might therefore include such techniques as:

1   The straight, didactic, teaching of quantitative subjects at a higher level, or a faster pace, to oriental students than Westerners.
2   Using them as resource people in quantitative areas – a technique which adds greatly to 'face' and allows them to cope more easily with weakness in other topics.
3   Use of case studies with long discussion periods of the careful encouragement of their views.
4   Use of cases with written answers based on pointed questions.
5   Practical exercises, particularly business games played 'for real', in a competitive spirit, but which force them to analyse the process involved as well as its results.
6   Structuring work so that there is enforced collaboration between western and oriental students on specific projects of some depth.
7   Demanding complex, written explanations in a contingency framework.

As a second concern, there is a need to develop in the Oriental a consciousness of the western paradigm, at more than the obvious superficial level. This will entail:

1   Explanation of the scientific method and justification for the use of abstracts, the idea of causation, the nature of models.
2   Attempts to deliberately force mental exercises in rationalisation. Use of open discussion to sponsor reasoning. Stress on examining for explanation using abstracts.
3   Stress on universality at least as an ideal. Use of cases to enhance understanding of universality of principles, as well as principles per se.
4   Stress on the fine tuning of subjective probability. Weaning away from fatalism.

Forms in which these processes can be presented will vary greatly. It is possible to build them into lectures. Certainly they ought to be markers for what to look for in case discussions. They can also act as guides to seminar discussions and as examination criteria.

What is involved here is the attempt to introduce the oriental student to what lies *underneath* the western textbook. It has to proceed on the assumption that the application of Cartesian logic to social reality is foreign in more senses than one, and may not be absorbed naturally. In this connection also, it is necessary to acknowledge the dual nature of this educational process, and the difficulty for the western teacher of stepping back and looking at his own subject-matter in perhaps a new perspective. Some awareness is essential of the processes of social science when it attempts to provide students with mental maps of reality or conceptual frameworks, whose eventual purpose is understanding, then control, then management, of that reality. An essential component at least of postgraduate management teaching should be an introduction to social science epistemology. If nothing else, it introduces perspective, caution — and perhaps humility in the teacher.

Two further points need to be made when considering management education and oriental students and they both relate to behaviour patterns which are deep in oriental cultures. They are self-effacement and learning-by-rote.

The ethic of self-effacement is very powerful and related to the prevalent Confucian value of modest behaviour. Open discussion in front of large numbers of others requires the oriental student to infringe this ethic, as he may be perceived by his peers to be placing himself above them, and, unless forced he will not do so. Classroom techniques cannot rely on lively discussion sessions if large numbers (say, more than 15) are involved. It is still possible to ask questions of individuals directly as this removes the onus of decision to speak, but debate as such becomes rather stilted. To counteract these tendencies, the use of small groups is highly effective. Practical exercises also are valuable contexts in which the pragmatic qualities of the oriental mind can be fused with an opportunity to make theoretical points.

The tradition of learning-by-rote is heavily influenced, in the Chinese case, by the nature of the language. Without an alphabet, or a standardised graphic representation of sound, mastery of the Chinese language involves a formidable test of memory. In the education process this brings a very early exposure to rote-learning, as a person cannot be literate without being able to recall some thousands of characters. This pattern of learning remains the norm and is practised in almost all subjects, whether apposite or not. In many branches of university teaching much effort has to be expended in changing, or adding an alternative to, the memorising of texts. A related aspect of this same tradition is an unwillingness to question the printed word or the ideas of the teacher. Flattering though it may be for a lecturer to have his word taken as gospel, it may not be what he intended if he were deliberately presenting one side of an argument, or attempting to be provocative, and such misunderstanding must be guarded against. It is advisable to dismantle the Confucian perception of the teacher as having very high status qua teacher if a real exchange of ideas is to take place. At the postgraduate level especially, and in the uncertain areas of contingency theory in which much management teaching takes place, this 'equalisation' process is a prime requisite. Again, the most effective means is the small group discussion which deliberately fosters the exchange of opinions and allows for the weighing of various options.

Finally, it must not be forgotten that a contributory factor to the reticence of the oriental student is the simple fact that English is usually a second language. In the case of the Chinese, the learning of their own language is so demanding that coping with a second one, of such radically different structure, presents difficulties which are not sufficiently appreciated. It is noticeable in the cases of Singapore and the Philippines, where English is the lingua franca, that their students are considerably less reticent than those from elsewhere, thus suggesting that the language barrier itself is a major factor.

There are clearly, and regrettably, few simple practical solutions to the general educational problem being considered here and, in the end, the mutual transfer of understanding and the building of the necessary bridges will depend more on the intellectual acknowledgement of the problem among the teachers who are handling it, than upon techniques per se. It is, however, hoped that some of the approaches suggested above may be tried in a spirit of inquiry and, if monitored carefully, lead in turn to refinements.

There are many questions still unsettled in this field and it has to be acknowledged that our knowledge of the relevant factors is still primitive. There are also considerations of values which have been avoided here, but which make for interesting points of debate in a future which will see more attention given to these issues.

Notes

[1] M. Masterman, 'The Nature of a Paradigm', in I. Lakatos and A. Musgrave (eds), *Criticism and the Growth of Knowledge,* Cambridge University Press, Cambridge 1970.
[2] F. S. C. Northrop, 'The complementary emphases of Eastern intuitive and Western scientific philosophy' in C. A. Moore (ed.), *Philosophy – East and West,* Princeton University Press, Princeton 1944.
[3] H. Nakamura, *Ways of Thinking of Eastern Peoples,* University Press of Hawaii, Honolulu 1964, pp. 185–9.
[4] M. Maruyama, 'Paradigmatology and its application to Cross-Disciplinary, Cross-Professional and Cross-Cultural Communication', *Dialectica,* 28, 3–4, 1974, pp.135–96.
[5] S. G. Redding and T. A. Martyn-Johns, 'Paradigm Differences and their Relations to Management Functions, with reference to South-East Asia' in A. Negandhi and B. Wilpert (eds), *Organizational Functioning in a Cross-Cultural Perspective,* Kent State University Press, Kent, Ohio, 1979.
[6] H. I. Ansoff and R. L. Hayes, 'Introduction' in H. I. Ansoff, R. P. Declerck and R. L. Hayes (eds), *From Strategic Planning to Strategic Management,* Wiley, London 1976.
[7] G. N. Wright et al., 'Cultural Differences in Probabilistic Thinking: an Extension into S. E. Asia', technical report 77–1, Decision Analysis Unit, Brunel University, 1977.
[8] Chan Wing-tsit, 'The Individual in Chinese Religions', in C. A. Moore (ed.), *The Chinese Mind,* University Press of Hawaii, Honolulu 1967.
[9] M. Cole, J. Gay and J. Glick, 'Some experimental

214

studies of Kpelle Quantitative Behaviour' in J. W. Berry and
P. R. Dasen (eds), *Culture and Cognition: Readings in Cross-
Cultural Psychology,* Methuen, London 1974.
[10] E. T. Hall, *Beyond Culture,* Doubleday, New York
1976.
[11] P. Sithi-Amnuai, 'The Asian Mind', *Asia,* Spring 78–91,
1968.
[12] F. L. K. Hsu, 'Psychosocial Homeostasis and Jen:
Conceptual Tools for Advancing Psychological Anthropology',
American Anthropologist, 73, 23–43, 1971.
[13] S. G. Redding, 'Some Perceptions of Psychological
Needs among Managers in South-East Asia', in Y. H. Poortinga
(ed.), *Basic Problems in Cross-Cultural Psychology,* Swets
and Zeitlinger, Amsterdam 1977.
[14] R. Benedict, *The Chrysanthemum and the Sword,*
Meridian, New York, 1946, p. 222.
[15] R. L. A. Sterba, 'Clandestine Management in the
Imperial Chinese Bureaucracy', *Academy of Management
Review,* vol. 3, no. 1, 1978, pp. 69–78.
[16] R. House and K. D. Mackenzie, 'Paradigm Development
in the Social Sciences: a Proposed Research Strategy', *Academy
of Management Review,* vol. 3, no. 1, 1978.
[17] J. Ford, *Paradigms and Fairy Tales,* Routledge and
Kegan Paul, London 1975.
[18] J. Child, *Organization: a Guide to Problems and
Practice,* Harper and Row, London 1977.
[19] T. Parsons, 'Weber's Methodology of Social Science'
in Max Weber, *The Theory of Social and Economic Organization* edited with an introduction by Talcott Parsons, The
Free Press, New York 1947.
[20] H. I. Ansoff, *Corporate Strategy,* Penguin, London
1965.
[21] Ansoff and Hayes, op. cit.

PART II
THE SUPPLY:
PRACTICE AND EXPERIMENTATION

13 A Strategy for Organisational Learning: The IVECO Experience

DESMOND McALLISTER

Introduction

This chapter describes an in-company management and organisation development programme in a newly formed pan-European multinational. The programme is still in progress, thus a more critical evaluation will have to wait till later, but it may be helpful to give a description of experiences half way through the process since it may be one of the few examples of the design and implementation of a comprehensive management development programme at the international level. It is an attempt to learn how to cope with new activities and new environments through an educational intervention at the strategic level.*

The complicated cross-cultural nature of the Industrial Vehicles Corporation (IVECO) is captured well by Robert Wilson.

> There would be nothing unusual about a truck manufacturer in Kentucky sourcing (procuring) axles from Ohio, engines and transmissions from Michigan, steel

---

* The author would like to acknowledge his gratitude to the participants of the IVECO management programme with whom it has been his privilege to work over the past two years and to all his colleagues on the staff of the programme. In particular he would like to thank Achille Cartoccio, director of in-company programmes of management and organisational development and director of the IMP, and Ivan Snehota, international management consultant, ISVOR-FIAT. Achille, Ivan and he constituted the core management group of the programme until summer 1979, and he owes to them not only a unique learning experience but also much of what is written in this chapter.

from Indiana, aluminium from Iowa and frames from Wisconsin. But let's shake up the apple cart. Let's say the people in Kentucky speak German, the people in Ohio speak Italian, the people in Michigan speak French. The people in Indiana have one kind of currency, the people of Iowa another and the people of Wisconsin still another. One currency is hard; another is soft; and the third is positively limp. Let's further assume these 'nations' have different political and economic conditions, different unions, different short and long term goals and different work ethics. But let's not assume that the logistics of producing a truck, having the right component at the right place and the right time and not a moment sooner, is any less important than it is in the real world. Having come this far, let's make one final assumption just to keep the proposition interesting. Let's market the truck in Brazil and to prove we are serious about the market let's adopt Portuguese as the official language of our company. This 'reductio ad absurdum' is not as far-fetched as it may seem. It is not so different from the business strategy of IVECO (Industrial Vehicles Corporation), a Common Market combine of five truck and truck component builders bent on penetration of the U.S. truck market. [1]

IVECO was born only in 1974, the result of a joint venture between FIAT, OM, and Lancia in Italy, Magirus Deutz in Germany and UNIC in France. It is essentially a holding company, incorporated in Amsterdam, owned 80 per cent by FIAT and 20 per cent by Kloeckner-Humboldt-Deutz. The company has some 60,000 employees, a turnover of $3.5 billion and a production of over 100,000 trucks and buses per year. About 40 per cent of its sales are outside the three national markets, and 30 per cent of turnover in 1978 was by sales outside Europe. It is now the second largest truck and bus company in Europe, after Mercedes-Benz, with considerable development and expansion in extra-European markets.

The purpose of the IVECO merger was to build up an integrated industrial system capable of survival in the European truck business. In competition with each other and with all other truck producers it was estimated that none of the partners could survive for long; united into one pan-European company, IVECO, they could become one of the leaders in the business by exploiting economies of scale and rationalising component production and truck assembly across all of their varied facilities in the three countries.

But while all this makes perfect sense from a logical and business point of view, making it happen has not always been smooth and easy. There have been real technical difficulties, which need not concern us here, and, not surprisingly, there have been difficulties in getting people to cope with change and adapt to a new environment with a more complex set of activities.

Each of the national companies which formed IVECO had had its own proud history of more than 50 years as an independent and successful enterprise with its own particular organisation, management style and culture. Before the 1970s each national company was more concerned with their own particular environments, markets and products, and only secondarily with what was happening in the wider context of Europe and overseas. Most managers had not needed to be international in outlook.

The situation changed dramatically in 1974. Managers from different national companies suddenly found themselves catapulted from a known company culture and business environment to a completely different and more complex situation in which they were expected to work across company and national boundaries by co-operating with colleagues from Italy, France and Germany. Moreover, the nature and dimensions of the new business in the league they had entered meant that many of them would have to operate at a multi-national level as *ambassadors* of IVECO outside Europe — with all the changes in behaviour and learning of new skills that this would imply.

The process of integration and internationalisation was helped initially by the creation of an organisational structure which put great emphasis on intercompany (and international) *functional working committees,* each composed of the IVECO functional director and counterpart managers from the national companies. These functional committees have been concerned with procedures and coordination: policy and strategy is decided by the top board, the *Management Advisory Committee* (MAC), which consists of the managing directors of FIAT, Unic, and Magirus Deutz, IVECO functional directors and IVECO's managing director. Considerable progress has been made by the fact that Italian, French, and German managers were obliged to work together within this organisational structure across their national cultural boundaries, communicating sometimes laboriously in the official company language, English, or some variation of it.

Even so the need was felt at the top from some kind of *educational* intervention in order to accelerate this process of integration, and to develop rapidly a truly international and professional IVECO senior management, who would then continue this process downwards throughout the organisation. The idea of setting up such a programme had been discussed in 1975, but it was not until mid-1977 that the IVECO personnel department requested ISVOR (the FIAT group's management development and training institute – the acronym means in Italian 'Institute for Organisational Development') to design a programme specifically tailored for IVECO. This author had been a consultant with ISVOR for some years previously and had run international management programmes for the FIAT group, and was invited to help design and run the IVECO programme.

The educational intervention

The problem had no apparent direct precedents. The objectives were to integrate the various management groups within the company; to help managers operate more effectively at the multinational level; to improve their professional skills; and to help create an IVECO company culture. In terms of international management development little could be found that responded to the specific IVECO problems, so a new model was evolved which was progressively modified and developed during the programme.

The planners wanted to create a microcosm of the company at work, a mini-IVECO, where they could experience the same conflicts, problems, and difficulties, which were hindering the company from working effectively; and then be able to work through these problems with participants. They wanted to create a *learning community* which would have its own distinct boundaries and yet be constantly related to the reality of the company. They wanted to help participants understand their past company histories and identities and those of their colleagues in order to be able to work together to create an IVECO identity and culture transcending all. They wanted to give them an opportunity to reflect on cultural differences and the implications and demands of operating in a multinational context. They wanted them to learn by *doing,* working together in mixed international groups on real company problems. They wanted this whole learning experience to stretch over a considerable period of time, so that participants would continually relate their learning experiences to their own organisational role. And they wanted to work with almost 200 senior managers in two years, so that the programme would constitute a 'critical mass' within the company and not be simply an opportunity for individual managers to learn; but also for organisational learning and development with key managers in close interaction with top management.*

---

* In 'Engineering Organizational Change', addendum to *The Levinson Letter,* 1979, Harry Levinson talks about the critical mass as 'those people who make or break the organization — the people who, whatever their titles, hold the real power'. The hypothesis here was that they would reach many of those key people in the ranks of their 200 senior manager participants, and that they would gradually be able to involve top managers as the process evolved. In effect, what Levinson says about his particular project holds true for what has happened in IVECO: 'Though many were anxious about becoming involved in a study which could criticize some management practices and offend some of their superiors ... the people in the critical mass were encouraged by top management's involvement. And, out of their own experience working on the project, these people were gradually won over to it. Politically, this was the place to be. People saw an unusual opportunity to shape the company's future. This was their big chance to make a difference and they didn't want to let it go.'

The design of the IVECO management programme (IMP)

A modular management development programme was devised, structured in eight separate 'editions' working with groups of 24 managers at a time. Participants come from each of the national companies and the headquarters. They are in positions where their responsibilities now have direct or indirect repercussions at the international level, and who have therefore become involved in problems of transnational business activities. Participants in each edition are as heterogeneous as possible, both in terms of national company origin and function. Each edition lasts about eight months, with five residential modules in various parts of Europe, and a series of project group meetings organised by the participants. Such a design allows ample time for reflection and testing of programme experiences back home. At any time there may be up to four different stages running in parallel.

IMP is based substantially on learning by experience. Participants bring to the programme real-life problems they have perceived or felt in IVECO. The aim is to use these company problems, and the experience of living and working together in international groups, as the principal learning vehicle. Thus the emphasis is on IVECO case studies and analysis of IVECO problems, rather than the use of external and inappropriate material. Externally-generated conceptual frameworks in organisational analysis, cross-cultural phenomena, and key functional areas such as marketing, production and management control systems is provided. There are some information-giving sessions related to the company itself, its strategies and policies, and to the major socio-economic and political institutions and issues in various European countries.

The IMP is articulated in two main phases, the first of which could be called 'classroom' work; and the second 'project' or field work organised by the participants with the support of the staff. There is a noticeable progression during the IMP from what might be termed teacher-controlled activities to the participants taking responsibility for their actions, learning, and the application to their work. Even in the classroom phase, though, the design offers a high level of participation with great emphasis on working in international groups.

The intention was to design a programme which would be
a learning opportunity for the deep analysis of key company
issues at the various organisational levels of participant's
responsibility, and which would help improve participants'
managerial skills. Through this educational intervention they
aimed to help improve the overall effectiveness of the company and contribute towards an organisational learning and
development *process* in IVECO. Consequently, an increasing
involvement of company top management was included
within the programme. This gave participants an opportunity
to understand better, and participate in the evolving company
strategies and to examine the implications and repercussions
of those at all levels. The continuous dialogue with top
management was seen as a learning opportunity for the
directors, ensuring that the IMP total effect is organisational
learning of a type where the process, contents and results
are closely related to the IVECO dynamic.

Implementation

How is all this done in practice? Perhaps the clearest explanation is to describe briefly the various parts of the typical
IMP edition, noting that each edition is flexible and able to
be modified in relation to the evolving company.

A programme like IMP clearly requires the active participation of managers disposed to share their perceptions and
experiences in the multi-cultural environment. This motivation
cannot be presumed, since participants have been selected by
their personnel managers and cannot be expected at the
outset to understand completely the objectives of the programme nor its usefulness for them. So a considerable
amount of energy is devoted at the beginning of each edition
to examining reciprocal objectives, motivation, and the
psychological contracts in this temporary learning organisation.
This is done at a meeting prior to the first module with a
member of staff and each national group. Originally there was
a two-day meeting with all the participants, which was
valuable but had to be discarded for logistical reasons. After

the introductory meeting with each national group the first day of the first module concerns the processes of socialisation, unfreezing and taking stock of expectations.

The first module is devoted to an analysis of IVECO's current situation. In national company groups participants develop an individual assignment, given at the introductory meeting, to make a qualitative historical analysis of their own national company until the time of the joint venture. This is then presented to their colleagues from the other two countries. The thinking behind this is the importance of an historical perspective in being able to grasp the social reality which exists in an organisation; the importance of understanding one's own roots at a time when one is being required to go beyond them and help create a multi-national organisation; and the need to begin to appreciate the differences and values in others cultures and backgrounds.

Participants then move into three heterogeneous *working groups* to examine the development of IVECO since 1974, and then to look at specific areas in the company, e.g. marketing and sales, production, or administration and control. The results of the groups' analyses are discussed in plenary session with the IVECO director responsible for that particular function. It is worth noting that the *process* of working together across functions and nationalities, together with the process of interaction with top management, is considered as more important in terms of *learning* than the concrete results of the group work.

The work of this first module is to a large degree the basis for all that follows, both in terms of clarifying one's individual and corporate identity, and of indicating present or potential problems within the company. This module is held at ISVOR-FIAT's facilities at Marentino near Turin.

The second module is held in London, and is designed to highlight the problems which arise when operating internationally both in the IVECO environment and in the wider external context. An attempt is made to deepen participant's understanding of management cultures and organisational behaviour and structures in Italy, France and Germany, and other European and extra-European contexts, and to improve participants' ability to understand and deal with those cultural mechanisms affecting managing in foreign environments. Furthermore a comparative study is made of significant socio-economic institutions and factors in Europe which have direct relevance to multinational company management — not unlike the kind of information John Drew suggests (see Chapter 5).

Much of the work on cultural differences is based on raw material furnished by the participants themselves in their answers to questionnaires developed at the Wharton Business School. Participants are also invited to prepare beforehand written 'critical incidents' — descriptions of real experiences in IVECO where cultural differences seem to have led to misunderstanding or even conflict. Thus the examination of cultural phenomena is constantly related not only to external research data but also to experience in IVECO itself.

The third module is held in either Italy, France, or Germany near one of IVECO.s production facilities. Its aim is to continue from the first module and analyse some key management issues in the company, developing a systematic working methodology, and improving participants' knowledge of practical frameworks in important functional areas. There is also an examination of interfunctional problem areas; for example, the launch of a new product, the approach to a new market etc. Since the contents depend upon IVECO's current situation, and this is continually evolving, this module has been subject to constant modification.

The second part of the module is dedicated to launching the field work, first of all developing together a work methodology, then choosing the project themes and groups, and then getting started. This is in many ways the core of the programme, and the concept was clearly influenced by the action learning movement.

The fourth module, therefore, is the field work itself in which an international, and partly interfunctional, self-selected group of five to six participants concentrates for eight to ten weeks on a specific problem within the company. The topics are chosen by the participants together with, and subject to, the approval of those members of IVECO's top management who will be the projects' 'clients'. Participants work on these group projects on a part-time basis and they take responsibility for their own work, including all logistical arrangements, client contacts etc. Typically each group would meet together four or five times alternating between Italy, France and Germany, combining these meetings as far as possible with other work commitments. Each group has an elected chairman whose task is to co-ordinate the group's work and liaise with the IMP staff who offer consultancy to the project groups.

At the end of this period participants meet again for two days at ISVOR-FIAT in order to finalise their draft reports and agree on a strategy for presenting these to their various clients. Some of the topics chosen so far have tackled such problems as:

Review of the boundaries of marketing and sales functions in IVECO with special regard to marketing strategy and field marketing.
Production planning.
Guide lines for a procedure for the development of new products.
Centralised construction of prototypes.
Definition of a range of trucks for developing countries.
Starting a new truck range.
IVECO HQ's location.
Improving district managers and salesmen performance.
Managing options for increased flexibility and profitability.
Management informations systems in IVECO.
Minimising risks in new IVECO initiatives.
Evaluating operational and economic performance of subsidiaries and branches.
Credit control function.
IVECO career planning system.
Congruence between commercial strategy and market communications.
Reducing production costs by extending purchase function.

The fifth module takes place some three to four weeks later at ISVOR-FIAT and includes a final meeting of each project group with its client to discuss the project reports and their implementation; a sharing of the learning experience of the field work with colleagues from the other project groups; an analysis and evaluation of their whole experience of the IMP; and finally a meeting with the managing director of IVECO, in which the results of the programme and in particular the field work projects can be discussed with the company's chief executive. This meeting marks the closure of each edition.

Figure 13.1 gives a schematic presentation of a whole edition of the IMP, while Figure 13.2 attempts to relate the main phases of an edition to the programme's objectives. Each edition is staffed by two to three tutors, whose task is to provide methodological support and assistance to participants, to co-ordinate the edition, and integrate the various contributions of external teachers, consultants and guest speakers. External contributors have come from a wide range of countries, including the UK, France, Germany, Italy, Switzerland, Sweden, and the USA, and they represent business schools, universities, research and consultancy organisations, and guest speakers from other multinational contexts. These international inputs seem to be an important contribution to a programme which has as one of its objectives the creation of an international management culture in IVECO.

Initial results

So much for the original structure of the IMP. But what about the process? What actually happened? What problems were there?

The programme has now completed four editions, and the fifth is already under way, so it is an appropriate moment to take stock of what has been achieved and judge what has to be improved. Two years have elapsed since the programme was first discussed with clients, and during this time some significant changes have taken place within the company and its business environment. It is impossible at this point to measure any kind of direct cause-and-effect relationship

Programme objectives:

To accelerate the process of IVECO integration.
To develop an international IVECO management.
To improve participants' knowledge of a practical framework in the IVECO key functional areas, in particular industrial marketing and control.
To improve managerial skills related to IVECO:
    analysis of complex situations;
    interaction and communication (group work);
    orientation to objectives;
    evaluation of results.

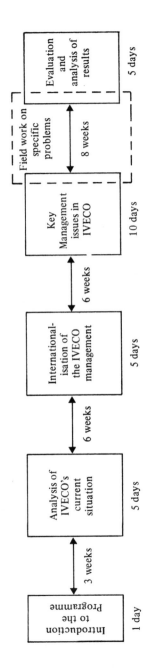

Figure 13.1   IVECO management programme

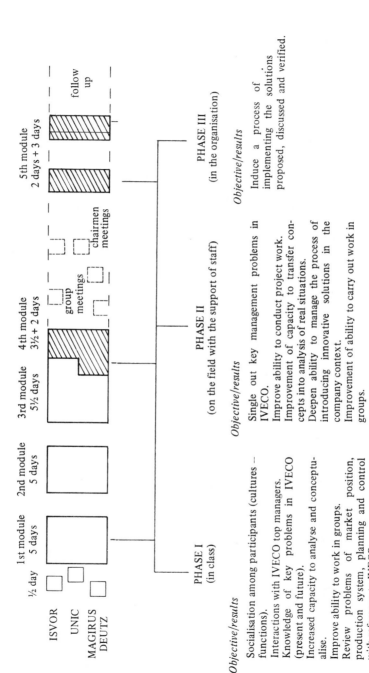

Figure 13.2   The original design

between the IMP and changes in IVECO, but at the very least IMP has been an important arena in which organisational changes could be examined and discussed critically by participants and top management.

In 1979 the Italian managing director, who had amalgamated the five companies, held them together during the first five years of IVECO's life, and who stamped his strong, charismatic personality on the company, retired in favour of a younger, more technocratic, Frenchman. The new managing director initiated a review of IVECO's strategy and structure and, thus, IMP has in this last six months been contributing to and examining the processes of a major organisational change by definition, since the intention was to create a programme focused on the real problems of the company. The external environment has changed too, and the company is going through a difficult period compared with excellent sales of two years ago. It is now proposed that the IMP be adapted in order to be able to respond more adequately to the present needs of the company. The aims of the programme remain essentially threefold:

1   To achieve a higher degree of cross-cultural and cross-functional integration.
2   To accelerate the process of internationalisation of the management of the company.
3   To improve those managerial skills required by IVECO management in the emerging company — characterised above all by an increased degree of complexity and interdependency.

In a programme maintenance and redesign meeting in July 1979 the programme was judged to have been reasonably successful with regard to the first two objectives but needed improvement with regard to the third. There follows a synthesis of the analysis of the different modules of the IMP and some comments of their present adequacy.

First module

This module has concentrated on an historical analysis of the constituent companies prior to 1974, and an analysis of the development of IVECO since then. It is recommended that the historical diagnosis and research aspects be completed by fuller considerations of the significant variables in IVECO's business development; particularly in the light of recent decisions regarding company strategy and new organisational structure. Understanding this will be facilitated by parallel reflections on the salient factors of business policy, strategy, and structure, in other multinationals. This module would be a better place for the meetings with the managing director.

Second module

The aim of this module is to highlight differences and problems involved in operating in an international dimension, and although it seems substantially in line with these objectives, there is room for improvement in looking at how companies become multinational.

Third module

This module has been the most problematic. The objectives were on the one hand to identify key management issues in IVECO, and on the other hand, in parallel, to improve participants' comprehension and analytical ability in the main functional areas. This was meant to help create a common conceptual frame of reference which would facilitate the project work in the fourth module. Although through various editions case material from IVECO itself was used (development of the 170 truck, the US project etc.) seeking to emphasise the interfunctional aspects of the material, this was never quite successful. Perhaps the set objectives were too ambitious, given the time at their disposal and the heterogeneity of the participants. In any event it is now proposed to move this module forward until *after* the field work has begun, when the time can be used not only as a support to the field work projects but also to provide conceptual inputs in functional areas at a point in the programme where such inputs seem more relevant and practical.

Field work (fourth and fifth modules)

There were two main objectives here:

1   To contribute to the problem-solving process within IVECO by attempting to deal with real life company problems and helping improve the company by recommending concrete solutions in specific areas.

2   To use this problem-solving process as an opportunity to help individual participants to learn, exercise and develop managerial skills by working across complex functional and national boundaries.

The evaluation is that they were more successful in the first than in the second; but that they have a long way to go in respect to both objectives. The major problems encountered have been with their inability as a staff to maintain constant support to the project groups — among other reasons because of the overlapping of various editions of the programme — and the difficulty in having access to the client system during the field work. The field work thus often became 'reports' to be 'presented', rather than an exercise in integrated efforts to initiate and *manage* change.

There are several factors within the field work that show the situation is improving. Top management have now realised the usefulness and importance of objective 1 above, and now suggest the kind of topics *they* would like project groups to tackle for them, and with them. The staff group and the IMP itself has achieved much higher credibility within the company. Staff now have better and more direct access to potential clients, but constant staff support during this phase seems essential.

The final meeting was intended to allow participants to test the results of their field work projects with their respective clients, share the learning experience of the field work with their colleagues, and evaluate the whole IMP in terms of a more effective future performance in the company. In fact it was always a confused meeting. The presence of the managing director was seen as an evaluation of the project work and of the participants leading to characteristic symptoms of regression to dependence. Eliminating the meeting with the MD and having the meetings with clients beforehand therefore seems sensible and would allow concentration on the sharing of the learning experience, and the application of the programme to the company and participants' own organisational roles.

During the period of field work there should in future be more explicit connection between the theme chosen and the strategic decisions of IVECO. This correction can also be reinforced by a greater involvement of top management in the choice of projects. There must be a greater effort to guide the field work projects towards *implementation,* involving the clients who have the power to make the proposals operational. There must be more concentration on the *skills* required by participants for this kind of exercise, as these are the kind of skills they require increasingly in the complex multinational system of IVECO. In order to do this staff must ensure their continuous support for each group in the various stages of the field work.

Proposals for the revised structure of the IMP can be seen schematically in Figure 13.3. There are three distinct phases with their own specific objectives. It will be noted that the major change regards the third module and the field work.

Follow-up

A series of follow-up meetings is planned for participants who have completed different editions of the programme. This would measure to some extent what impact the programme has had on individual participants' capacity to manage their organisational role, and more generally what effect the IMP has had on the company culture. It will be an opportunity to check on the progress of the various field work suggestions, and a chance to allow participants from different editions of the programme to socialise and exchange experiences. It will be also an opportunity to understand better and reflect on IVECO's new organisational structure and its implications; and a chance for participants to look at their own career development within the company and possible need for further training.

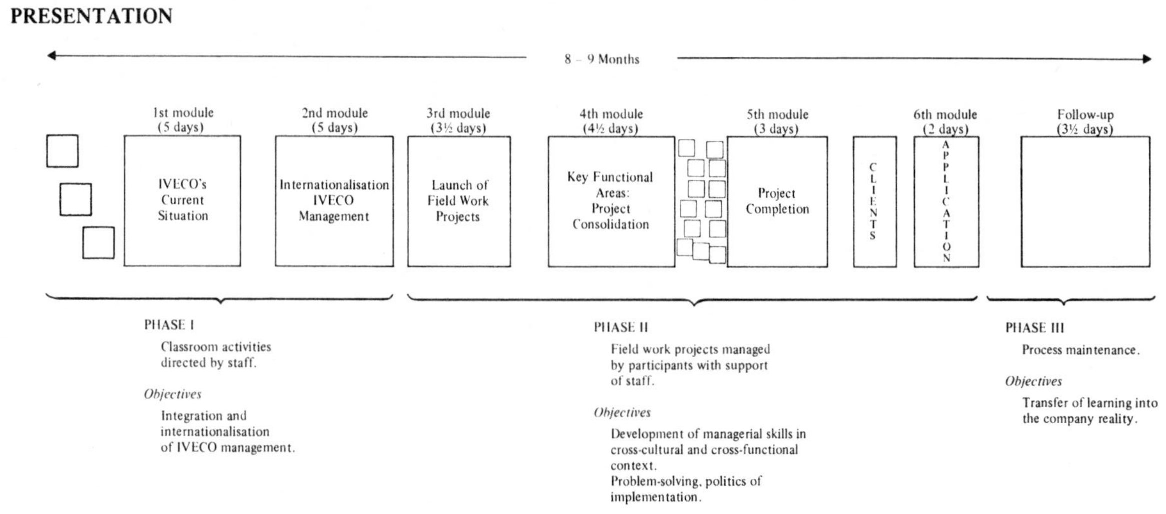

PRESENTATION

8 – 9 Months

| 1st module (5 days) | 2nd module (5 days) | 3rd module (3½ days) | 4th module (4½ days) | 5th module (3 days) | 6th module (2 days) | Follow-up (3½ days) |

IVECO's Current Situation

Internationalisation IVECO Management

Launch of Field Work Projects

Key Functional Areas: Project Consolidation

Project Completion

C L I E N T S

A P P L I C A T I O N

PHASE I

Classroom activities directed by staff.

Objectives

Integration and internationalisation of IVECO management.

PHASE II

Field work projects managed by participants with support of staff.

Objectives

Development of managerial skills in cross-cultural and cross-functional context.
Problem-solving, politics of implementation.

PHASE III

Process maintenance.

Objectives

Transfer of learning into the company reality.

Figure 13.3   Revised general structure, September 1979

Reflections on the wider company issues

To some extent the IMP can be seen contributing to the
search for an IVECO culture which would transcend, though
not destroy, the pre-existing cultures of the constituent
national companies. The effect of working with more than 100
senior managers over the past eighteen months has been to
build up a critical mass of significant actors within the
organisation. Their experience of working together in the
project-based programme is judged by themselves as leading
to more effective interactions at work. 'In order for organizational learning to occur, learning agents' discoveries,
inventions, and evaluations, must be imbedded in the organizational memory'. [2] This is ensured in part by the field
work projects, by continuing commentary on the progress
of the IMP in the company newsletter, but above all, by the
considerable growth of an *informal* network among participants. Cross-cultural friendships have developed and people
have grown to respect the differences of behaviour of their
colleagues in other countries. All this has contributed to
more rapid solutions of related problems as they occur. There
is a new kind of 'esprit de corps' which binds Turin, Paris and
Ulm and enables former IMP participants to continue their
collaboration with each other through building on their
experiences in the programme while carrying out their
normal company activities. As always, knowing the right
person to contact in order to get something done can short-
cut cumbersome procedures.

But above all there is a greater understanding and tolerance
in IVECO. The multinational manager needs to be flexible
working in cultures and situations alien to his own; he needs
to have the capacity to accept in a personal way a certain
cultural relativity, the ability to accept differences, not in
terms of right or wrong, but as perfectly legitimate patterns
of behaviour in contexts different from those to which he
is accustomed. In Charles Handy's terms, 'to develop a
situational sensitivity, being able to recognize different
paradigms and move in and out of them with some degree
of facility and even comfort'. [3] Learning to do this cannot
happen through books or lectures. There is no substitute for

living and working abroad in a foreign culture. The IMP simply recreates a multinational situation and gives participants working in mixed groups the opportunity to reflect and learn from this experience, to cross a lot of complex boundaries and cope with radically different situations swiftly and rapidly.

The original request from initial contacts with the personnel department was for a more or less traditional management development course similar to that designed and implemented by ISVOR-FIAT for the whole FIAT group in the four years prior to 1977. What they eventually succeeded in implementing, was of course, much more ambitious.

They were aware that they needed to broaden their base, to have more access to other significant actors within the company apart from the personnel department to test out their and others' perceptions about company needs. This, at the outset, was not easy, and in retrospect it is disappointing that they did not succeed in conducting more widely based research into the kind of training and development needs that existed within the company. The preanalysis was based on a number of interviews with representative persons within the company, and the experience of two short technical management courses with a sample of the client population who would be working with the designers in the IMP. But as the programme has continued there has been a significant improvement not only in their understanding of the company situation and training and development needs, but also of the credibility of the IMP itself and the staff vis-à-vis the company, both top management and participants.

Dealing with top management

After some difficulty, a series of meetings with members of the board was successfully built into the programme and thus as the programme developed they were able to involve top managers more and more in the change process. These meetings with participants changed from being an added engagement in their already full diaries taking up three hours of their precious time into opportunities for top management to explore with their immediate subordinates how to solve particular problems in their own area or look at the relevance of company strategy. From having to convince the board to find the time to come, and having to brief them on what to say, they soon found themselves in a situation where they were being approached by the board. The board were giving feedback about the effects of the programme, offering suggestions and relevant topics to be looked at, and generally entering into the learning process themselves in a collaborative way. Thus they were succeeding in broadening their base away from the 'personnel/training' label, and establishing their credibility as being concerned with *business* and people development simultaneously. A close link with top managers was developed gradually by working with them in trying to keep the IMP in line with the company's needs and in seeking to implement the most important results of the field work projects.

Steering committee

At present they are trying to set up an IMP *steering committee,* a point of reference for the programme staff which would have a wider basis of power and credibility, and perhaps also impartiality, than the personnel department alone. So often at the beginning they were confronted by situations in which they were told by personnel managers that such and such a course of action would be impossible because of a supposed negative response from the MAC or some member of it. These were often found to be the projected and untested fears of the personnel managers themselves which nonetheless prevented them from following a preferred course of action! As they have broadened their own power base and credibility, and gained direct access to most of the MAC, this situation no longer exists. Yet there still seems to be a strong argument for some kind of steering committee, as a guarantor, sponsor, and advisory body for the staff of the programme and the MAC itself. Members of this committee must be people of the highest standing within the company if its role and that of the programme are to have sufficient credibility within the company. The steering committee will be composed of the director of corporate planning, personnel director, director of production and perhaps also director of administration and control (all members of the MAC) together with the management development manager, director of ISVOR-FIAT, and two representatives of the staff of the IMP. They expect to meet with this committee every six weeks to take stock of the development of the programme and ensure its coherence and adequacy with respect to developments in the company and the outside world.

Tutors' role

The question is often asked, What is the role that trainers have to take up in a programme of this kind? What particular kind of professionalism is required? What training should the trainer have? It is not an easy question to answer. An international and cross-cultural staff group is important in a programme of this kind. It makes no sense to try and help participants to work better in a multi-cultural context if tutors are unable to do so themselves. As IMP staff members, their professional backgrounds have been quite varied, the common denominator being their commitment to 'live' management education and organisation development. One must take the risk of learning how to be comfortable about working across functional boundaries and tackling technical problems from an overall company perspective. The staff group needs to have a behavioural competency, to be sensitive to process issues and to the political implications of organisational interventions; it needs to have the technical skill of business analysis; and the conceptual and teaching ability to provide frameworks for the analysis of various company problems. Last, and not least, it needs to have a linguistic ability in a programme of this kind. The official language of the IMP is English, although simultaneous translation is provided when necessary; but their ability to communicate with participants both on the formal sessions and perhaps more importantly in the informal discussions over meals or at the bar when often the really important learning can take place, in Italian, German and French, has enhanced our effectiveness as tutors immeasurably.

Languages

Those who are involved in teaching in international manage-ment development programmes have to some degree to provide a model of behaviour which others can adopt, so it would seem important that they are seen to be able to operate effectively at the multinational level.

It is important that such a teacher be able to speak and work in at least one other language than English. It has been possible in the past for US and British managers and teachers to 'get away with' speaking only English according to the accepted ethnocentric, colonial model, but those days are rapidly drawing to a close. We have to place more importance on language training and skills in the development of our future managers and teachers. [4] This is not because a foreign language is always *necessary* in the strictest sense. It is not. Most of our senior foreign colleagues are more exposed to foreign languages and at the multinational level they *have* to speak English. Apart from it being extremely useful to be able to understand what people are saying without recourse to simultaneous translation — and for the different kind of relationship one can establish through knowing someone's language — a second language is a key to a deeper knowledge of another culture and thus to a *qualitatively* different kind of communication. The possession of a foreign language and the resulting understanding of the specific national culture, gives the possibility of further insights into differences in other cultures. [5]

There is another very simple and usually underestimated point. Knowledge of other languages also helps one to be clearer in speaking English to foreigners, both in terms of the vocabulary used and also clarity of diction. Knowledge of foreign languages enables one to speak an English which is more intelligible to non-native English speakers as one is more aware of using colloquial expressions and thus of the need to explain them. This might sound trivial and amusing to English readers, but non-English speakers who have been subjected on international education programmes to English-speaking teachers without the advantage of another language would consider this an important point.

If multinational management teachers do have to offer a model to their clients, then it seems difficult to see how this can be done without having worked in a foreign culture themselves and experienced the problems and challenges of having to operate as multinational managers. [6] It is difficult to help people learn to do something which one doesn't really know how to do oneself.

Notes

[1] Robert A. Wilson, *Automotive Industries,* June 1978, p. 44.

[2] C. Argyris, *Organizational Learning: A theory of Action Perspective,* Addison-Wesley, 1977, p. 19.

[3] C. Handy, in note to ATM Conference, Cambridge, 1979.

[4] See, for example, Judy Lowes' chapter in this book (Chapter 6) and her recent book *The New Euromanagers,* Woodhead-Faulkner, Cambridge 1979.

[5] Jules Ambrose makes some relevant comments to this point in 'The Middle East Mirage' in *International Management,* April 1979: 'An expatriate's ability to understand and accept these differences is one way of measuring his cultural empathy'. The importance of having this affinity is spotlighted in a survey of Egyptian and Saudi Arabian executives attending a conference at the University of Maine in the US several years ago. The Middle East executives concluded that cultural empathy was the single most important requisite for the successful conduct of business in their countries. 'It is not enough any more for culturally sensitive people at mid-management level to carry the ball in these countries', say the authors of the survey, Professor Guvenc Alpander and Professor Jacob Naor. 'Top management must itself possess a cultural sixth sense to achieve effective business outcomes.' The two academics note that there is no easy way to determine in advance the extent of a manager's cultural empathy.

However, one indicator is his language learning ability. 'It is important for a manager to know one or more foreign languages or the language of his host country', they say. But his aptitude and desire to learn should be considered more significant, they add, as it shows a willingness to assimilate. [6] See, for example, Vern Terpstra, *The Cultural Environment of International Business,* South Western Publishing Co. Cincinnati, Chapter 1, 'Language'.

14 Mobil's System for Organisational Improvement

ALAN BARRATT

Most multinational companies find it difficult to ensure that good standards of effective training and development take place in companies, affiliates and subsidiaries around the world. The development of managers and supervisors (chief executives) to improve their on-the-job performance provides a continual challenge to the developmental function in Mobil. Over the past four years Mobil has been designing, testing and implementing a system which seeks to integrate the need to improve the performance of the individual with the needs of the organisation.

The Supervisor Development System (SDS) is a departure from the approach to supervisory training taken by many organisations. The title is misleading: SDS is a system that deals with *organisational* improvement at all levels; however, as in most organisations, once named, always named. The system is designed to improve measurably upon the training results achieved by more traditional methods, while reducing the time and costs by as much as 50 per cent. It combines training with methods and actions to improve the effectiveness of organisations. Managers who have used this system report increased profits, reduced costs, and improvements in numerous areas of organisational functioning such as supervisor — subordinate relationships, communications, role clarification etc.

If the system is applied in accordance with the prescribed guidelines, it provides opportunities to change the training function from a cost activity to one that generates measurable and attributable profits.

System concepts and rationale

The conceptual underpinnings of the system rest on findings in adult learning theory, successful applications of the behavioural sciences and organisation research. Tables 14.1 and 14.2 summarise these issues. The SDS design is a response to the growing accumulation of data concerning the lack of effectiveness of many management/supervisory programmes. On-the-job and within-the-work-group training are key operational concepts. With the exception of the initial workshops to introduce the system, no training actions are taken until specific data have been collected relevant to individual, group and organisational needs. The system fosters the participation of individuals in the analysis of their own needs and in the decisions which are made about meeting those needs.

The key elements or components within the system follow a modified action-research model of survey-guided development. The original model was researched and tested by the Institute for Social Research, University of Michigan. The research extends over twenty years, includes over 30,000 managers in a wide range of organisations and to date has cost well over two million dollars.

Following a problem identification session which involves the entire management group and less than two days of workshop activities, supervisors are given an opportunity actively to participate in the process of clarifying and solving the problems which they have identified and which are getting in the way of improved performance. Knowledge, methods and disciplines acquired during the initial workshops are used during all problem-identification, problem-solving and action-planning activities which occur throughout the life of the system.

SDS

The Supervisor Development System contains methods to identify and meet all the training and development needs of supervisors, worldwide. It is flexible enough to encompass

Table 14.1
How adults learn

Adult learning starts only when the individual recognises a significant difference between what he/she should know and do, and his/her actual knowledge and performance.

Adults learn best on the job or when the learning situation closely approximates the job context.

Adults learn best at their own pace with and among their peers.

Adults learn best when they are involved in the learning needs assessment process and in the training decisions to meet those needs.

Table 14.2
Research results

Productivity often improves when employees are involved in decisions about work and change.

Data collection — feedback — problem solving can improve productivity and organisation effectiveness.

Behaviour modification programmes can improve business results quickly and inexpensively.

Timely performance feedback from the job itself improves performance and productivity. Timely and appropriate feedback from the supervisor can also be helpful.

Employees at all levels have data and can contribute to problem solving and improved decision quality. Appropriate involvement improves decision implementation.

Motivation can be measured and taught. People and jobs can be matched.

Elements of organisational functioning impact on business results.

and include locally sponsored supervisory training activities which are compatible with the data based system; local managers have found it effective in bringing about sought for, job-related behaviour change. These needs include supervisory skill programmes and approaches that deal with personal growth and coping with change.

In addition to reducing training time and costs, the system virtually eliminates the need to send managers and supervisors away for training. The primary training emphasis is on-the-job, within the job context, or within natural work groups. The process involves employees in the identification of their own learning needs and in the decisions taken to meet those needs. Unnecessary and ineffective training is eliminated because the identification process focuses *solely* on job-relevant, documented training needs. As a result of employee involvement in the process, the responsibility for learning and for changed job behaviours shifts primarily and naturally to the employee. Training results are improved because employees feel ownership of the needs they have helped identify and for the training decisions which they helped to make.

Training methods

Training needs are met largely through the following training actions:

> On-the-job coaching, by the supervisor.
>
> Job knowledge coaching labs, conducted by local employees who are qualified in the knowledge area covered by the particular lab.
>
> Mini-workshops, confined to four hours or less, designed and packaged under the direction of the central training group, to be conducted by the local system project leader.
>
> Skill improvement workshops and job knowledge seminars of up to two days' duration, conducted by training and/or consulting resource people from outside the affiliate.
>
> Developmental, rotational or orientational assignments.

System design considerations attempt to recognise organisational realities and the diverse cultures in which the system will be applied. It is intended that within clearly stated guidelines, the system be installed, monitored and maintained by *local* people. This applies specifically to affiliates that have no training persons on their payrolls. Thus, methods and concepts within the system are expected to greatly reduce the emphasis on professional trainers, external consultants, classrooms and off-site exposures. With the exception of the mini-workshops required to install the system, workshops and other training actions are conducted only after specific learning needs have been documented through the use of surveys.

Whenever possible, workshops and other training actions are restricted to four hours or less and are conducted on site by local employees. Given the range of individual and organisational needs that the system is designed to identify and meet, this will not always be possible. From time to time, longer workshops conducted by professional trainers and consultants are needed. Coaching and interpersonal skills are typical needs met by longer, professionally conducted workshops.

The focus of the system-combining methods and activities to improve the competence of managers and supervisors with approaches to improve the effectiveness of their work groups means that the emphasis gravitates between individual knowledge and skill, and the effectiveness of vertical or natural work groups and horizontal work teams.

Through self-designed and administered mini-surveys, it provides employees at all levels with methods to collect data about how well the organisation is functioning and how effectively individuals and groups deal with one another. With this data in hand, it provides the people in the organisation with methods to analyse and cope with the data and decide what actions they wish to take to improve individual and organisational performance. As a result, organisation improvement activities are also data-based, job relevant and directed solely at identified needs.

During the initial application of the system, managers and supervisors are given a series of up to five mini-workshops.

These brief, concentrated workshops provide the participants with the methods, knowledge, and to a limited extent, the skills, which they need to install effectively and maintain the system. Initial inputs cover these topics:

Interpersonal communications — some useful concepts and vocabulary.

Coaching methods.

How to write an objective and an action plan.

Problem clarification, problem solving, action planning. Leadership.

Following the workshops, groups are formed to clarify and solve problems which were identified in the initial problem identification session as interfering with the ability of individuals and groups to improve their performance. The problem-solving mode continues with additional brief workshops conducted locally based on the problems and/or needs identified by employee groups. Typical workshops which might be required would include time management, reading improvement, report writing, delegation, motivation, coaching skills, listening skills, conference leadership etc. Modules for mini-workshops and longer *skill* development workshops are made available for local administration as required. Self-study programmes are also utilised.

Occasionally, resource people from outside the affiliate may be needed to support local training and development efforts. Training assistance will be needed by some affiliates to conduct functional programmes and supervisory skills workshops, i.e. coaching skills, communications skills etc. Occasionally, organisational issues are identified that will have a level of difficulty or risk which will demand outside help. Typical examples include role conflict, team functioning, goal issues, high-level interpersonal and intergroup conflict, interpersonal communication skills etc. Occasional use of local outside consultants is encouraged where professionally qualified people are available and are willing to work within the framework of the system.

As the SDS is implemented and develops in an organisation, experience shows that the organisation will become more effective. Some of the outputs found are: increased levels of trust; improved communications; better relationships between groups, supervisors and subordinates and among peers; increased individual competence; and improved policies, procedures and practices. In addition to increased organisational effectiveness, one has developed a qualified and experienced coordinator (high-potential line manager) to guide and control the transition.

Thus, in addition to cost effective training to meet documented needs, the system helps managers' supervisors and other members of an organisation to cope with the increasing pace and impact of change. This is a major reason for the success of the system. Expressed in a slightly different way, the system combines a proven method for measuring job-related learning needs — and brief, cost effective, on-site learning exposures — with actions to measure and modify elements of organisational functioning.

Extensive research and application by reputable researchers and consultants has shown that these elements have an impact on training results and on business results. Figure 14.1 is a model of the system. The left hand side of the model deals with individual data and individual requirements and actions. The right hand side of the model deals with group and organisational data. These two areas are kept quite separate during the initial stages of the system application. The two come together for the core process of feedback and action planning and then separate for implementation. Here, however, the separation is not clear cut. Implementation steps on both sides of the model can be concurrent and will, on occasion, overlap. It is one of the strengths of the system that individual development and organisation improvement are linked and expected to take place simultaneously. A typical application sequence is outlined in Figure 14.2.

The benefits

Mobil believes the system will show an early payout in terms of management/supervisory practices; improved problem identification and problem-solving abilities; general efficiency;

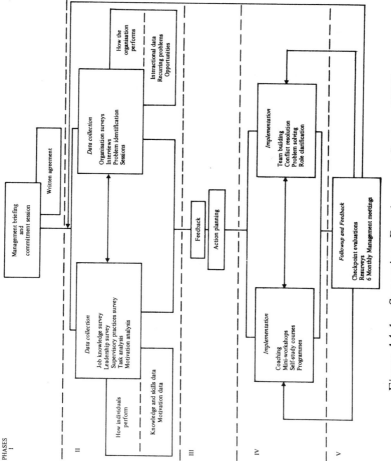

PHASES

I

II

III

IV

V

Management briefing and commitment session

Written agreement

Data collection
Organisation surveys
Interviews
Problem identification
Sessions

How the organisation performs

Interactional data
Recurring problems
Opportunities

Data collection
Job knowledge survey
Leadership survey
Supervisory practices survey
Task analysis
Motivation analysis

How individuals perform

Knowledge and skills data
Motivation data

Feedback

Action planning

Implementation
Team building
Conflict resolution
Problem solving
Role clarification

Implementation
Coaching
Mini-workshops
Self-study courses
Programmes

Followup and Feedback
Checkpoint evaluations
Resurveys
6 Monthly Management meetings

Figure 14.1   Supervisor Development System (SDS)

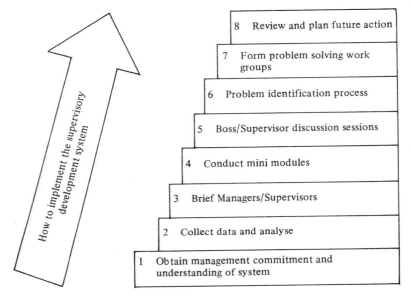

Figure 14.2   Typical application sequence

and improved interdepartmental relationships. The initial benefits have been:

Improved communications and relations between supervisors and subordinates.

Improved communications between departments.

Greater understanding and agreement between managers, supervisors and subordinates of their actual workload and responsibilities.

Streamlining of paperwork requirements.

Increased consciousness of supervisory responsibilities in the field of coaching and counselling.

Development of a more systematic approach toward problem analysis and problem solving.

Development of a better understanding by participants of how they are perceived by their fellow employees.

In addition, affiliate (local) supervisors learned how to write quantifiable objectives with performance standards, and an action plan to meet those objectives. The problem-solving workshop was based on current *local* problems which were identified by the participants as getting in the way of improved performance. Developing solutions to these problems required participants to utilise heavily the inputs from the mini-workshops on communications and objective setting. These solutions provided a direct payout to the affiliate which were quantifiable.

Figure 14.3 shows how the internal consultant/project leader's time was spend in a recent intervention.

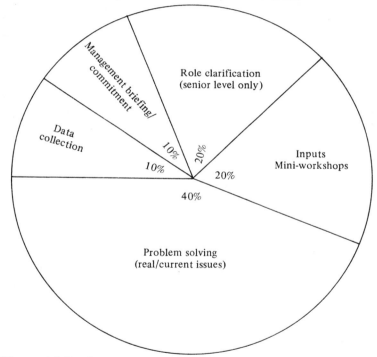

Figure 14.3   Internal consultant/project leader's time utilisation

Many organisations are seeking new innovative ways of improving the utilization, development and growth of their employees and their business. The SDS approach is designed as a company do-it-yourself system with minimal external assistance and produces *bottom line* results!

15   Dunlop in Nigeria

DAVID C. STEEL

Historical background

Following World War II it was not until the mid-1950s that
European manufacturers of consumer and industrial goods
were able to meet their customers' demands in their home
countries and, subsequently, develop export markets in
developing countries. The growing availability of goods
created a growing demand in countries like Nigeria, which
the manufacturers were keen to satisfy. Manufacturing
companies had to reconsider their policies. This led the larger
multinational manufacturers to establish local manufacturing
facilities to cover their main products in the early 1960s.

Until then 'Training' had been going on quite easily in
Nigeria since the business activity was that of trading, and
trading has been a natural occupation in Nigeria for centuries.
It was very much a part of their culture. Such training and
development had been very much 'on-the-job' training passing
on from 'father to son' or, 'master to apprentice' in the
various craft activities.

However, with the advent of local manufacture using mass
production techniques, this format of training was inadequate
both in quality and quantity. The training required now was
vastly different, due to the technological demands, and the
demands for these products to compete immediately in the
market with imports in terms of quality and durability. This
situation heralded the change from a trading economy to the
beginning of the industrial revolution in Nigeria and, subsequently, towards a consumer-based society.

This period forced the Dunlop company to identify a number of training problems which would seriously affect the business efficiency of this enterprise:

1   The technical know-how covering the manufacturing processes was often patented or protected in some way by the original European-based manufacturer. So the number of Nigerians who may have studied or even worked overseas were: (a) unlikely to have the required experience in industry, or (b) likely to be in such small numbers as to be insignificant in meeting the needs of new local industry.

2   The education system in Nigeria had been established to meet administrative occupations, particularly the Civil Service, so the local labour market was extremely short of science-based industrial personnel.

The resultant effect was that this vacuum of technology was filled by the importation of expatriate expertise at nearly all staff levels above that of operative. These expatriates were briefed to pass on their skills and knowledge to local personnel, but they were faced with many simultaneous problems:

1   The majority of manufacturing companies had neither the expertise nor the facilities required to run co-ordinated manpower development and training schemes.

2   The external management development and training programmes available locally were very limited.

3   The expatriate specialist found it difficult to do two jobs; that is, to ensure that his unit was operating efficiently and, *at the same time,* implement adequate training schemes.

Unfortunately, these facts were overlooked by the emergent companies, mainly because the concept of manpower development was still in its infancy, even in the so-called 'developed countries'. This situation continued with very few exceptions. Such exceptions were represented by a handful of companies, mainly large, who readily accepted that co-ordinated manpower development is an essential part of the organic growth of *any* enterprise.

It seems that many directors and senior managers have attempted in the past to solve such problems by training based only on superficial symptoms of local problems not the root causes. These root causes revolve around appropriate selection, organisation structure, job descriptions etc., to suit the local working environment.

Only during the last decade, with pressure from governments through the establishment of industrial training legislation, has industry and commerce in the 'developed' countries begun to feel a 'wind of change' and accept a much greater professionalism in the total field of manpower development. The result has changed the attitude of western management to manpower development but this is only beginning to percolate through to the developing countries. However some, such as Nigeria, have been quick to realise the need for highly trained personnel, and these countries have promulgated various forms of legislation covering industrial training and development.

The assignment — general introduction

In relation to the historical background, a similar situation faced the directors of Dunlop Nigerian Industries Limited in the early 1970s, with the ending of the Nigerian civil war. These directors and senior management, together with their superiors in the London headquarters, recognised that the company was in a stage of accelerated expansion and it was necessary to identify the manpower development problems, to facilitate the transfer of management know-how and skills to the local indigenous Nigerian staff. Unfortunately, because of the management climate previously mentioned, the problem was accepted at board level but their perception tended to be rather vague, i.e. only that it was necessary with the expansion of the company to have a co-ordinated training and development activity.

Both groups of directors thought the solution was to recruit a senior experienced staff development specialist to go to Nigeria and begin solving these problem areas relatively simply. This plan, whilst understandable, was not easy to

implement due to the lack of staff development specialists
who had any overseas' experience.

It was at this stage that the author was offered by the
UK company the chance to go to Nigeria and solve the
problems. He immediately asked what were the specific
identifiable areas of the problem and was given rather vague
information. It was only after much detailed discussion that
the UK management were persuaded of the need for an in-
depth survey of the problem before any further action should
be taken. It is necessary to emphasise at this stage, the
importance and need that such a preliminary survey should
be carried out before any action is taken.

The outcome was a survey of the current and planned
business situation, the state of planning for staff development,
the available facilities, and the trends in training and development policies used by large local companies. It soon became
clear that the main emphasis placed by *other* companies in
the field of training was on technical, e.g. engineering,
training; and that co-ordinated management development had
largely been overlooked. Management development consisted
then of sending Nigerian managers back to the UK to learn
how to be a manager *in the UK* as distinct from how to
manage in their own country. This state of the art was not
adequate for the company's needs, as the recommendations
drawn from the survey indicate (see Table 15.1).

Table 15.1
Report on survey of staff/development within
Dunlop Nigerian Industries Ltd

General recommendations

1 To establish a training and development department to
   implement and co-ordinate all types of related training.
2 An accurate budget to be run on all costs that training
   incurred and channelled through to the training and
   development manager for his approval.
3 Within six months of the training development manager
   commencing work a Nigerian local would be recruited
   to understudy this manager.

(Table 15.1 *continued overleaf*)

(Table 15.1 *continued*)

4   A complete general reassessment of staff recruitment procedures within the company should be undertaken to evaluate the differential between Dunlop and other large companies.

5   To attract to the company the best staff so the widest possible search techniques should be used.

6   The establishment of a staff selection panel to vet all short listed candidates on their potential and initiative.

7   Appropriate management trainee schemes should be created as required in various departments. Such programmes to be tightly co-ordinated through continuous assessment systems, mutually done by the training department and the various functional departments. Also all trainees would eventually work for the training department so avoiding salary differentials etc.; once confirmed in a position they would receive job title and salary etc.

8   Regarding the development of managers by sending them on UK or overseas trips, prior to any departure, an agreed in-depth programme to be written with a clear objective in mind and also greater effort must be given to validation of any such development programmes.

9   Consideration should be given to creating a Dunlop scholarship system up to and including degree level or beyond.

10   The establishment of a company training centre which, when commissioned, should employ the best tutoring staff, even if that meant external consultants etc., to ensure proper staff development on site.

11   To create as vital the establishment of systematic training systems within the company covering the engineering department, with a special emphasis possibly on the creation of an engineering centre.

12   Every effort should be made to maintain and develop good relations with all outside agencies involved with training and development in the country.

Table 15.2
Staff development definitions

The term 'staff development' has such a broad meaning that it is important to identify a few practical definitions to ensure complete clarification.

1 *Industrial training*
   The systematic procedures and methods which prepare any individual to perform a job to specific target/methods or objectives laid down by his superior/company.

2 *Industrial education*
   The procedures and methods which acquaint the individual with the technical professional knowledge required to perform any specific activity, and the understanding of the concepts and principles of modern management techniques.

3 *Industrial (career) development*
   This is the self-development of any individual in a systematic manner, with the assistance of the company, and to the benefit of the company.

Common staff development problem areas

With the benefit of hindsight, it now seems that there are many common problems that confront the staff development specialist going overseas. These problems and their possible solutions are as follows:

1 It is essential that a clear development policy towards local company staff exists for reference purposes. Such a policy will differ in its mechanical implementation in different countries but should be integrated with a complementary headquarters policy.

2 Within such a staff development policy, the general term of 'training' should be defined, since it is clearly misused and often misconstrued. (See Table 15.2) for suggested definitions as written for Nigeria.)

3   The concept of manpower development must never be divorced from the business objectives. It is, therefore, essential that a detailed *manpower* plan (not a training plan) appear in the company management plan.

4   Every effort must be made to correct the lack of an original manpower plan. Currently overseas companies have mainly promoted staff on the basis of seniority and, therefore, many indigenous persons are in the wrong jobs or have been over-promoted. This situation leads to job frustration and an inability to meet objectives. So efforts to create a balanced *succession* of staff must be given a high priority together with appropriate individual management development.

5   Expatriate managers responsible for an adequately trained staff tend to be very entrepreneurial. Unfortunately, such people tend not to recruit entrepreneurial nationals to their staff. They prefer to have as subordinates those who will do as they are told. In a climate of indigenisation it is better to have as an expatriate manager an older man who, by inclination, is a teacher/tutor/catalyst, willing to develop his local staff rather than the younger man with a name and a career to make.

Establishment period

During this six-month period there were a number of areas which turned out to be of great significance in planning the implementation of staff development in Nigeria. Because the company was a subsidiary of a large multinational company with a London headquarters, the overall problem had some of its origins in the HQ management climate and style. The following areas needed exploration as they directly affected that management climate.

Overseas staff development fundamentals

It is essential that all staff development programmes are conducted in the appropriate business language. The depth of content, place and presentation must differ according to the local national trainees. In the early stages controlled, co-ordinated, *in-plant staff development programmes* are preferred to any form of external courses regardless of the level of staff involved.

Shortages of quality local manpower encourage 'staff piracy' between private companies and the local civil service etc. Thought should be given to controlled 'over-staffing' in key areas to ensure essential long-term manpower planning.

To counteract loss of staff from natural wastage, early efforts must be made to recruit at school-leaving age and then to provide sponsored programmes, of all types and levels related to the industry, up to and beyond degree level. The best potential employees can then be attracted to work for private industry, instead of joining the educational conveyor belt and subsequent 'brain drain' overseas.

To establish a common educational base, careful assessment of each territory's educational *system* is required. With this clarified, suitable training can be more easily co-ordinated, especially in the science-based functions, i.e. engineers, technologists etc., and then related to Western European standards.

A deeper understanding of the indigenous cultural upbringing is vitally important to identify possible problem areas. For example, the current generation of Nigerian men, as children, never had any chance to play with toys like Lego, Meccano etc., so their slight grasp of simple mechanics, compared to their expatriate colleagues, is understandable and excusable. Another common example in Nigeria, seems to be the lack of 3D perception. This was easily illustrated during a craft apprentice selection test. Boys scoring over 90 per cent in maths and English were scoring less than 40 per cent in 3D perception due to the West Africans valuing roundness rather than perspective. These two facts played a vitally important part in the selection and training of technical support staff.

Technical training is not too problematical. If it is required, arrangements can be made with an appropriate establishment either locally or in a developed country. This type of training is normally *one-off* so it does not encounter the problems of *continual* development as with management training.

At levels of management training and development the traditional solution of external courses does not stand up to evaluation in a developing country. Why? It would seem that the critical factor of effective management training is basically the encouragement and development of teamwork. An external course does not help in improving an individual's effort in relation to his co-workers. It is essential that management training and development be done on site and from the top down.

Mechanics of establishment

The starting point was with an architect in the UK who was given the task of redesigning and reconstructing a large new personnel block for the Lagos factory. This was an excellent start as it allowed a 'green field' site within the factory to be designed specifically for the future task.

From the outset it was agreed that on-site training and development was preferable to any external activity. This is often a fact of life in a developing country as local hotels and conference centres are rare. Therefore, the company had to have its own complete facilities. The outline of the training centre consisted of two Floors:

(a) Lower floor — training staff officers/reception area,
  — two case study/reading rooms,
  — small library area;
(b) Upper floor — large, fully equipped lecture room,
  — small canteen facility,
  — toilet facilities.

If one thinks of this layout in a European situation is should be quite simple to construct and equip such a building. However, it turned out more difficult than anticipated and it took the best part of six months to achieve workable facilities.

During the construction period one is faced with a legion of problems which one can only try and solve with the construction company as they occur. Be prepared for all eventualities! On reaching the equipping stage, further unforeseen problems may come to light, e.g.:

1   Furnishings and wall fittings had to be made locally, and it took three attempts to find the best carpenter — so different from the UK where one chooses from a catalogue with the immediate advice of the equipment sales staff.

2   The normal air conditioning units were too noisy so time was spent tracing suitable units; it was also necessary to ensure that local servicing for these units was available and of reliable quality.

3   It was found necessary to import all visual-aid equipment; eventually it was assembled after a number of pieces had been stolen at the docks, airports etc. Ensure that such equipment can be serviced by a reliable firm of long standing.

4   Black-out curtaining had to be imported since it was impossible to purchase locally. These were found to be essential due to tropical light penetration etc.

When working in an overseas environment one has to take into account various services, or the lack of these, during the design of the training centre — electricity supply, water supply, both of which could vary in strength and availability. The training centre must be of a design which is flexible enough to allow for the non-availability of these services, which could sometimes cease during the running of a management course. This list may seem pedantic but the lack of national infrastructure means one must return to basics.

Whilst the author was overseeing the construction and equipping of this centre, we agreed with the directors of the company to look at an overall company manpower audit. This audit was a follow-on from an original survey carried out a few months previously. The audit covered each department in terms of the current manpower available and its level of competency. Also required was staff development information which had not been kept. This lack of information was due directly to the expatriate managers not being aware of the specific need to develop their staff, but just to ensure the present job was done practically. Throughout the initial period of the audit and basic information collection, the following manpower development system was envisaged:

1 Link in with the corporate planning of the company; identifying the key areas of business; relating to the environment; assessing the corporate strategy; and, subsequently, both the long and medium-term business objectives.

2 Consider and develop manpower planning in terms of these objectives, i.e. using examining manpower audits, personnel information systems and manpower forecasts.

3 Consider and develop compensation planning, i.e. the salary/wages structures; and the various all-in packages which are so important in a developing country where economic and social infra-structure are often missing.

4 Develop a system of recruitment and training; considering selection methods, systematic training, course planning, job analysis etc.

5 Assess career development, understanding local career influences. Consider succession planning, identifying, where possible, potential for future training/development. Assist work rotation and work enlargement, to develop the local people. Re-examine with expatriate managers the organisation structure in terms of the local environment requirements, and re-design as required.

6 Evaluate the true performance of staff using the normal appraisal systems and check whether the expatriates have counselled and developed in any way, their local subordinate staff.

Staffing and training centre

Throughout this period the staffing of the training and development function was not fully considered until a clear picture of the company objectives had emerged. Having established what the department was set up to do, advertisements were placed on the open market for suitable training and development specialists. This was a real problem area since in a developing country there is not a pool of training and development specialists. The early conclusion was reached that the company must recruit the most suitable applicants and take on their training and development.

Training/development function status

The next point of importance was to establish the status of the training and development function in the company. This was important in the cultural situation in Nigeria, since the status of being seen to be working directly for the directors in the organisation gave the author's department much more credibility to plan and achieve their objectives. The chain of command was structured so that he worked for the managing director instead of any specific functional director. This was quite deliberate since it was vital that staff development was seen to be unbiased.

Training/development department structure

The outcome of the manpower audit led to the basic structure of the function. This was:

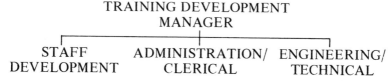

TRAINING DEVELOPMENT
MANAGER

STAFF DEVELOPMENT   ADMINISTRATION/ CLERICAL   ENGINEERING/ TECHNICAL

It was decided not to implement the engineering training area at this early stage but to consolidate on the staff development side first. One must remember that technical/engineering training had been a continuing activity so it was more important to change the overall attitude to training and development. This could be done through the provision of sound staff development which would then lead on to more specific areas of training, e.g. the engineering apprenticeships etc.

Essential PR aspects

Throughout this establishment period a deliberate policy was pursued of good external PR with all interested parties, i.e. local manufacturers' associations, other large companies and various government agencies. It was necessary that everyone was aware of the efforts the company was making to achieve a co-ordinated manpower development system. This objective went some way to giving back to the local nation, skills and expertise that may have been otherwise attracted overseas.

With the completion of the training centre it was decided to hold a grand opening ceremony to which all the TV and press media were invited, along with all relevant people involved with staff development in the country. To perform the opening ceremony, the Secretary of the Home Affairs Department of the government officiated — this ensured good PR coverage.

On reflection, this PR activity, though hard work at times, played an essential role in illustrating the good intent of the company and ensured long-term credibility for the whole training/development activity, to the mutual benefit of the company employees and the host nation.

Comments on the establishment stage

It is important for the new expatriate training/development specialist to allow himself at least six months to assimilate his new working environment, especially national cultural characteristics, and the management climate of the company.

With the pressures for achieving results, it is too easy for the relatively inexperienced expatriate manager to cling to his old work format and standards. This is unrealistic in a developing country; one must clear one's mind of UK-type activity and take an objective view of the local conditions.

It is worth noting that during the specific period of the assignment in Nigeria there was little effort on the government's part to involve itself in the mechanics of industrial training and development within the private sector. This was to come later, through legislation, and the creation of their own Industrial Training Fund. The working of this organisation was similar to the British ITBs and was set up with the assistance of the British Industrial Training Service.

Finally, at a time like this one should never attempt to set up such an organisation in isolation. Every effort should be made to work in liaison with all interested parties, both in the private and public sectors. One always needs support from each other especially in a developing country, where one tends to be very isolated from the UK services. Forging links with all these differing organisations does nothing but good, and goes a long way to the satisfactory establishment of a sound training and development base of operations, both inside one's company and in the host country.

Implementation period

The implementation period began with the successful opening of the in-company training centre and lasted approximately nine months. The problems of planning the implementation of such a staff development scheme now had to be thought out in detail. This was based largely on the manpower audit, which threw up a great number of individual and group needs. It was clear from the audit results that virtually no one in the management staff had any background of management training, apart from the few exceptions – staff who had been sent to the UK, or who had been educated overseas, and had acquired a western management veneer. Unfortunately, these men had not been allowed to adapt and use their managerial skills in their local environment. As the basic management principles used in management training in the UK and Europe were generally unknown, it was now clear that one had to start from basics. Therefore, prior to designing any formal courses, it was necessary to discuss in depth possible programme content with Nigerian colleagues at all levels to ensure appropriateness to the local culture.

Trainees' cultural aspects

The target population of this new staff development programme were all indigenous nationals of Nigeria, and *they were all first generation industrial workers.* This means that they had no knowledge of the kind of work and self-discipline required in industry. *This fact is of vital importance and is often misunderstood by the new expatriate trainer.* Cultural aspects were of prime consideration during the whole of the period in Nigeria and affected to a greater or lesser extent all activities.

The successful overseas trainer must try to understand the 'role' of people moving into industry, i.e. on one hand being a manager in an industrial organisation and on the other hand being a vital link in a well-entrenched extended family system. Loyalty to the extended family system in a country like Nigeria is much stronger than the loyalty any company could command. The company, through the training and development activity, can attempt to shift some loyalty away from the family unit but should never expect company loyalty to supersede family loyalty in the foreseeable future.

This *does* affect the day-to-day efficiency of the individual worker, at all levels. It is often confusing for the new expatriate to encounter this situation since the exact opposite is usually the norm in western society, i.e. the paramount loyalty is to the workplace often at the expense of family life. One must be aware of this and remember also that within the national culture there are a number of ethnic backgrounds, i.e. specific tribal associations. It is important to understand this when planning a programme, since one has to be extremely careful in considering which people can attend programmes and to ensure that no one is missed for any training opportunity.

Initial training courses

It was eventually decided for the first six to nine months to create a modular approach in terms of a training plan, totalling six specific modules:

1   Effective business communication, a two or three-day course.
2   Leadership training (based on an industrial society ACL, packaged but re-written for local use), a two or three-day course.
3   Financial/costing appreciation, a three-day course.
4   Management of men, a three-day course.
5   Marketing appreciation, a three-day course.
6   Manufacturing appreciation, a three-day course.

The primary objective of running these initial courses as *modules* was to ensure that every member of staff from supervisory levels upwards could attend — by repeating the modules as many times as required. This objective was achieved and it provided a whole new attitude to training as well as a good basic foundation of how a business operates, covering everyone and ensuring no misconception within the differing groupings.

Prior to beginning these programmes every effort was made to communicate the objectives of the scheme, by calling together different levels of staff in briefing groups, and personally going round the factory and the offices discussing objectives. This involvement allowed the programmes to be mounted quickly and with immediate effect, rather than having reluctant trainees turning up on courses with their minds full of suspicions etc.

Initial course tutoring

It was realised that neither the tutor nor his new staff could afford the time to design, write and mount all these programmes so some alternative method was necessary. It was decided to hire external consultants from the United Kingdom to come to Nigeria and write from scratch the specific programmes covering the first three modules. This was found to be quite difficult since the majority of consultants approached decided to send their standard programmes which were not suitable for the local situation. Eventually consultants were retained who were willing enough to come to Nigeria, review the situation, understand the culture, and then sit down and write or re-write original programmes to suit. The remaining three modules were created and written by the company's training staff in conjunction with the local senior managers, both expatriates and Nigerian. This achieved two of the objectives, i.e. the involvement of the local senior staff in training and development and also the beginning of existing staff involving themselves in course production covering the staff development within the company.

External involvement

When considering using any external overseas training consultants there are a number of points which should be considered, i.e.:

1   Do not try to take a European-type programme and transfer it straight into an overseas situation. One can expect the content of a programme (and the pace of presentation) to differ radically from that in the UK/ Europe.

2   Guard against visiting consultants who are attempting to sell their own specific training methods into the growing market in developing countries. A number of these consultants felt that they could do a tremendous amount for training but lacked any form of experience in developing countries and wanted only to push their standard products.

3   When considering any type of programme it is wise to undertake a great deal of liaison with local educational and staff development agencies and with local companies in the same sector, with the objective of assessing their offerings against one's own objectives. Also run a number of joint programmes with other companies as a group training scheme in staff development. This scheme was initially very successful, but did not continue due to the large back-log of work for one company. During the initial build-up period there was discussion with senior staff development people in other organisations and this continued in Nigeria.

Training and teaching methods

The complete method of training presentation had to be rethought for the modular programme. The teaching process most used in Nigeria was the lecture method of chalk-and-talk. Understanding of the more participative methods of training was practically nil. This realisation came rather as a shock, since a number of the modular programmes required a large amount of participation because of their belief that *training is by doing*. It was therefore, necessary for the staff and the external tutors to continually amend the various training methods. Gradually the trainees were converted to the participatory style but never to the level that participation is used as a training method in Europe.

To quote a few examples, first a number of exercises used in the leadership module in the UK ignored local culture. These were the use of Lego and jigsaw puzzles. Both items were virtually unknown at that period in Nigeria so the tutors were forced to rewrite exercises using local items. Second, in business communication the style was very different between UK and Nigeria. This seemed to emanate from Nigerian teaching practice which tends towards the essay-type of written communications. Such a tendency encouraged verbosity so one had to teach layout, precision and presentation suitable for the concise communications needed in modern business management.

Consolidation period

With the series of modules completed it was felt that the first stage had provided a basic foundation — bricks upon which each trainee could build his appreciation of business and, through this, his attitude towards management training and development.

It was time to move forward to introducing a much broader-based *industrial manpower development system,* with specific emphasis on management staff development. This part of the assignment lasted a further two years and was based on the concepts shown in Figures 15.1 and 15.2.

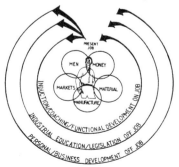

Figure 15.1   Concepts of staff development

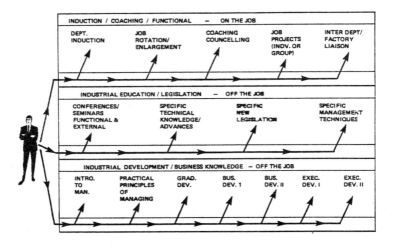

INDUCTION / COACHING / FUNCTIONAL — ON THE JOB				
DEPT. INDUCTION	JOB ROTATION/ ENLARGEMENT	COACHING COUNCELLING	JOB PROJECTS (INDV. OR GROUP)	INTER DEPT/ FACTORY LIAISON

INDUSTRIAL EDUCATION / LEGISLATION — OFF THE JOB			
CONFERENCES/ SEMINARS FUNCTIONAL & EXTERNAL	SPECIFIC TECHNICAL KNOWLEDGE/ ADVANCES	SPECIFIC NEW LEGISLATION	SPECIFIC MANAGEMENT TECHNIQUES

INDUSTRIAL DEVELOPMENT / BUSINESS KNOWLEDGE — OFF THE JOB						
INTRO. TO MAN.	PRACTICAL PRINCIPLES OF MANAGING	GRAD. DEV.	BUS. DEV. 1	BUS. DEV. II	EXEC. DEV. I	EXEC. DEV. II

Figure 15.2   Paths to staff development

Annual training and development plan

It was necessary to bring staff development into *direct* contact with the business objectives, so that training could make its contribution to the efficient running of the organisation — and this was then possible, with the new positive attitudes at all levels of staff. The members of the training department were able to hold coherent discussions with functional managers about their business objectives, and identify if action was required in the training of departmental staff to meet these objectives. This analysis resulted in needs, both individual and group, being identified and assembled together, allowing the creation of an annual training and development plan directly related to the annual business objectives (see Table 15.3).

During the creation of the plan, detailed costings were presented for directors' approval prior to being circulated to all levels of management. With involvement of all parties during the creation of the annual plan, the implementation was *automatic* since it was accepted as an essential part of the total company business plans.

Table 15.3
Training and development plan 1976: annual programme
and course timetables

Section 1	Policy objective 1976.
Section 2	Training centre, internal full-time programme:
	(a) January to June;
	(b) July to December;
	(c) outline of general course contents.
Section 3	Training centre, internal part-time programme:
	(a) general short courses;
	(b) department workshops;
	(c) 'ad hoc' lecture/sessions.
Section 4	External courses, central training co-ordination.
Section 5	Company/external overseas development programme:
	(a) January to June;
	(b) July to December.
Section 6	Engineering staff training and development programme.
Section 7	Graduate staff trainee scheme.

Management trainee scheme

This was by then well established, using the format described
in the initial survey report. There were intakes of new trainees
every six months who were given basic company induction
for a month and then given a 'trainee' job in the appropriate
area. This second period would last between six to nine
months during which time they were continually assessed
and counselled as to their career choice. Once a trainee had
proved his ability and a suitable position arose, the trainee
transferred from the training department to his first real
position. Trainees were generally recruited in three main
groupings, marketing, manufacturing and commercial. This
general grouping allowed time within the scheme for the
best use of the man, by going to a mutually agreed career
area. The number of trainees for the company was built
into the annual plan so every one was quite clear. It is worth
noting when operating such a scheme overseas, never turn

any potential applicant away — always interview them since good men are continually returning home from overseas' courses of study or work and are ready to take up employment.

Administration aspects

One must be aware in a developing country of the geographic difficulties in communications. An *agreed* annual plan is vital. Managers at the outstations can then take the necessary responsibility and action to nominate for the appropriate programmes. Due to the great distances to be covered and the irregular transport facilities available, appropriate and flexible time-tabling and planning are also of great importance.

Once agreed, the continuing training and development plan allowed the trainers and line managers involved to continue to review the programmes and take remedial action as required. One must remember the varying educational levels between people of differing ethnic backgrounds. It is important therefore to plan, in the long term, to get appropriate groups together to review the contents of the training. By doing it through the annual plan, the main objective was ensured, i.e. 'density of thought' across the appropriate levels of management in the organisation.

Use of manpower resources and manpower planning

After the creation of the first annual training and development plan it was found necessary to examine in much greater depth the company manpower resources, department by department, in terms of future company plans.

The outcome of this, was the creation of the *staff development co-ordinating committee* which met monthly and was an off-shoot of the main local directors' board. The standing members of this committee were: managing director (as chairman), director of administration, and training/development manager (as secretary).

The Committee operated with minutes being issued for appropriate action, but due to the nature of the contents of these minutes, they were restricted in circulation and held under a 'staff in confidence' file. An average monthly meeting worked in the following manner:

1 A function department manager was co-opted to the committee accompanied by his responsible director.
2 The manager revealed his current manpower organisation to meet on-going business objectives, identifying strengths and weaknesses.
3 A long term (three years) manpower plan was then shown by the manager, and all staff movements required discussed in great depth.

Very often the action required from the committee's discussions necessitated a review of various organisation structures. Any department manager only received one month's notice of his attendance at the committee. This encouraged full co-operation by the functional senior managers and the training and development manager.

A further development resulting from the working of the above committee was the decision to create an annual *social plan*. This plan was to be a supplement to the company business plan. As its title implies the social plan detailed all facets of employee relations and development. The contents included the current status and the future plans in areas such as staff salaries and wages, welfare, sports and social activities, health and safety, union agreements, training and development plans, and all fringe benefits. This plan was a rolling plan and was updated each year with the annual company business plan.

The creation of this social plan highlighted the necessity of accurate manpower planning and associated manpower resources. The plan itself was of immense use and formed a vital part of the overall manpower development system. One must bear in mind in the creation of such a plan that manpower statistics in a developing country should be treated with the greatest caution. It is essential to check the government statistics and compare them with one's own figures for your industry.

Specialist technical training

With the positive attitude towards training confirmed and the acceptance locally of both external and internal involvement with training and development, it was time to move forward and take constructive action on the specialist technical training problems. This move towards the training problems surrounding engineering and rubber technology was much more easily achieved due to the sound foundation of training already in existence. So much could not have been achieved, in terms of training and development, had the specialist training problems been approached first, as advised by the UK headquarters. Unfortunately it seems that the majority of large companies overseas attempt to tackle their manpower development problems in this way. Adopting the technology-first approach allows the activity of management development to be seen as second best with the resultant inability to improve overseas management quality.

The total training problems within the engineering area were approached two years after the initial establishment period. This assignment was undertaken in a similar way but in much greater detail and specifically within the engineering function alone. The survey and the initial establishment of the engineering training centre was carried out by an engineering training manager from the UK. The eventual result of this assignment was the design, construction and equipping of a tailor-made engineering training centre on the factory site.

Training in rubber technology followed a similar pattern to the engineering area. This resulted in two main types of programme:

Rubber appreciation course. This was designed in ten separate modules each lasting one afternoon, and was aimed at *anyone* within the company who felt they required such training. This programme was run totally by the local training staff in conjunction with their technical colleagues.

Basic tyre technology. Such a programme was essential in a developing country due to the lack of suitable local educational facilities. It was a difficult programme to design since the detailed tyre technology was very company orientated. This problem was overcome through the creation of the course contents in the UK using CCTV video cassettes. It assisted identifying suitable potential technical staff who were then sponsored up to, and including, degree level in Nigeria or in the UK.

Public relations aspects

With all the internal activity discussed during this period, i.e. staff development committees, social plans etc., it was necessary to extend the expertise of the department by becoming involved with external agencies. This improved the PR image of the company in terms of training and development. The following are examples of external agencies in any developing country.

> *Local employers' association* — This involved attending their training and development committee and assisting with the running of their programmes.
> *Local institute of management* — This involved attending meetings and supporting their training courses.
> *Government training agencies* — Working in liaison with the ILO training advisors attached to these units, on national policy matters, and assisting programmes as the need arose.
> *Junior management competition* — This competition was initiated and sponsored by the company, administration details being made by the local institute of management.

It is clear that a large multinational company in a developing country should ensure that a good company image is portrayed in terms of training and development activity. Such an image goes a long way to coping with the difficulties often experienced with regard to expatriate work quotas and associated problems, and the same image definitely attracts the returning nationals from their overseas courses and has immense leverage in the local labour market.

Assignment conclusion

By the fourth year the manpower development activity was

well established with the company and implemented with direct relevence to the local environment. There existed a well co-ordinated staff development function complemented by well designed technical training activity. The function was now accepted fully into the business and contributed towards overall efficiency. The assignment assisted in the general good public relations image of the company and this was naturally of great value to the enterprise.

The author's assignment was completed when his role was taken on by a senior Nigerian manager, who is still running the function. He continues to create a sense of sound management team-work in the exciting environment of Nigeria.

Practical considerations

Finally, from the author's experience working overseas, he has compiled a checklist of practical considerations under three headings: culture; technical education; and training mechanics. These considerations apply principally to work in developing countries, though many of them will no doubt apply equally or with only minor modification to work in developed, industrialised countries.

Cultural aspects

1   Any expatriate working overseas must not be 'colonial' in attitude, he must learn to adapt to his new environment.

2   The expatriate must avoid discussion of local politics, considering his position as a foreign national, even when drawn into such discussion by indigenous colleagues.

3   As an expatriate he must learn to accept the differing aspects of daily life as compared to his home country's standards without making criticism, especially in emphasising differentials in standards of living between societies.

4   As a visiting specialist one tends to be held in high regard by the local work force. This situation carries consider-

able responsibility and one must therefore set a good example by leadership. Through this role, one will best motivate his local work force by good personal example and earn respect.

5   There is usually a lack of tradition in the mechanical skills in a developing country, and this must be quickly understood and appreciated in the terms of local technical education otherwise the expatriate may become very frustrated with his new students.

6   'Loss of face' in a developing country, is of greater importance than in western society and the new expatriate manager must understand this situation and make every effort not to allow any of his students to lose face in the presence of their colleagues.

7   In a developing country the trainees expect their tutors to have absolute knowledge. Consequently, constructive 'question and answer' sessions are very rare, putting the expatriate tutor at a great disadvantage in establishing class feedback. This situation is extremely frustrating and can be alleviated by continuous written assessment until the tutor is eventually accepted as an approachable person.

8   Due to the lower salary and wage levels in developing countries it is not uncommon for people to have a second job to improve their standard of living. The trainees could easily fall into this category which makes extramural learning very difficult, if not impossible.

9   Where English is used as the normal teaching language, all tutors must refrain from using vernacular terms and keep to basic English.

10   The value placed on education varies with differing cultures so one must understand the local values and learn to work slowly from them to where you want to be.

11   When one visits an overseas country, one must be aware that different cultural values mean that thought processes used in learning can differ remarkably, e.g. sequential logic might not be considered of great importance.

12   Different cultures have a vastly different appreciation

of time and thus precise time-keeping expected by the European does not play such importance in a developing country.

Technical education aspects

1   It is very difficult to persuade those who have had any accademic background to do practical work, this causes immense difficulties in achieving training through practical activity.
2   Appreciation of mechanical comprehension varies amongst cultures and poses further technical training problems.
3   Training technical manpower statistics can be variable in the developing country so making relevant technical training planning difficult.
4   Over-production of arts degrees has aggravated the lack of specialised science-based degree education. This often causes difficulties in staff recruitment for specialised positions.
5   The general lack of textbooks in technical education produced locally, means that such stocks have to be obtained from Britain or the USA often disrupting training continuity.

Mechanical training aspects

1   All programmes must be supplemented by clear course notes and well laid out for the trainees' future use. It was often found useful to have a course handout with the heading only given to the trainee at the beginning of any sessions, this would allow him to complete the notes in whatever language he wished.
2   The overseas tutor should ensure his course content and presentation is flexible enough in pace to suit the local environment, i.e. a UK course usually runs approximately 50 per cent faster than one in Nigeria.
3   Course time-tabling should not include any evening work as this could cause problems as previously discussed in the culture section.

4   Specific presentation techniques beyond that of lecturing must be chosen with great care and full knowledge of whether the trainees have had any prior experience of such techniques.

5   To establish trainee feedback it is sensible for the tutor to conduct short written or verbal tests. These tests should be used either at the end of each section or the beginning of the next. This will allow learning to be monitored and increase trainees' motivation.

6   Trainee groups should be chosen carefully from similar levels within the company, this will ensure minimal educational/status problems.

7   It was found advantageous to have available suitable course certificates for presentation to all successful trainees at the end of their programme — regardless of level of course content.

16 Designing International Post-Experience Development Programmes

TONY ECCLES

'International' is a great word. It carries hints of sophistication and mystery. The internationalist clearly has his or her mind on more impressive matters than the boringly domestic trivia of the stay-at-home. No management developer worth his machismo could fail to rise to the challenge of internationalism. But what is the international ingredient in management development? Conventionally it is used to refer to such dimensions of programme design as the faculty, the subject matter, the participants' home countries, or the participants' work countries. One additional dimension which is of particular concern to programme designers is the question of programme focus. Should the development activity concentrate on issues faced by managers in one organisation, in a consortium of companies − perhaps in one industry − or should it be an open programme with participants from a wide variety of organisations?

Dimensions of programme design

These five dimensions taken together lead to many alternatives for the basic construction of a programme. They can conveniently be considered in the form of a simple matrix (see Table 16.1). Allowing for a few combinations which are scarcely international, this matrix generates upwards of 108 possible modes of international management development. However they are rarely discrete choices, because each dimension is more of a continuum than a set of separate items, as can be seen from the following brief comments.

Table 16.1
Dimensions of basic programme design

Faculty from:	Run programmes with material which is:	For managers from:	Employed by:	Who work in:
Several countries	International	Several countries	Many organi-sations	Several countries
		Another country	Several organi-sations	Other country
One country	Domestic	Same country	One organi-sation	Own country
2	2	3	3	3

Dimension 1: the faculty

This dimension ranges from a single-country faculty with only domestic experience and interests, through single-country faculty with increasing proportions of international experience and interests, to a multinational faculty with wide ranging international experience and interests. Certain institutions (such as CEI) and programmes (such as TIO) [1] insist on the faculty being multinational to a high degree.

The management development programme designer knows that it is the international orientation of the faculty which is important rather than their nationality or country of residence. (See, for example, Chapter 8 by Lee Nehrt for a US perspective on this issue.) An international faculty is not necessarily useful if each member has interests which are predominantly domestic within his own nation. However, an internationally orientated faculty from a variety of cultures is undoubtedly powerful in terms of the breadth of their insights which can be brought to bear on particular issues.

Client organisations are often impressed by the, sometimes illusory, quality of a faculty which is flown in from all parts of the world: clearly the planet has been scoured for the best, the very best. This comforting feeling may only disappear if the various teachers appear to have little connection between them or if they are evidently less helpful than locally available faculty. In that case the main benefit may accrue to airline revenues. A competent programme designer can often cope with these problems by careful selection and briefing of faculty or by persuading the client that the grass is not necessarily greener elsewhere and that the management development effect which he desires can be achieved by using local people — who may indeed be better for the purpose if they are more readily available for follow-up action, as well as being more committed to the programme if their local reputation depends on it.

Dimension 2: the material

Even the most domestic programme with international aspirations would be likely to use some cases, projects or other material from abroad and the international perspective could grow until the programme contained nothing which could be labelled domestic.

Indeed, specialist domestic programmes without international aspirations often use international comparisons to open the minds of participants to new possibilities and to fresh interpretations of their domestic circumstances and experiences. This is not simply to help people to tackle immediate problems. If attention can be focused on international matters so that people are better able to deal with cross-cultural issues, then it should be easier for them to deal with cultural clashes and changes within their domestic society. A consideration of, say, Japanese management systems should sensitise even the most incurious European manager to the possibility that there are other ways to run an enterprise than his own existing recipe.

Dimensions 3 and 5: manager's nationality and workplace

The managerial dimension incorporates domestic managers

who work in their own country but in jobs with increasing amounts of international liaison, travel and responsibilities. Alternatively, they may have domestic jobs now, but have had previous international experience.

It is helpful to distinguish between the various types of international manager — as does Judy Lowe in her discussion of the 'polyvalent' manager. (See the Introduction and Chapter 6 for alternative means of categorisation.) Managers may be 'international' in some senses even if they never leave their domestic desks, provided that international matters impinge on their jobs. You do not have to live abroad, whether for a career or for an assignment, to be international. A manager may have an international liaison role or be a 'boomerang manager' who has a domestic base but who goes and returns from foreign trips which occupy a major part of his time.

Such managers are as likely to be technical as they are to be commercial in their activities, though no less 'international' for that. Retrieving a large transformer which has fallen off its delivery truck and blocked a bridge in Colombia may require just as much international management competence as the commercial negotiation which led to its original sale.

Conversely, the manager who resides and works in a foreign country is not necessarily international in any significant sense. He may be a foreign national with a domestic job. There is little inherently 'international' in the framework of a Frenchman married to a Canadian and living and working in her country rather than his own.

The internationalism which results from job location is related to the usefulness of other work experiences which can be brought to bear on the man's current job. A variety of work experiences in other countries can hardly fail to modify a manager's perceptions of his current work tasks, though it should not be assumed that these will be automatically helpful. Anecdotes abound about managers from one culture who find it very difficult to accept the work habits of their new colleagues in the new culture.*

---

* For some such anecdotes, see Chapter 18.

Dimension 4: the organisation

The participants may come from one organisation now, but have had previous careers in other companies. The participants may come from a few companies or be on an open programme with perhaps 40 different organisations represented out of 50 participants.

This dimension is a key determinant of the programme focus. The single company format will require the designer to maximise 'relevance' as it is agreed, sometimes uneasily, between himself and the client company. Faculty may be unprepared to undertake the considerable investment required to concentrate on the organisations' particular problems. The client may find it difficult to accept that reinforcement of local beliefs and shibboleths may be the result of excessive concern to keep within the organisation's existing horizon.

International management development choices

If each of these five dimensions is a near continuum it does imply that, in combination, an 'international' programme can vary from token gestures of non-domesticity all the way to a level of variety of faculty, programme material, participants' nationalities, work countries and organisations such that the common bonds are little more than the internationalism itself, particularly, if 'organisation' is interpreted widely to include non-business enterprises.

The key measure which distinguishes each of the above dimensions from the purely domestic is that of economic and cultural complexity. From mono-culture (be it of nation or of organisation) to multi-cultural mixtures, the internationalism increases from a base of domestically oriented faculty teaching domestic material to domestic managers who are in one organisation's domestic jobs, to a thorough mixture of cultures on all five parameters. Of course a management development programme for members from all parts of a large multinational company is not mono-cultural in nationality, though it may sometimes be so in terms of organisational style and system.

Perhaps we could find examples of all 108 combinations

of the five dimensions if we cared to look hard enough at the management development world. Fortunately there are a few combinations which are found more frequently than others and they help to show the implications of the mono/ multi cultural dimension for the development of international managers.

Executive development programmes (ED)

The most common is the senior management programme which is open to executives from any relevant organisations. Such open programmes are run, in some form, by most leading post-experience management education establishments. These ED programmes usually involve managers from many organisations and several countries in an event which incorporates significant amounts of international material, partly taught and partly experiential — though experiential usually in terms of exercises rather than projects on organisations. The faculty is usually part domestic (albeit with varying degrees of international experience and interest) and partly from other countries (some with third country experience).

Single organisation programmes (SO)

A frequently encountered variant of the ED programme is the SO programme which is broadly similar in construction but which is run for international executives from one organisation only. By removing the organisational variety which is inherent in the ED programme, the SO programme can concentrate on the company situation and the central issues which are of concern to the organisation. The programme can be designed round work-related projects and tasks. Cross-cultural coordination can be enhanced, and mutual agreement and understanding can be improved between different parts of the organisation. This kind of programme can be very useful for team building and for the development of under-standing and commitment to more effective organisational policies.

International institute programmes (II)

The next identifiable type of programme is the activity where the internationalism is enhanced to the maximum degree. Multi-cultural variety is increased by putting an upper limit on the number of participants who can come from one industry or company, and lower limits on the nationality of faculty and participants, so that the variety of backgrounds, companies and jobs is maximised. These are often deemed to be very senior courses, though the executives coming on them may be no nearer the top of their organisations than on a good, international strategy-oriented SO programme. The variety in an II programme can be impressive, particularly if the event is designed to help the multi-cultural managers to learn from each other. It is not so clear that a multi-cultural faculty is such a benefit, particularly if the faculty members come and go rapidly and leave little in the way of continuity. Staging a revue is not always superior to staging a play with a plot which unfolds logically.

Action learning programmes (AL)

The last discrete programme type is that where the teaching/ learning mode is a central determinant of the programme design. Because AL programmes are primarily designed round work projects which often last several months and which are expected to result in organisational action, the logistics of AL activities make it difficult (though not impossible, as the IVECO programme in Chapter 13 shows) to run a significantly international action learning programme. The focus on the work place also affects the substance of the projects and, apart from some of the AL programmes which involve the exchange of managers between organisations, it is rare for action learning groups to have a significantly multi-cultural focus. Indeed current experience suggests a simple rule. The more work-experience based is the management development programme, the less international is it likely to be.

Experience also suggests that the more international is the programme and the more culturally varied the participants, the faculty and the nominating organisations, then the more the programme will be concerned with generalities and universal issues; exposition, cases and classroom exercises; and personal development rather direct organisational usefulness, and the less will it be work based. This can lead to the generalities seeming to be anodyne or inoperable.

It is logical for a management centre running an II programme to want the most senior people to come as participants, because that increases the chance that the generalities could be relevant. If the participants are senior enough there is also the possibility that their power in the organisation will mean that their personal development can be put to direct organisational use. Using the mono-cultural—multi-cultural dimension again, it can be seen that the typical profiles of the four programme types are quite different (See Figure 16.1).

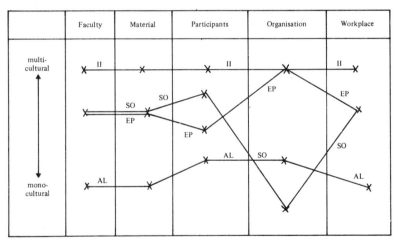

Figure 16.1   Cultural dimensions of four types of programmes

The underlying premise is that a fully international programme is likely to be strongly multi-cultural on all five dimensions and that such programmes occupy a distinctive position in the management development world. It suggests that action learning programmes can be very useful but not easily arranged with a major international orientation in their projects. There are, of course, programmes, such as the

Swedish TIO, which have located most of their dimensions on a line somewhere between the II and the SO/EP profiles.

A further premise is that action learning programmes are likely to be quite different in kind and in form to other international management development programmes. This could be a useful distinction as well as something of a relief. There have been too many tiresome arguments about the respective merits of action learning programmes as contrasted with formal management programmes, as though one or other had some monopoly of virtue. For those academics who are involved in both types of activity, the arguments have seemed somewhat tedious as well as misleading.

This point is worth discussing because the differences between formal programmes and experience learning have become destructively exaggerated by some management education practitioners. It would be an odd course which did not tap the varied experiences of the faculty, even if it is substantially taught. Only the most modest experience-learning programme would have no exposition of analytical frameworks, descriptions of organisational systems, inputs of specific technical skills or coaching in the ways in which people can work together fruitfully. [2]

It is not clear that these two approaches are so distinct. Nor is it clear that one system produces sturdy self-reliance rather than dependency; nor that one method induces more successful interventions; nor that one approach leads to a more acceptable synthesis between organisational goals and personal development.

One charge by action learning's advocates is that formal courses are so concerned with talking about action that they have forgotten the need for managers to take action and to have greater experience of taking action.

Formal management programmes are also criticised for not using the experience of the participants and for not helping them to learn from each other, though this is exactly what is intended in the effective use of case studies. Programme participants also persist in having the expectation of learning from each other and each other's experience. Indeed, this is often their strongest prior expectation, and one of their major reported benefits from programmes. For example, at

Harvard, Andrews found [3] that the major benefit came from discussion with participants' groups rather than from the faculty or with sessions involving faculty. Whilst this is a sobering thought for faculty who might prefer that the major benefit comes from their inputs, it does suggest that all but the most dedicatedly didactic courses do give participants the opportunity to bring their diverse experiences to bear usefully on issues which the participants see as important.

The counter charge would be that experiential learning has become so interested in the process of development that it has ignored the need for content, i.e. knowledge and skill techniques. Managers who are being invited to take risks need more than social supports.

Considerations for client organisations

Despite the commonalities between action learning programmes and executive development courses, they are still distinctively different approaches to the task of developing more effective managers. This suggests that certain types of management development activities are not alternatives but are complementary. One practicable blend of management development programmes is for a company to use the international institutes to expose its senior managers to the diversity of multinational attitudes and practices, whilst using action learning programmes for other managers to effect change in the operating organisation at the mono-cultural level.

Alternatively, the company might choose to run a development programme for its own managers alone, in which there was considerable attention to work issues as well as mixing of executives from different parts of the world and different elements of the enterprise, as in the case of London Business School's senior programmes for Cadbury-Schweppes. Only a mixture of different company cultures would be missing from this choice. It would then be possible to send some managers also to open programmes which would compensate for this omission if it was felt to be important.

A third choice would be to patronise the programmes

which (like TIO) deliberately enhance the multi-cultural nature of the design whilst retaining some of the work relevance of less complex programmes.

The lesson is quite clear. Any company wishing to develop its managers and its own operations to greater levels of understanding and effectiveness would be wise to consider having more than one mode for its international management development. The market is segmented and claims by management developers or client organisations that their chosen way contains all known beneficial ingredients should be treated with certain amount of caution. Developing international management competence can be a subtle business.

The task for supplying institutions

The task for management development institutions is also reasonably clear. The training of international managers certainly demands a faculty which is internationally-oriented and which can use a variety of teaching and learning approaches to help the managers to learn both from the staff and from each other. The institutions' reputation can be enhanced by having a thoroughly international mix of faculty. For many centres, this would mean using visiting faculty or people on short-term contracts. Visitors however, make it more difficult to create and maintain stability and programme continuity, but this is the inevitable price of having this variety of international reputation.

Certain institutions also have an advantage which is gained from their student body. Doctoral and masters degree students increasingly undertake projects which have an international focus. Their findings (as well as their demands on the faculty) propel their own institutions' staff into greater understanding and awareness of international management issues. It follows that there may be an experience curve for an institution's internationalism. The larger and more internationally focused is the student body, the more rapidly will there be an accumulation of international experience and exposure by the faculty, who will be driven on by their students' requirements as well as by their own inherent interests.

It will also help the cause of international management development if institutions nurture the small number of company executives who have a deep commitment to international development. It seems likely that the bulk of 'normal' development work will continue to be that of training at a none too multi-cultural level. Yet education for those involved in cross-border transactions may be critically important for the client organisation's overall competence. In other words, policies which are exclusively at either extreme will not be good enough.

Consequently, the successful supplying institution will have to assist the process of international management development by offering a product mix which enables its clients to select the appropriate mixture of development activities up and down the mono/multi-cultural dimension.

It seems likely that such institutions will need to expand their efforts to develop sound reputations for the international work which they already do, but their performance would have a more convincing foundation if they were to augment their faculty with people having extensive experience of international management issues. This experience is not just a question of travel or of variety of workplaces. It relates to subject interest, research activity, information networks, consulting focus and, in particular, to the degree to which faculty members have stepped beyond the boundaries of business and become involved in those wider geo-political issues, institutions, and movements which increasingly affect corporations from outside the business domain.

The specific task of the international programme designer is always to use such experiences in ways which help client organisations. The key job of the designer is to utilise his own and his institution's experiences to build the best blend of focus and time sequence into the management development programme with two key objectives. The participating managers should come out of the programme more able to handle international management issues: their organisation should emerge from the activity with the determination to implement appropriate organisational action.

Notes

[1] Centre d'Études Industriels, in Geneva; and Training for International Operations, a programme in Sweden sponsored by Stockholm Economics Institute (IFL).

[2] Charles Handy, 'The Learning Manager', unpublished working paper, London Business School, 1978.

[3] Kenneth Andrews, *The Effectiveness of University Management Development Programmes,* Harvard Business School, Boston, Mass. 1966.

17 The Transfer of Management Know-how in Asia: An Unlearning Process

HENRI-CLAUDE DE BETTIGNIES

From north-south dialogue, to UNCTAD conferences, through 'non-aligned' meetings, many devices and recipes are proposed to handle one of the most critical issues of the next decades: how to deal with the widening gap between one-third of humanity, which benefits materially from the most tangible results of technological progress, and the other two-thirds which suffer from a process of continuous impoverishment. Proposals are many, sometimes contradictory, even though everyone claims to pursue a superordinate objective: 'development'.

'Development' — the elephant for the blind — means different things to government, business, intellectuals, the rural masses or the foreign experts. However, for all, 'development' seems implicitly to be the new name for 'progress' applied to the whole of humanity. And yet is the 'western' defined model of 'development' the only one? With its dominating technostructure (the 'megamachine' of Lewis Mumford), is our western model going to be the new entity where technology and power combined will not be controlled by national decision-making bodies which nevertheless depend on it for their prosperity?

The craftsmen of the 'megamachine' — the managers — attribute their success both to (a) a thorough understanding of 'systems' functioning, and (b) an efficient and effective handling of the systems' interdependent components. They call this 'management'.

Today, whether management is defined as a science, an art, a difficult mix of both, a product (packaged, sold and bought), an ideology with its values and action principles, or a religion (with its churches or even cathedrals), it is perceived as a critical ingredient of the development process. Omolayole, chairman of the Nigerian Institute of Management, emphasises:

> Since management is an essential ingredient of the process of economic development, economic development plans of developing countries have little chance of successful implementations unless and until deficiencies in the supply of managerial manpower, both in quantity and quality, are made good in these countries. [1]

This emphasis on the need for 'management' has been widespread throughout the developing world:

> In the last decade there has been a tremendous awareness in developing countries of the role of good management in the affairs of the nation. This awareness has led to the formation of institutes of management, acting in these countries as the source and symbol of professionalism in management. Many of these institutes run short courses in management appreciation, functional management, and general management. [2]

It seems then that we live in a world where everyone wants development because it is progress. Everyone thinks development goes with 'management', and that management can be acquired and transferred. Throughout Asia the same comments are heard; the same institutes offer identical packages, courses, seminars; the same management paraphenalia. But is this transfer of management knowhow effective?

This is an issue of such complexity that it has not been investigated rigorously. Many years ago following the pioneer comparative study of Haire, Ghiselli and Porter, [3] others such as Davis, [4] Newman, [5] Webber, [6] and de Bettignies, [7] emphasised the interdependence between 'culture' and management effectiveness. These works had little or no impact on the actual transfer of management knowhow from north to south, from the west to less developed countries (LDCs). As Mendoza, the dean of the Asian Institute of Management said, in his thought provoking presentation at the Bellagio conference:

Today, what is known as management theory in most of the world consists basically of the American interpretation of the teachings of the classical school of Fayol and Taylor, with some gleanings from the works of the better known behaviourists and operations management theorists. It is also almost generally accepted that the 'principles' of management used by the Americans with so much success are universally applicable, that they are transferable, with some minor 'fine-tuning', from country to country and from one organisational type to another. As one consequence most management training and education is done today all over the world, often by rote, from American text books. [8]

The consequences of this situation are serious if not dramatic, in terms of cost—benefit analysis. It is only in the last decade that the transferability of western management models has been seriously questioned. Mendoza traces the Japanese success to the beginning of the challenge of the universality of management principles: 'It is this Japanese management system, radically different from that of the West yet equally effective, that now prompts a re-examination of the premise, the assumption, the long held conviction, that the 'principles' of management discovered by the West are universally applicable'. [9] It is true that the Japanese have crystallised a much needed reflection on the transferability of management principles and practices. As early as 1965 attention was brought to the pedagogical role for the Western management communities of the Japanese management example. [10] Fifteen years later, at a time when both Japanese and westerners (e.g. Johnson and Ouchi, [11] Thurley, [12] Kraar, [13] Tsurumi, [14]) are carefully investigating the possibility and/or the results of transferring elements of the Japanese system to the West one is still hoping that a solid body of knowledge on international transfer of management know-how will become available.

Today, in our increasing small global village, this problem of the transferability of management knowhow is of a paramount importance. It is so for both developed and developing nations alike, for international corporations, for management researchers and consultants who are supposed to produce and disseminate relevant knowledge and who therefore should be concerned by critical issues of real life.

This chapter looks at one side of the issue: the transfer of management knowhow to developing countries, and gives illustrations from Asian environments. The transfer of management knowhow seems to rely implicitly upon four assumptions commonly held by elites both in South East Asia and in the West:

1   'Effectiveness' is the means of achieving development and growth (ideology).
2   'Management' is the privileged means of achieving organisational effectiveness (functionality).
3   'Management' can be easily transferred: we can *learn* it and, therefore, become effective in solving problems and in reaching cororate goals. The media is training, i.e. courses, seminars etc. (transferability).
4   'Management' carries the idea of 'modernity', as it is an element of the modernisation processs and is therefore socially desirable (desirability).

In other words, in today's changing world effectiveness is the condition of survival. Whether one is from the right or from the left, working within one of the many brands of socialist economies or in a liberal capitalist society, one tries to organise and use resources in order to achieve goals and be effective. A kolkhoze, a kibbutz, a sogo shosha, an MNC, are each in their own way trying to be effective, to reach their goals. Effectiveness (organisational effectiveness in particular) is therefore not considered a choice, but a *necessity* for survival. Management, perceived as 'instrumental' for effectiveness becomes the privileged and readily accessible tool one needs in order to be endowed with the power of making things happen. For ideological reasons, for its functionality, transferability and desirability, management seems to be perceived as a deus ex machina of development.

Seen in these terms, management is in great demand in developing countries and educational systems have been, and are being, organised to satisfy the demand. In South East Asia there are many public and private universities which have 'departments' or 'schools' of 'economics', of 'commerce', of 'accounting' and many institutes (e.g. Lembaga in Indonesia or Malaysia) of management attached to campuses. Outside universities, there are a number of institutes (public and private, national, provincial or local) for civil servants, or private sector employees. One observes a growing number of South-East Asian young graduates applying for admission to the regional Asian Institute of Management (Manila) or to American, European or Australian schools of business. Western academics and consultants are passing through the region preaching, with the aura of 'gurus' luring new disciples to the western management gospel. But is there only *one* way to manage effectively?

What is the outcome of this multichannel transfer of mono-cultural management knowhow. Is it cost effective, or effective in any terms? Does it really increase the managerial competence of firms and individuals in the region?

Most observers in the ASEAN region agree on the dire shortage of managerial talent. The situation varies from one ASEAN country to the next, although when looking at the region there seems to be a consensus on the gap between: (a) the tremendous needs for management talent necessary to develop and exploit the wealth of existing resources in each country; and (b) the availability of appropriate skills to monitor and control efficiently and effectively that development process.

The transfer of management know-how

Educational systems

There are some significant differences between each ASEAN country's management education system and their comparative efficiency. The focus of this chapter, however, is not 'comparative'. Thus only those features common throughout the region are identified.

INSEAD carried out a study of an ASEAN country management education system in 1976. They identified, with their professional colleagues of the country, some system's dysfunctions (observed later elsewhere) and they proposed alternative change strategies over time. Essentially their study — confirmed by other reports and observations — linked the causes of inefficiency both to the 'actors' and to the 'system' tied together in several vicious circles. The efficiency of management education can be assessed through a number of ratios (e.g. teacher/student, student input/ output, pedagogical production, cost per student, actual number of years spent per degree awarded) and through clinical observations of the system (or some subsystems). It appears that in a less developed country *if*:

    (a) management training is much in demand;
    (b) the supply of teachers/trainers is scarce;
    (c) academic salaries are low;
    (d) working conditions on campus are poor,
then members of the academic community (the know-how transferors):

    (e) tend to spend much time 'moonlighting' (earning the income through lecturing and consulting — they feel appropriate to their needs and to their status);
    (f) devote a limited amount of time to student groups or individuals' guidance;
    (g) do not produce pedagogical materials (developing indigenous teaching material from their local experience);
    (h) do not engage in research (to produce indigenous management knowhow);
    (i) run the risk of progressively becoming stalled;
    (j) over time get used to the system which has a number of individualised benefits.

Even such a system can be considered inefficient when one assesses its poor use of internal resources. Its production in terms of graduates, teachers, educational materials, ideas, contingent models, is limited. Furthermore, the actors and the system, in a synergistic way, tend progressively to produce ineffectiveness. From inefficiency to ineffectiveness, the helpful transfer of management knowhow becomes increasingly less evident. Not only does the university produce a small number of management graduates, at a comparatively high cost per student, but not all the graduates can find a job (while many drop-outs are keen to become successful entrepreneurs or managers-cum-entrepreneurs). In other words, the products available from the educational market do not seem to meet market needs. The management graduate has learnt 'dependency' (listening to a teacher transmitting knowledge through an often inefficient teaching technology), 'irrelevant' knowledge (learning from American textbooks — not always translated in his own language — written for students from different socio-economic environments, with different thought processes and learning models), or 'obsolete' knowhow (since the pedagogical tools used are 10 or 15 years old from the time the teacher had the opportunity to study abroad). The few educational institutions which have tried to escape from such pernicious systems have found it very difficult and costly financially and socially because they have had to break norms well maintained by those who benefit from status quo.

In spite of the considerable demand for managerial talent to monitor and control effectively the socio-economic development of the region, one observes an inefficient and ineffective transfer of managerial knowhow built into institutional systems whose actors and mechanisms mutually reinforce each other's ineffectiveness. The transferors, local educators (sometimes trained abroad), do not have environmental conditions (psychological, professional materials):

(a) to produce the relevant knowledge and knowhow — through research within their own socio-economic environment — to train students and managers with models well fitted to local conditions;

(b) to think through what they learnt yesterday and *adapt* it to today's particular (but changing) conditions;

(c) to develop appropriate educational technologies (e.g. teaching materials, notes, exercises, cases) specifically designed to local students and managers' profiles.

This lack of knowledge production combined with a shortage of efforts to produce relevant transfer methods and tools, limits considerably the effectiveness of the management education and its developmental processes.

Foreign firms

Foreign firms also contribute to the transfer of management knowhow. Their impact spreads far beyond the in-company training programmes they organise. Expatriate managers through role-modelling play a significant educational function on the indigenous managers, while imported management systems and procedures attempt to shape local employees' managerial attitudes and behaviour. Transfer of knowhow takes place empirically through daily operations at a pace which varies according to both transferor and transferee's skills. Inevitably conflicts on this difficult road of transfer tend to be solved according to the expatriate's fund of cross-cultural experience, his insight in understanding local cultures and his skills in communicating and negotiating. Empirical research in six developing countries has established 'the feasibility and utility of transmitting advanced management practices and knowhow into industrial enterprises in developing countries', and has illustrated the role of MNCs in fostering such transfer. [15] Today no-one would deny the role of multinational firms as a powerful management transfer agent in South-East Asia, along with international technical assistance programmes and foreign management education institutions. However, MNCs contribution to local management development remains usually limited to the firm's internal needs.

The process and outcome of the MNCs' transfer should be further researched to identify 'at what cost such a transfer is feasible and whether the costs of transferring management practices are commensurate with the benefits derived from them'. [16] Such research would produce more understanding into the transfer process itself and provide guidelines not only for multinational corporations operating in developing countries, but to management educators whose task is to transfer effective management know-how.

Multinational corporations operating in South-East Asia, currently under host governments' pressures to 'localise' (often with tight schedules), are exploring alternative ways of transferring the management knowhow *they* think their operations need. Trade-offs between local ad-hoc training courses or public seminars on the one hand, and corporate training centres back home or international management institutes on the other are carefully assessed. Studies (in process) to facilitate the design of educational, training and development strategies and their implementation are much awaited to make current practices more 'cost effective' or merely 'effective'. [17]

Foreign education

The third common means of transfering management knowhow is professional education and training abroad, through foreign educators. This transfer method is one of the oldest, one of the most expensive and maybe, one of the least cost-effective and least appropriate. For many years the elite's children have used the possibility of being educated abroad, bringing back home (if they return) knowledge, skills and attitudes the mix of which may not necessarily be conducive to effective management of change in the home environment. Assumptions, underlying models, methods and tools learnt abroad are often taken for granted and transferred whole to be imposed upon local conditions for the sake of 'effectiveness'. Disillusionment and frustration of the PhD or DBA returning home after four to seven years abroad could be avoided or limited if a few important conditions had been accounted for in the transfer process. Let us explore this further as it takes us to the core of the transfer of management technology issue.

The Japanese economic growth, as suggested earlier, has emphatically demonstrated to the gurus of western management tradition and to their disciples that the management process was not following 'universal' rules. The gospel of management as taught at Harvard or Stanford has not been the bible out of which Japanese managers have drawn principles of management action and administrative procedures. They have organised *in their own way* people and tasks to efficiently and effectively reach corporate goals in international environments fast changing for them as for the rest of the world. The particular way in which the Japanese defined 'management', 'goals', the way they implemented 'strategies', to manage constraints and opportunities seems however, to have worked successfully. The Japanese case exemplifies the observation that management is a 'product of culture', though management is 'a still evolving mix of concepts and subject matter drawn from diverse disciplines, and there is not complete agreement on what the components of that mix ought to be.' [18] Acknowledged as a critical component, the 'cultural' element has now been operationalised, and its critical role in managerial effectiveness has been demonstrated.

As a product of culture, management knowhow becomes a much more difficult product to export, to transfer, than westerners naively thought. As Moris says: 'Our image of 'management' as being *Western, rational* and *efficient* is probably a better indication of our idiosyncratic needs within Western society than it is a tool for the comparative analysis of other administrative systems'. [19] The western business schools' academic community tends to be 'culture blind', believes in one rationality, one logic and therefore implicitly 'one best way'. Streeten [20] makes the point: 'It is a strange fact that social scientists whose special interest is social reality, are exceedingly naive when it comes to examining the social origins of their own theories and models'. Ethnocentric, prisoner of our models, we believe that management 'rationality' is one, while as Moris emphasises [21] 'the notion that western management is intrinsically rational strikes many non-western observers as strange since to them the patent irrationality of our arbitrary procedures is strikingly obvious'. Under such circumstances, it is not surprising that the transfer of management knowhow to developing countries has had such disappointing results.

There is often an unfortunate connivance between the 'foreign' management teacher or the expatriate manager and the local professor, student or employee. The western 'expert' (professor or manager) is convinced he knows how to apply (his) rationality to local problem solving for achieving organisational effectiveness. His partner (professor, student, employee) in the learning situation, is convinced that management coming from the developed countries of the West brings 'modernity', and must be somewhat 'scientific'. He therefore accepts them and adapts his models and tools, realising soon afterwards that it does not produce the expected results. For instance, he may soon become aware that deeply-rooted attitudes towards authority and assumption about communications negate the intended impact of many western managerial approaches. [22] The foreign expert unwillingly often maintains this state of affairs. Many *weaknesses* he sees in assessing the functioning of South-East Asian bureaucracies, and management systems, are 'weaknesses' only from the standpoint of *his* peculiar western managerial assumptions about administrative and organisational effectiveness. 'Viewed as functional prerequisites in a social system, these same traits become organisational *strengths* that help to explain the extraordinary persistence of traditional bureaucratic forms under adverse conditions. The system retains the capability to perform certain social functions effectively, so that viewed from within, the organism appears in *normal health'*. [23]

Many examples of these so-called 'weaknesses' in ASEAN countries' managerial processes are often not understood within the local system functional rationality. Management, change, transfer of knowhow, not based upon an understanding of the particular local environment tend to be ineffective. Many experiences emphasise how identification and understanding of the local system's cultural components become of paramount importance for effective transfer of management knowhow. It is only through a comprehensive understanding from the inside of how the system appears to work, that we will discover the rational causes (which can be analysed and perhaps acted upon) of what, too often, we tend to label 'irrational weakness'. There is evidence that the effective transfer of management knowhow is likely to remain somewhat cost-ineffective as long as, managers and academics alike, the cultural dimension in the transfer strategy is not introduced, on both sides by the transferor and by the transferee.

'Culture': as 'catalyst' for transfer of management know-how?

The international management transfer is indeed imbedded into cultural issues probably at the three classical levels:

> Management *knowledge,* i.e. the conceptual tools and techniques concerning management (e.g. operation research, quality control, systems analysis, linear programming). The knowledge is drawn primarily from economics, statistics, business administration.
> Management *skills,* i.e. the ability to implement and effectively use management tools and techniques (e.g. environmental analysis, problem diagnosis, systemic thinking, integrative skills, decision making). The skills draw mainly from political science, sociology, anthropology, economics, law.
> Management *attitudes,* i.e. points of view of managers concerning managerial tasks, human beings, environmental settings (e.g. perception of hierarchical authority, structures, functional specificity of roles, of 'rational' norms and procedures).

It is often assumed that the transfer of conceptual 'knowledge' and 'tools' is the least difficult transfer, since it is free from cultural problems. There is now evidence, however, that such is not the case. [24] Accounting tools and procedures, budgeting practices [25] are culturally influenced; they rely upon implicit models and assumptions. Semantic differences in concepts (e.g. 'time', 'responsibility', 'group', 'leadership' etc.) make the transfer of concepts their translation entangled with cultural differences. [26] Not only culture permeates through concepts and models, but prior to the transfer of a technique the transferor often fails to test its relevance or possible use in the transferee's environment (e.g. training in the use of elaborate cost-benefit techniques in a context where data are unavailable, true costs unknown, and benefit incommensurate; training in the use of sophisticated marketing models, in countries where reliable market information just does not exist).

At each level of transfer the transferor must account for

the 'administrative culture' into which the transferee is going to operate. Effective managerial behaviour can be achieved exclusively when consistent with given, though changeable environmental-cultural settings; effective management implies a 'fit' between tools, skills, attitudes and the cultural environment in which they are used. Furthermore, organisation effectiveness implies a thorough understanding of the enterprise's external environment, of it's dynamics, to be able to monitor the firm/external environment interface.

If one accepts this hypothesis, the implications both for the transferor T (academic or manager, foreign or local) and for the transferee t (student, manager or civil servant) are principally:

1   T must have a good understanding of both the cultural dimension embodied within the management principle, or tool to be transferred; the administrative culture into which he wishes to transfer; his own cultural role as perceived by the transferee. As a transfer agent he is an essential part of the transfer process. ('The medium is the message'.)

2   t must be (or be 'made') aware of the 'foreign cultural component' of the knowhow transferred. With western management transfer we often observe a massive accompanying cultural penetration. This must be made explicit.

3   The transfer of management knowhow is far from 'neutral', it influences the distribution of power in the system: both T and t should be clear on the consequences. Transfer of management knowhow in that sense is a political process, and dealt with as such.

As 'transfer' is so difficult, some have suggested the creation of local management systems, congruent with and evolving from local cultural environments. Mendoza again raises interesting questions in this respect: 'This comparison of the Japanese management system with the American management system, the Japanese culture with the American, almost inevitably raises several very fundamental questions regarding management in the developing countries of Southeast Asia'. [27] In trying to answer these interesting questions, Mendoza identifies profiles of managers, specific competences needed in the region, and suggests upon which cultural components to build up the development process.

A research direction: the INSEAD Euro-Asia Centre experience

In Europe, the INSEAD Euro-Asian Centre is engaged in a research effort precisely along these lines. They are developing a pool of competence in assessing the cultural components of ASEAN socio-economic environments, of each country's administrative culture. From their system understanding of South-East Asian administration cultures, they might be able to identify *what* can be anchored on the local environment and possibly *how*. Programmes, specifically designed, tailor-made, to enhance management effectiveness in given ASEAN countries rely upon a process of limited transfer of management knowhow. It capitalises as much as possible upon the manager's understanding of his own management systems, and of its cultural component.

The Indonesian senior executive programme, a three weeks' seminar held annually since 1976 at Fontainbleau for a group of 30 managers, has been developed along the lines suggested above. The objective is not as such to transfer European management knowhow for Indonesian executives' use, but rather to increase participants' capacity to solve *their* administrative problems, through an intense reflection upon *their socio-economic and cultural* environment. The management of such a learning process is very difficult due to both participants' expectations and faculty professional experience. On the faculty side, two common pitfalls exist: (a) complying with participants' insistent demands to be given sophisticated models, tools and recipes from the 'bible-like management-science textbooks', and (b) avoiding questioning faculty members' own assumptions and models about what they do, why they do it and how they do it.

In their endeavour to prevent the *faculty* team from becoming victim of such dangers (e.g. complacency, ethno-centrism, intellectual comfort) they should engage in a costly, time-consuming investment in learning about and understanding the Indonesian environment. They should both (a) encourage teachers' involvement in learning about, in and from the Indonesian environment, through stays, language learning, field research etc, and (b) provoke among the teachers a critical self-assessment of their implicit and explicit models, theories and tools. Such a 'remise en cause' of one's own professional knowledge, though difficult, has personal spin-offs much beyond the task of transferring management knowhow from Europe to developing countries.

In this process of learning about their own 'rationality', their own 'cultural' biases, they review the last 15 years of European experience in transferring, accommodating, adapting, assimilating US management research, teaching, writings, practices. This painful 'acculturation' of US management knowhow to the different managerial cultures of Europe has produced some learning: it could prepare them better to deal again with the transfer issue.

On the *participants'* side, they also learn how to increase the transfer of 'efficiency' and possibly its 'effectiveness':

> Participants were very carefully selected, 5 months prior to the beginning of the programme.
> Participants had to write a paper describing managerial issues they had to deal with in their current firm operations. The paper reviewed by the faculty team, initiated a dialogue between a faculty member and the participant. Such a procedure had many functions, in particular it obliges each participant to explain *his own* conceptual way of defining problems. It gave the faculty, over time, a feeling for the world of a Javanese businessman. It produced a rich pedagogical material for the seminar (and beyond) to ensure the issues dealt with were 'relevant' and in their real context.
> Participants were told (and soon had to 'experience') that the seminar would not give them 'recipes', 'modern tools', unless the learning community (teachers and participants together) had tested their relevance within the specific conditions of the Indonesian environment. Participants were warned that such a learning design, perhaps frustrating at times, was likely to produce more relevance, more validity, in the transfer process.

The results of this concept are currently being assessed in relation to the objective of increasing participants' capacity to *define* issues and problems in ways which make *culturally acceptable solutions* easier to identify clearly and to implement. Their approach attempts to overcome some of the shortcomings tied to the often complacent teacher-learner interdependence, apparently inherent in transferring management knowhow. They learnt in the process the invaluable resource of a Euro-Asian team, where European and Asian academics work together, muddling through, to increase the emergence of contingent management knowhow and of effective acquisition of transfer methods. The European experience is, in this respect, a precious, but insufficient capital. This work is but one small contribution to the wider debate about the transfer of technology.

Because technology transfer is a 'hot' issue in today's new international economic order, the transfer of management knowhow (a 'soft' technology) will become increasingly a key feature of the difficult dialogue between the EEC and the ASEAN. It will oblige national educational systems, foreign investors in LDCs, academics and consultants of developed countries and international agencies to rethink (if possible together) how to become more cost-effective. Within the ASEAN academic community one can hope to find the relays, the 'multiplier' effect, so much needed to rethink *what* has been or has to be transferred and *how*. This will indeed involve 'unlearning' before we can be sure we are asking the right questions.

Notes

[1]   M. Omolayole, 'Management Education Needs in Developing Countries', in *Management Education in the 80s,* AIESEC International, Brussels 1979, p. 17.
[2]   Ibid., p. 24.
[3]   M. Haire, E. E. Ghiselli and L. W. Porter, *Managerial Thinking — an International Study,* Wiley, New York 1966, p. 298.
[4]   S. M. Davis, *Managing and Organising Multinational Corporations,* Praeger, New York 1979.

[5]   W. H. Newman, 'Is Management Exportable?', in *Columbia Journal of World Business,* May-June 1969, pp. 7–18.

[6]   R. A. Webber, 'Convergence or Divergence?' in *Columbia Journal of World Business,* May-June 1969, pp. 75–83.

[7]   H. C. de Bettignies and S. H. Rhinesmith, 'Developing the International Executive', in *European Business,* no. 24, Paris, January 1970.

[8]   A. Mendoza, 'Management Education for Development Transferability of Western Management Concepts and Programmes', discussion paper prepared for conference on public management education and training, Bellagio, Italy 1976.

[9]   Ibid., p. 2.

[10]   H. C. de Bettignies, 'Japanese *vs.* European Top Management', paper presented at the Business in Japan Workshop, Osaka, 4 March 1965.

[11]   R. T. Johnson and W. G. Ouchi, 'Made in America — under Japanese Management', in *Harvard Business Review,* September-October 1974.

[12]   K. E. Thurley, M. Nanaku and K. Uragami, *Employment Relations of Japanese Companies in the UK: A Report on an Exploratory Study,* British Association for Japanese Studies.

[13]   L. Kraar, 'The Japanese are Coming — with their own style of Management', in *Fortune,* March 1975.

[14]   Y. Tsurumi, *The Japanese are Coming,* Ballinger Publishing Co., Cambridge, Mass. 1976.

[15]   A. Neghandi, 'Transmitting Advanced, Management Practices to Industrial Enterprises in Developing Countries', paper presented at the International Institute of Management, Berlin 1977.

[16]   Ibid.

[17]   A. Neghandi, *Quest for Survival: A Comparative Study of American, European and Japanese Multinations,* Praeger, New York 1979.

[18]   L. D. Stifel, J. S. Coleman and J. E. Black, *Education and Training for Public Sector Management in Developing Countries,* The Rockefeller Foundation, New York 1977.

[19]   J. R. Moris, *The Transferability of Western Management*

Concepts and Programmes and East African Perspective, p. 75.

[20] P. Streeten, 'The Use and Abuse of Models in Development Planning', in *The Teaching of Development Economics,* K. Martin and J. Knapp (eds), Frank Cass, London 1967.

[21] J. R. Moris, op. cit.

[22] Ibid.

[23] Ibid.

[24] S. G. Redding and T. A. Martyn-Johns, 'Paradigm differences and their relation to Management, with reference to South East Asia', in *Cross Cultural Studies in Organisation,* A. R. Neghandhi and B. Wilpert (eds), Kent State University Press, Ohio 1979.

[25] A. J. Enthoven, *Accountancy Systems in Third World Economies,* North Holland Publishing Co., Amsterdam 1977.

[26] A. J. Enthoven, *Accounting and Economic Development Policy,* North Holland Publishing Co., Amsterdam 1973.

[27] S. Ferrari, 'Transnational Analysis in Developing Countries', in *Journal of European Industrial Training,* vol. 3, no. 4, 1979, pp. 12—15.

18 A Ten-Step Model for Multinational Training*

MELVIN SCHNAPPER

Many trainers, both neophyte and experienced, are discovering that their notions of how to design, implement and evaluate effective training for their normal client populations are not always effective when applied to multi-cultural or multi-national trainee groups. They are discovering that hitherto valid assumptions, approaches and techniques create vastly different reactions and dynamics when applied to culturally different or heterogeneous populations.

In this chapter, the terms multinational corporations/ international organisations are used generally to apply to organisations in the public and private sectors such as profit-oriented businesses, international development agencies, bi- or multilateral military forces, international exchange programmes, educational institutions and even multi-cultural, multi-racial or multi-ethnic organisations which are domestic in staffing and focus. The common feature of all of these being that the trainer and trainee populations include a heterogeneous cultural background.

The literature is rich with examples of wasted effort, money and time because of inter-cultural misunderstanding. The expanding size and impact of multinational companies and international transactions will increase the potential and magnitude of such waste. After identifying some of the unique challenges facing the multinational trainer, this

---

* This chapter is an abridged version of a monograph entitled 'Multinational training for multinational corporations/international organisations', originally published in 1977 by The American Society for Training and Development, P.O. Box 5307, Madison, Wisconsin 53705, USA.

chapter explains some general goals of training as proposed by the experiential/cognitive approach and why this approach is uniquely appropriate for training people to cope more effectively with cultural diversity. A basic ten-step training module is described and some cross-culturally relevant concerns highlighted. The need for such training is clear, but the demand remains low, for reasons discussed later.

Multinational training is intended for the multinational manager who must be knowledgeable and skilful in a number of areas. Therefore, multinational training must include an appropriate blend of training areas which are typically mutually exclusive:

1   *Managerial training* focuses upon the managerial functions of leading, controlling, planning and directing, regardless of the language, cultural differences and the business.
2   *Intercultural training* focuses upon cultural differences such as values, perceptions, assumptions and style, regardless of the language, managerial role and the business.
3   *International business training* focuses upon business practices/functions across national boundaries such as production, marketing and financing, while international agencies will focus upon the technical expertise supporting this particular purpose or goal. Both will typically give less than adequate attention to the managerial role, language or preparation for cultural differences.
4   *Language training* focuses upon developing language fluency in the social and technical areas regardless of the managerial role or the business purpose, though some attention may be given to culture.

All these areas, as parts of a total comprehensive development programme, are necessary for adequately preparing the multinational manager. The comprehensive foci of multinational training is summarised in Table 18.1, where 'Yes' indicates that the area is focused upon and 'No' indicates typical neglect.

Table 18.1
Multinational training foci

Focus / Training	Managerial role	Cultural differences	Technical/ business purpose of organisation	Language
1 Managerial	Yes	No	No	No
2 Inter-cultural	No	Yes	No	No
3 International/business	No	No	Yes	No
4 Language	No	No	No	Yes
5 Multinational	Yes	Yes	Yes	Yes

Need for multinational training

The literature is replete with case after case of wasted effort, time and huge amounts of money due to cross-cultural misunderstanding. Businesses and governments at all levels have suffered because of waste.

A Venezuelan vice-president of marketing for an American-owned multinational was fired by the president because he refused a promotion, which would have meant abandoning his parents in Caracas and moving to Boston. In Venezuela where children are expected to take care of their parents, 'abandoning them' would be shameful. The American president of the company was angered and confused by the Latin American's 'lack of appreciation and loyalty'.

A German engineer, thinking he had successfully negotiated a joint venture with a Japanese firm, returned home to await the Japanese signatures on the contract and discovered several weeks later, that the Japanese had not agreed to over half of the contractual conditions. While in Tokyo the Japanese had smiled and nodded approvingly all during his presentations. They also wined and dined him very graciously and never hinted at being resistant to his proposal. He had no idea that during the brief time of their acquaintance, they were not yet ready to disclose their serious reservations.

A British supervisor of a bridge-building project in Nigeria was shocked when his team of Nigerian workers refused to continue the project after he had encouraged them to pick their own team leader. He knew that his Nigerian work team was a mixture of several tribes, but he did not expect that tribal rivalry would be so significant that competition for a leader role would bring work to a halt.

Mistakes like these occur daily in some parts of the world, be it Caracas, Tokyo or Lagos. These misunderstandings result in needless wastes of time, effort and money that one or both sides of an international transaction must bear. Very often entire projects/programmes get wrecked on the shoals of the inter-cultural misunderstandings. Careers are often ended abruptly because managers interpret cultural differences as personal and attitudinal manifestations of 'disloyalty', 'lack of proper leadership' or 'poor judgement'. Contracts are often concluded based on faulty assumptions and on misinterpretations of the legal, personal and cultural aspects of the negotiation process.

All these factors contribute to multinational managers becoming frustrated, angry, and even racist, because they have little appreciation of how cross-cultural differences affect managerial style. Frequently these feelings result in an early return for the manager and his/her family, causing a waste of managerial talent and money.

Goals of multinational training

There are too many variables to allow any one training approach to be valid across different nations, cultures, organisations and departments. The trainer must hold lightly to models, techniques and philosophies of training and select the appropriate blend of each to fit the needs of the organisation, trainees and training staff. Nevertheless there are certain basic goals which must be achieved.

What multinational training must accomplish

Perhaps a brief aphorism will establish a framework for the multinational training model.

> Telling is helping to know.
> Teaching is helping to know and to grow.
> Training is helping to know, to grow and do and inevitably becoming a different person.

Thus, training must have an element of doing and 'inevitably becoming a different person'. These 'becoming' processes are not occurring very much in programmes that are largely didactic in nature. The nature of effective training demands that the person not only:

(a) *know* about the cross-cultural management differences, inter-cultural communication skills, both verbal and non-verbal and business – markets, laws, economics etc.;

(b) *grow* – have awareness of self and others in the environment, knowing how managerial behaviour affects others; and

(c) *do* – effectively fulfilling the job mission, making friends and satisfying personal needs; but the manager must also

(d) 'utilise different behaviour' – as a result of inter-cultural adaptation, the manager learns to internalise and/or accept new values, assumptions, perceptions, and to risk different and more appropriate behaviours. All these processes will in some way help the trainee cope more effectively than the person who first entered the programme.

These necessary personal change processes are often ignored by programmes intended to help prepare the multinational manager for the inter-cultural encounter. Such programmes often present a great deal of necessary and useful information about the laws, business practices, employee expectations, government regulations, taxes and profit issues as well as important data for almost any business function. These seminars may also include detailed discussions about history, customs, and cultural data about working and living successfully in the multinational/multi-cultural environment. Most companies will give the employee an adequate orientation related to the terms and conditions of the assignment including compensations, travel and shipping arrangements, special allowances and employment conditions, overseas and upon return home.*

All this information is necessary but not sufficient. In almost all cases this information is presented in a traditionally academic manner. This approach will not enhance the manager's personal/cultural self awareness, will not develop specific inter-personal/inter-cultural skills and will not help to initiate and/or facilitate the personally profound insights, awareness and dynamics that will change a domestic manager into a truly competent participant in the multinational management world. This kind of preparation has marginal utility and does not meet the previously identified criteria of effective training.

Experiential training

There is growing evidence [1] to support the contention that in the hands of skilled, inter-culturally sensitive and empathic trainers, the experiential or laboratory method of training will accomplish these personal change processes which were identified as so critical for effective multinational management.

> A new form of interpersonal training is emerging. Its technology is borrowed from organizational development efforts, and many of its tools are taken from the laboratory techniques of the behavioral scientist. It is possible to expose the future expatriate to training sessions on relating authentically to people in different cultures, the value of candor and interpersonal feedback in cross-cultural communications, and how to understand what your foreign counterpart is really saying. [2]

---

* See Chapter 2 on how even basic briefings on matters other than purely 'housekeeping' details are often absent.

However, the trainer must be very cautious about which techniques to use and how to make them appropriate for a specific or multi-cultural group of managers. The next section which explains the ten-step multinational training model will suggest how to make this happen.

Ten-step multinational training model

Ten steps

There are a variety of training approaches that span the continuum from purely academic to purely experiential. Preferably the training is an appropriate balance of the two. Whatever the approach, this ten-step multinational training model (see Table 18.2) will help ensure an effective programme. Unique considerations for the multinational context will be posed for each step.

Table 18.2
A ten-step multinational training model

Steps	Focus
1 Client request 2 Performance analysis 3 Training needs 4 Training objectives	Organisational diagnosis
5 Training design 6 Training of trainers 7 The training itself	Design/implementation
8 Training evaluation 9 Performance evaluation	Evaluation
10 Support/maintenance systems	Organisation development

Source: Bellman [3]

Step 1   Client request. Generally a client (individual, group, department or total organisation) will request training as a solution to a problem, even when the problem does not have a training solution. Often problems of poor performance, low morale, breakage, waste and conflict have a systems-wide source and may originate with poor procedures and policies. The trainer should not respond to the client's request with immediate delivery of a training programme, for no matter how well the training is performed, it may be irrelevant. The trainer should explore the needs behind the request, define mutual expectations, mutual and mutually exclusive areas of responsibility, seek for 'hidden agenda', and identify critical managers who need to approve and support a training intervention.

Multinational considerations

Poor performance in a multinational situation may have causes that are very different from those expected. Employees may not perform beyond a certain level because to do so would make others 'lose face' or embarrass 'elders' or other high status individuals.

Training may be seen as 'meddling' in very private or intimate areas or will be seen as futile since the status quo is seen as unalterable.

The trainer/consultant may be seen as working for the requestor in order to ensure the requestor's control over employees.

On the other hand, employees may overwhelmingly accept new training norms which will be disruptive of the organisation.

In many transitional societies like Nigeria where middle-level managers may be more educated and innovative than senior managers, immediate adaptation may lead to greater organisational conflict and the training may be blamed.

Step 2   Performance analysis. Most training requests are a result of perceived discrepancy between what *is* and what *should* or *could be* better performance. Performance analysis, sometimes referred to as 'front end analysis' or 'task analysis', is a process of observing the work itself. Performance analysis focuses upon identifiable behaviours and not upon hidden thought processes such as attitude or motivation. All conclusions should be tested with the employees, supervisors, peers, and any customer of the performance. Perhaps 'poor' performance was really a question of misunderstanding between these persons.

Multinational considerations

Very often performance deficiencies in a multinational result from traditional practices and values and not from inadequate training or unwillingness to cooperate. For example, a new product's poor performance in the consumer market (though extremely successful in another country) could be due to its image and/or need for consumers to change habits. Assuming that the salesmen need to improve their selling skills would be invalid and unproductive.

Observing performance may be impossible and/or very discomforting to employees who do not have familiarity nor tolerance for a 'fishbowl' experience.

Open discussions about 'poor' performance may be very inappropriate, as in Japan where not embarrasing fellow employees or being embarrassed by them is very important.

Step 3 Training needs analysis. Many different methods have been developed to identify training needs (see Johnson [4] for a good list). The choice of method depends on the familiar set of such criteria as cost and required degree of subtlety and the need to ensure that proper feedback is given to the client to engender commitment and ownership of the ideas.

Multinational considerations

Often persons unfamiliar with questionnaires will try to respond with the 'correct' answer instead of describing a work situation. If questionnaires or any paper and pencil instruments are to be used, they must be explained in depth, even by going through a trial run.

Interviews also must be designed to elicit critical data without offending existing norms and values about not betraying one's boss or the company. This is especially true where companies provide lifetime employment and encourage high levels of boss-subordinate loyalty patterns.

Group analysis where employees publicly identify their own and company shortcomings may be a nearly impossible approach, as in Vietnam where company, familial, social and political considerations are so intertwined.

Step 4   Training objectives. Training objectives are the specifiable, measurable and attainable statements about the training outcomes. They can be stated in terms of what people will know, be able to do, and even feel/think about something. The more specific and observable they are, the better training can be evaluated. Objectives must also be realistic in terms of systems support. If not, trainees with new skills, knowledge and awareness will feel frustrated and discouraged as they try to use what they have learned. Objectives must be limited to the few of many which may have been identified. These critical objectives must be accomplishable within the limits of time, energy, resources and budget.

Multinational considerations

A paradox of including key managers in the objectives-setting process is that the trainer's expertise may be seen as lacking, since so much help was needed. In many cultures the consultant is expected to act like 'l'expert' as in France.

When managerial training has objectives related to 'successful confrontation or feedback skills', these skills and their inherent values may be anathema to certain cultural norms.

Objectives must be stated in language that is understood by the client group, even though they are stated in ways generally unaccepted by the training professional.

Step 5   Training design. Though it was stated previously that training must inevitably facilitate change in the trainee and that the experiential approach is most effective, the variables in any particular situation may indicate that the most appropriate approach is to focus on knowledge and concepts with a non-threatening and low risk-taking discussion approach. The design must always be appropriate for the trainer's skill level, style, and comfort while challenging to the trainee population. The number of techniques that are available to the knowledgeable trainer are many, and by modifying, synthesising, and sequencing these techniques an almost infinite variety of training experiences can be provided. [5] To get the greatest mileage out of the training, the design ought to include supportive material which the trainee can use after training. Ideally the design would include a project to demonstrate application of training objectives with a follow-up session for trainees to share their project experience and learn new skills and/or sharpen old ones. Also the design might include cooperative and supportive action from the trainee's supervisor to build system support.

Multinational considerations

All aspects of the design need to be scrutinised to ensure that intercultural misinterpretations do not occur. Experiential group dynamics may be seen as a 'brain-washing' attempt; film produced in one country may communicate a very different message in another; media colours, shapes, symbols, images may provoke a very different response from that intended; using pictures of people may be offensive in a Moslem culture; the whole notion of attending a training session especially if more than one level of management is present, may be so different as to influence all responses no matter what the design!

Frequently the logistics of travel and lodging will determine the length of training programmes and even individual sessions, especially when a multinational has small offices in several neighbouring countries and training requires staff attendance from each office.

Step 6   Training of trainers. Though often neglected as an integral part of the training process, training of line managers or participants to train may be the only way to ensure the survival of the initial training efforts. The programme they have been through can do a lot to increase the credibility and desirability of the training function. This is not only a good strategy for gaining organisational credibility but allows a trainer to multiply potential training efforts. When training of trainers is accomplished by using the model described here and when the potential trainers are also graduates of the trainee group, the training itself is more likely to be acceptable, appropriate and effective.

Multinational considerations

As a developmental opportunity for the trainer, this level of training legitimises more detailed and intimate feedback while having a 'laboratory' to experiment with host national* reactions to his/her own training style.

Multinationals typically have few internal training resources, especially for managerial training. If training is to be seen as valid and useful, persons other than those in the training and development department ought to be involved. This will help ensure that all training aspects have the greatest input from a wide variety of staff and line management. Using line managers may ultimately support the survival of the training function.

Since training with host national trainers presents a lot of dilemmas and paradoxes, this area will be discussed separately in the next section.

Step 7   The training itself. All the best preparation in the world will go by the wayside if the actual implementation of training is poor. It is important to check and double check all facilities, equipment, provisions for refreshments and

---

* The term host nationals refers to the majority of the nationality of the local company or division personnel, e.g. a company headquartered in Ottawa with a subsidiary in England would refer to the British employees in the UK office as host nationals.

norms around starting and ending times of each session. Seating may also be a critical variable, especially if done in a way which departs from the typical classroom style which still dominates in so many training facilities. The staff must attend to the learning climate to ensure that expectations are identified and clarified and all learning objectives are understood. This will help the trainees take responsibility for their own learning and clarify mutual and mutually exclusive areas of staff and trainee responsibility. Since the design may have lacked some critical inputs from the trainees themselves, the staff must always entertain the possibility of changing the design midstream and be sensitive to trainee reactions to each part of the training as it continues.

Multinational considerations

The training itself is the area where many of the unknowns surface as trainees interact with and react to the staff and each other. When the trainee group is multicultural, certain training techniques such as simulation, role play, encounter, and feedback which are comfortable for some groups/individuals may be discomforting to others. The multinational trainer will have to make special inquiries periodically to maximise everyone's comfort and attention. Host national co-trainers, are a good source for this kind of data.

The trainer must also attend to his/her language even when speaking the trainees' language which he/she learned in a different country. Just as 'America and England are two countries separated by the same language' so do varieties of Spanish and French differ from country to country.

Also, the trainer must attend to non-verbal behaviour which differs widely from culture to culture. [6]

Step 8 Training evaluation. Evaluation of training is typically the weakest link in the whole training process. Evaluation which usually occurs either during or immediately after the training programme will measure either knowledge, skills, and/or attitude. Typically evaluation is in terms of reactions to staff and particular sessions. A more valuable approach would be to evaluate the actual skills and knowledge learned by the trainees. When learning objectives are a clear part of the initial design phase of the training, these objectives can readily become the evaluation criteria for successful training. Different techniques can be designed, such as role playing, observation of trainees during a subsequent task, or more conventional paper and pencil techniques to evaluate the actual learning. Clear objectives also enable the trainees to evaluate their own success or achievement. When evaluation is done within the training programme itself, feedback can enable the staff to further emphasise something not learned well or to change their approach to some subsequent objective.

Multinational considerations

Evaluation in a multinational setting is subject to all the same mistakes as Step 3 and the techniques must be selected appropriately. Very often trainees will see the evaluation process as reflecting solely upon their learning abilities as opposed to reflecting upon the skills of the trainers. The author's experience with Samoans and Swazis bears this out.

Participants may also be 'polite' during the evaluation phase and give the responses which they believe are expected. The evaluation approach must be designed to filter these responses out and/or trainees must be convinced that the *staff* are the focus of the evaluation process.

In a multinational context all the variables which are higherto unknowable may suddenly surface, e.g. the training was good, the objectives were achieved, but because of factors related to the selection process, the learning is irrelevant to the trainee.

Step 9 Performance evaluation. Though training evaluation is seldom done, performance evaluation is hardly done at all. It is very challenging to try to see what actual changes come about in a person's performance as a result of training experience. Sometimes these changes are so subtle, that change is almost impossible to observe and must be reported by the participant.

Ideally, part of the training design includes supervisory or peer ownership for giving the participants and/or staff feedback about changes on a post-training basis. At the very least the staff should build long-term follow-up interviewing into its plan.

One way of evaluating post-training performance is to assign on-the-job projects for trainees to complete after the training is over. In this way, the trainer knows that at least the project itself represents new performance. Hopefully, the participant can relate improved performance on the project to the training experience.

Multinational considerations

This kind of evaluation is very difficult to accomplish in a multinational, especially when so many corporations have an inadequate system for evaluating any kind of regular performance. So often the idea of supervisors evaluating, discussing and planning for improvement of training is very rare; and to expect this to occur because the training staff needs the data to evaluate its training is often unrealistic.

In one multinational European setting it was only after a second training programme that participants engaged in a candid evaluation of the organisation.

Cultural norms, apart from organisational norms, may prove very punishing to the participant who returns to work and tries to implement the new learnings.

Step 10 Support/maintenance systems. If training is to be truly effective, it must be supported by reward systems which are part of the trainee's environment. The skills for example, from a session on 'evaluating subordinate performance' are much more likely to be carried back to the job if the organisation has a formal performance evaluation procedure that forces the supervisor and subordinate to examine the subordinate's performance. One way to get some system support for training behaviours, when such supportive systems are generally absent, is to build in the support and cooperation of the participant's supervisor. Designing new support and maintenance systems is a challenging and often frustrating activity and requires a whole other set of skills usually referred to as organisation development or OD. A good trainer should have enough OD skills such as survey feedback and analysis skills, and making structural changes to help the organisation support the training objectives.

Multinational considerations

Since many multinationals do not have the appropriate support systems overseas, this area may be truly vexing. The need for OD skills in a cultural setting is therefore strong.

Since the multinational's environment is so fraught with unpredictable change, utilising OD strategies requires a great deal of flexibility and patience. Also general OD strategies are very value-laden and may be very inappropriate for the multinational environment unless drastically modified.

Paradoxes of multinational training

The ten-step model presents many dilemmas and paradoxes when applied to multinational training. Many multinational trainers ignore the paradoxes of preparing persons for working and living together in a multi-cultural setting, especially when such preparatory activities include different nationalities.

The paradoxes which exist within the goals and the processes of training are:

When managers who make requests for training are not culturally representative of the vast employee population, such training may be insensitive to and unwelcomed by the trainees thus setting up dynamics for failure.

If cultural relativism (the idea that all cultures are equally valid patterns of survival within their environment) is a 'truth' held by multinational trainers, then preparing managers to help their culturally different subsidiaries change (typically in the direction of buying into the value and belief system of North American behavioural sciences) is a violation of this 'truth'.

The 'belief' that multinational training is valid and accomplishable is a basically North American belief which, like other North American beliefs, is being sold to other countries.

When host nationals are used as part of the training staff, they typically have little decision-making power about training design and implementation. The message to trainees is subtle but profound — these nationals do not share 'valid' perceptions of what is important in their culture. This is often what Ivan Illich would call the 'hidden curriculum' of education/training. Is this what the training staff wants to communicate?

Host nationals have not been adequately used. They have more potential for serving as culture role models that managers can observe, interact with, become sensitive to and learn to cope with. Even though allowing and encouraging host national involvement in decision making may result in the compromise of basic experiential training beliefs/values, confusion, and entail lengthy negotiations, the resultant training model could have impressive and truly multinational outcomes.

Some trainers have even advocated that host nationals share an intense T-Group (or sensitivity training) experience with the trainees.

Human relations training for overseas work can probably be enriched by incorporating foreign nationals into the training groups. T-Groups of mixed nationalities, for example, may represent a microcosm of a cross-cultural encounter that can provide an in-depth cultural learning experience for the participants. Under skilful guidance, such a strategy may integrate the substantive content of cultural learning with the situational requirements for behavioural change. [7]

This approach, using a modified T-Group, has often been used successfully for integrating many Peace Corps training staff, though in some cases it has proved traumatic for host nationals, especially if they have not been familiar with experiential techniques. (Though the Peace Corps is a unique phenomenon with an unusually strong emphasis on inter-cultural competency, multinationals could benefit immensely from Peace Corps' multinational staff integration experience.) On the one hand, if host nationals are involved completely with all aspects of training, they will be forced to engage in processes that may be prohibited in their culture. In other words, to the extent that host nationals become truly respon-sive to the North American agenda for the training programme, they become less congruent with and/or authentic to their cultural origins.

If, on the other hand, the host national staff have ultimate decision-making power about the training programme, the design might well resemble a highly structured, academic lecture/discussion approach void of innovative experiential group-process training techniques. Is the gain of host national cultural biases worth the loss of what most experientially-oriented trainers consider to be effective training?

These questions with regard to training goals and processes are always implicitly or explicitly posed for every multi-national training programme. Unfortunately, many trainers do not recognise these issues or are uncomfortable in dealing with them, even though they do not have the choice *not* to deal with them.

There is no way to escape the 'double bind' posed by the paradoxes raised here, but one can benefit from recognising them and discussing them with the host national members of the training staff.

Sources of resistance

Much of the cause of the continuing low priority accorded to training of the type discussed here can be attributed to assumptions made by senior managers. Few managers in multinationals have a clear understanding and appreciation of cultural differences. Table 18.3 describes some of the more commonly articulated reasons for resisting multinational training with the underlying assumptions, and also the contrasting assumption which is more supportive of training.

This table is not assumed to be exhaustive. Feldman observed: [8]

> Many key management and HRD specialists either failed to recognize a need for cross-cultural training, or if they did, did not provide training in a way that took advantage of the available research, knowledge and experience for conducting effective HRD programmes designed to improve cross-cultural adjustment and interaction.

Nevertheless a trend towards greater awareness of the problems seems to be emerging. A survey of 33 major US international companies recently released by the Conference Board, a non-profit research organisation, indicated that they were putting greater emphasis on executives' ability to adjust to the customs and environment of foreign companies.

Table 18.3
Contrast assumptions which support and confront
resistances to multinational training

	Statement	Assumption	Contrasting assumption
A	'Our people have already proven they can work with people, no matter what their race or culture.'	Evidence has already been demonstrated that the person has proven his inter-cultural skills by working with a variety of fellow nationals. People are not so radically different, at least on the job.	Professional and/or interpersonal success in one's own country does not guarantee similar success in a different culture. The cultural differences between people are so profound that significant new skills and behaviours are necessary for effective inter-cultural interaction.
B	'Nothing can be done for the person until he is overseas and is in the actual situation.'	Only the reality of the job situation will produce learning. People will not accept the 'reality' of the training situation.	People can learn these new skills and behaviours before they get into the actual setting. Training which emphasises new behaviour in a supportive environment will help the trainee carry these behaviours into a new work situation.
C	'We're sending mature adults whose basic personality is already set.'	Mature adults cannot learn or unlearn behaviours even when such changes are to their advantage.	Though the preparatory activity cannot attempt basic personality restructuring, even mature and 'set' persons can change and modify their behaviour when they see it as serving their purpose. So-called set personality traits such as sensitivity to others, creativity, tolerance for ambiguity and ability to cope with stress can all be strengthened by a training process.
D	'Our personnel will get along with the host nationals by living and working with them.'	People learn to like each other and work together by being together.	Working and living with people who are different does not mean that people will learn to love each other or cooperate. There are numerous examples that indicate the contrary.
E	'There is no proof that any kind of preparation makes a difference.'	This is largely true. Most studies have either evaluated change immediately after training itself, or lacked controls or other 'hard research' essentials.	There are data that effective training can improve the functioning of managers.
F	'People are about the same everywhere.'	People differ only superficially in regard to foods they eat, the language they speak and the clothes they wear.	Beyond the obvious differences of clothes, physical appearance and overt behaviour are differences of how the world is experienced, of assumptions, and of cognitive structures.

Greater emphasis alone does not mean that these companies would support greater training efforts. They could rely on more sophisticated selection procedures. Unfortunately, when a foreign subsidiary or office is demanding a manager to fill a vacant slot, and that slot requires rare business, technical and/or managerial skills, multinational managerial sensitivity is seldom the key variable in the decision to fill that slot. Thus a large part of the burden is still on the training function to help managers manage more effectively, but to do so trainers need to understand what multinational training should accomplish, as has been previously discussed.

Conclusions

The world of the multinational is too vast, complex and changeable for one training model to have universal application. Multinational training must however focus on four major areas: managerial, inter-cultural, business and language. No one of them alone is sufficient to cope with all the complexities involved in each area. Yet all too often multinational managers receive lopsided preparation that leaves out at least one of the four areas and most often only includes the business preparation.

There are several things the multinational trainer can do to improve the position. Some of these were mentioned in the training model: (a) include line managers as trainers; (b) make sure that management (at least the next level above the trainees' level) supports the training; (c) design, implement and evaluate training using an organisation development strategy; (d) look for and initiate systems-wide leverage to support training goals; (e) follow all steps of the training model to ensure effective training that trainees will support; (f) include work-related projects so trainees will apply newly acquired knowledge and skills to their job; (g) have trainers show cost-savings results of applying learnings from the training; (h) have follow-up training sessions to reinforce knowledge and skills; (i) become knowledgeable about the business; (j) become an articulate advocate for multinational training using the language of business and avoiding jargon.

This chapter contends that experiential training is the most effective way to confront managers with the inter-cultural coping and personal change process so critical for the multinational working and living situation. Unfortunately 'proving' the relationship between multinational training and effectiveness is difficult. There are usually too many uncontrollable variables to draw sound behavioural science conclusions. Training nevertheless can ultimately have an appropriate fit with organisational norms and generate support. A great deal of critical information about the employees' contract, business issues and conditions, foreign laws and regulations, multinational regulations and procedures can appropriately be presented by the traditional approach utilising lectures, discussions, readings and case studies. There are many foreign language learning approaches which are very effective.

The ten-step multinational training model represents a logical and disciplined way to develop sound and credible training which attends to the particular needs of the multinational. The examples of multinational considerations for each step are not nearly exhaustive and are meant to suggest some of the many pitfalls for the unwary.

Currently most multinational trainers with a training or behavioural science background tend to use an experiential approach. Many values and techniques of this approach may not be supported by the host national culture. The multinational trainer will have to decide how to use host nationals as co-trainers and as trainers who may eventually assume full authority for training. The multinational trainer will have to resolve how to train them appropriately. There is, however, no substitute for the trainer's own skills and capabilities for designing the best possible programmes.

Notes

[1] Melvin Schnapper, 'Experiential Intercultural Training for International Operations', unpublished Ph.D. dissertation, University of Pittsburgh, 1972.
[2] David M. Noer, *Multinational People Management: A*

Guide for Organizations and Employees, Bureau of National Affairs Inc., Washington, D.C. 1975.

[3] Geoff Bellman, *A Ten Step Training Process,* G. D. Searle & Co., Skokie, Illinois 1977.

[4] Richard B. Johnson, 'Determining Training Needs', in Robert L. Craig and Lester R. Bittel (eds), *Training and Development Handbook,* McGraw-Hill, New York 1967.

[5] Melvin Schnapper, 'Culture Simulation as a Training Tool', in *International Development Review,* vol. 15, no. 1, 1973.

[6] Melvin Schnapper, (1975) 'Nonverbal Communication and the Intercultural Encounter', in John E. Jones and J. William Pfeiffer (eds) *1975 Annual Handbook for Group Facilitators,* University Associates, La Jolla, California 1975.

[7] Robert J. Foster and Jack Danielian, *An Analysis of Human Relations Training and Its Implications for Overseas Performance,* Human Resources Research Office, Washington, D.C. 1966.

[8] Milton J. Feldman, 'Training for Cross-Cultural International Interaction in the Federal Government', in *Training and Development Journal,* November 1976.

Further reading

Thorrell B. Fest and James G. Robbins, 'Cross-Cultural Communications and the Trainer', monograph prepared for the International Development Session ASTD National Convention, New Orleans, Louisiana 1976.

Cecil G. Howard, 'Major Personnel Problems of U.S. Multinationals Abroad', in *The Personnel Administrator,* May 1975.

Raghu Nath, 'Training International Business and Management Personnel — An Overview', paper presented at third annual conference of the Society for Intercultural Education Training and Research (SIETAR), Chicago, Illinois, March 1977.

Anant R. Neghandhi and Daniel Robey, 'Understanding Organizational Behavior in Multinational and Multicultural Setting', in *Human Resources Management,* vol. 16, no. 1, University of Michigan, Graduate School of Business Administration, Spring 1977.

Stephen Rhinesmith, 'The Development of Intercultural Sensitivity Through Human Relations Training', University of Pittsburgh, Graduate School of Public and Intercultural Affairs (mimeograph), 1967.

Marchall R. Singer, 'Culture: A Perceptual Approach', in David S. Hoopes (ed.) *Readings in Intercultural Communication,* vol. 1, Regional Council for International Education, Pittsburgh, Pennsylvania.

C. Wickham Skinner, 'Management of International Production', in *Harvard Business Review,* September-October, 1964.

Charles M. Stabler, 'Talk of the Globe', in *Wall Street Journal,* 18 April 1973.

Leopold S. Vansina, 'Improving International Relations and Effectiveness Within Multinational Organizations', in John D. Adams (ed.) *New Technologies in Organization Development,* vol. 2, University Associates Inc., La Jolla, California 1975.